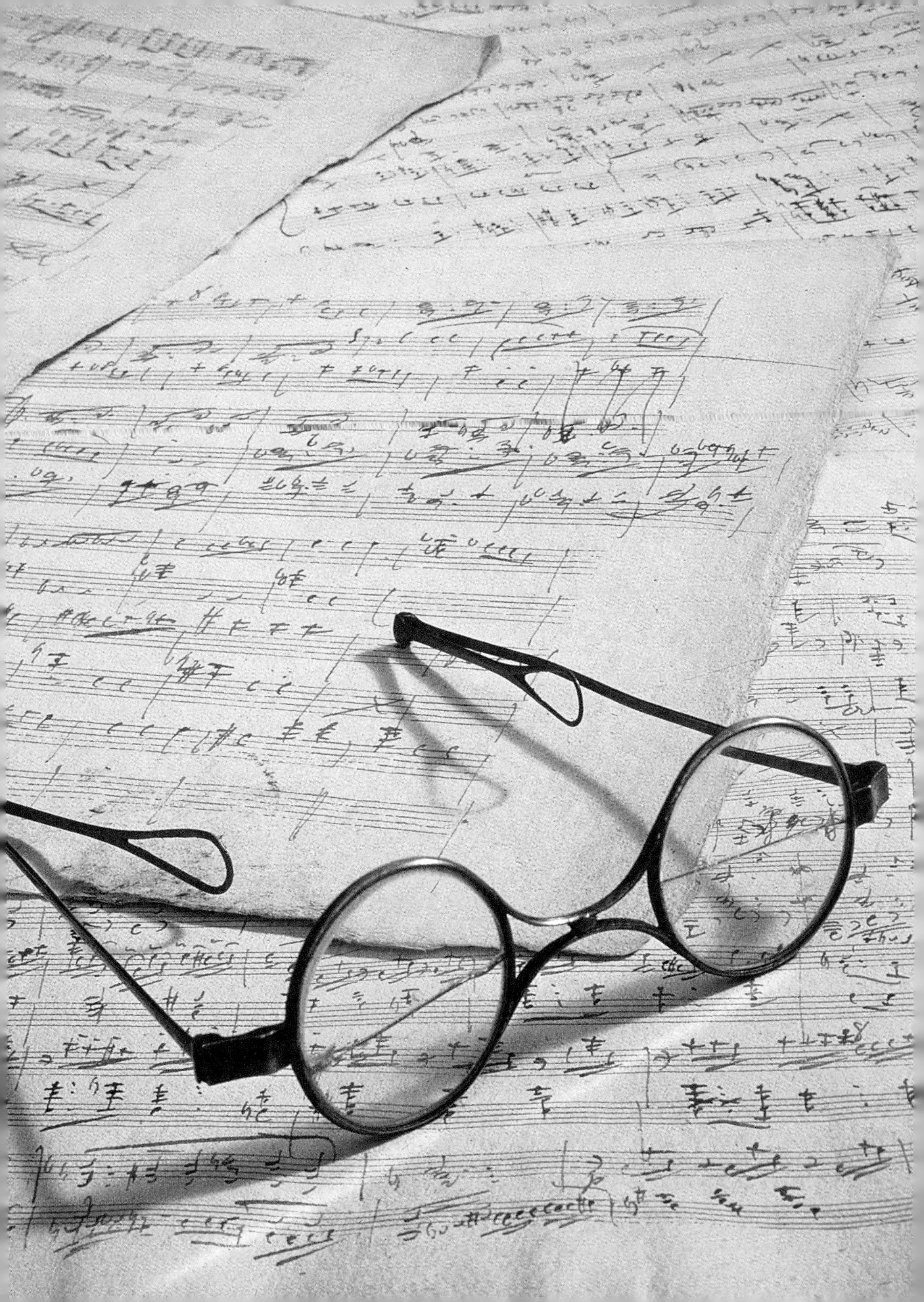

MARK ROWLINSON

Schubert

EVERYMAN–EMI MUSIC COMPANIONS

GENERAL EDITOR MICHAEL ROSE

Copyright © David Campbell Publishers Ltd.
and EMI Records Ltd., 1997

Music compilation ℗ and © 1997 EMI Classics (USA)
Text copyright © Mark Rowlinson, 1997

ISBN 1-85715-605-6

Published by David Campbell Publishers Ltd., 79 Berwick Street,
London W1V 3PF

Distributed by Random House (UK) Ltd., 20 Vauxhall Bridge Road,
London SW1V 2SA

A CIP catalogue reference for this book is available from the
British Library.

Front endpaper: 'A Schubert Evening at Josef von Spaun's':
sepia drawing by Moritz von Schwind made in 1868
(Historisches Museum der Stadt Wien).
Back endpaper: key to the above.
Frontispiece: Schubert's spectacles resting on original scores
at the Schubert House in the Kettenbrückengasse,
Vienna (AKG London/Erich Lessing).

Design by Anikst Associates
Picture research by Helen Ottaway
Typeset by AccComputing, Castle Cary, Somerset
Printed and bound in Germany by Mohndruck Graphische Betriebe
GmbH, Gütersloh

Preface

Schubert, that tubby little figure in round glasses with a shock of black hair, is an obstinately elusive figure, and is likely to remain so despite the many reassessments of his life that have emerged to coincide with the bicentenary of his birth. Of all the great composers he is probably the one about whom, personally, we know least. It is perfectly true that the eminent Schubert scholar, Otto Erich Deutsch, has filled a stout volume with descriptions and memories by the composer's friends and contemporaries, but many of these were written long after Schubert's death, often when rivalries or disagreements between the writers had arisen to influence what they remembered. Though they tell us a good deal about the surroundings in which Schubert lived, and about the famous Schubertiads, those convivial gatherings of friends which were such an important feature of his life, they tell us surprisingly little about the composer himself. Deutsch's even stouter complementary volume of letters and other documents relating directly to Schubert's life and work reveals a few tantalizing glimpses – but how we long for a correspondence of the kind Mozart had with his family! Schubert's life was even shorter than Mozart's, he travelled much less so there was less reason for extended correspondence, and his energies were more easily dissipated – the Schubertiads and nightly meetings over coffee or wine in the inns of Vienna were so much easier than letters as a means of communication.

It is much the same with the music. It is easy enough to analyse it, easy enough to demonstrate his absolute mastery and extraordinary invention in song, his frequent fallibility in creating instrumental structures, and his powerful originality when he succeeds. Yet these are hardly the things which touch us in Schubert. Where did he find those uniquely fluctuating harmonies that enrich the untiring flow of melody, and underline the sadness that is never far from the heart of his work? Why did he leave so many works unfinished – not just the famous symphony, but songs, at least one uniquely promising string quartet and no fewer than ten piano sonatas?

There are no substantiated answers to these questions, though many more or less credible attempts have been made. Today, when sex is seen as the root of so many human problems, all those genial meetings in male society are inevitably seized on as evidence of homosexuality, the melancholy quality in his music as a product of its unhappy realization – or lack of it. The terms of endearment that he used in his letters, the ambivalence of comments about him by his acquaintances, and the gossipy hints dropped later in life by some of his less reliable associates have added fuel to what is a relatively unimportant fire. Of solid evidence pointing in one direction or the other there is very little, and any there is suggests that whatever its orientation Schubert's sexuality was probably a timid and fitful one.

With so much unknown, or (worse) guessed at, there has been an inevitable tendency to speculate and romanticize, and layers of myth and legend have had to be peeled away by those seeking the truth. The image has grown up of a jolly little man – like Richard Tauber in *Lilac Time* – a simple child of nature, adored by the artistic *cognoscenti* of Vienna, pouring out songs over the dinner-table, scribbling them down so fast on the back of a menu card that a week later he had forgotten them. It simply was not like that. In this book I have tried to present an objective picture of Schubert that avoids the pitfalls of romantic fantasy, and relies on evidence for which there appears to be a reliable source. And when memories from long after his death have to be quoted, at least I have given the reader fair warning.

A word about the numbering of Schubert's works. As with most composers, Schubert's published compositions were assigned opus numbers more or less in the order in which they were published. These numbers give no guide to the actual dates of composition, and in Schubert's case such a small number of important works were published during his lifetime that the list is misleading: 170-odd solo songs out of a total output of more than 600; a few part-songs; a handful of church music; the 'Wanderer' Fantasy, the *Moments musicaux* and about 150 assorted dances for solo piano, plus a good many of the more popular works for piano duet. But only two out of the eight impromptus, only three of the eleven completed piano sonatas (and not the last great three at that), two or three out of that magnificent list of chamber works, and none of the orchestral works at all.

Many of Schubert's most significant instrumental compositions, therefore, did

(page vi) 'Game of Ball at Atzenbrugg': detail from coloured etching by Ludwig Mohn (c. 1820) after a drawing by Franz von Schober (landscape and architecture) and Moritz von Schwind (figures). Schubert is sitting in shirt-sleeves in the centre foreground with a long pipe, Schober (with stock) to his right, Vogl (in hat) on his left.

not appear in print until long after his death, and then in a haphazard order (with haphazard opus numbers) which bore no relation to their true place in his creative life. This may have been partly responsible for the lack of understanding with which a number of his greatest works were received, and it certainly contributed to the chaotic muddle which existed where the chronology of his compositions was concerned. It was not until 1951 when, after years of dedicated research, the indefatigable Otto Erich Deutsch published the first edition of his *Schubert: A Thematic Catalogue of his Works* that this situation was finally rectified – and it says a great deal for the quality of Deutsch's work that very little amendment has been necessary as the result of more recent scholarship. Since then the opus numbers have become more or less redundant, and each of Schubert's individual works is best identified by its 'D' (Deutsch) number, which gives for almost all Schubert's compositions an accurate indication of its place in the chronological series. However, in order to avoid loading the text with too many intrusive figures, I have used D numbers only where a work's title is not sufficient to identify it precisely.

For similar reasons I have tried to reduce footnotes to a minimum, and again Deutsch has been the inevitable resource. Except where otherwise indicated, all quotations used in this book have been taken from *Schubert: A Documentary Biography* and *Schubert: Memoirs by his Friends*, published in London in 1946 and 1958 respectively.

Finally, it has been my good fortune to have been supervised by not only one but two splendid editors, Michael Rose and Jane Holloway, to whom I should like to extend my thanks.

M. R.

Himel Port Grundt

CHAPTER 1

The Early Years

(left) Schubert's birthplace: detail from the bird's-eye view of Vienna and its suburbs, 1769–74, by J. D. von Huber. Himmelpfortgrund is the main street running across the middle of the map, number 72 ringed.

Statistically it is a wonder that we have any music at all by a composer called Franz Peter Schubert: he was one of only five children to survive from the fourteen born to Franz Theodor Florian Schubert and Elisabeth Vietz between 1785 and 1801. Franz Theodor came from a family of Moravian country people, farmers, smallholders and woodsmen; Elisabeth was the daughter of a Silesian master locksmith. They met in Vienna where Franz Theodor was an assistant schoolmaster to his brother Karl. When Franz Peter, their twelfth child, was born on 31 January 1797, the family was living at 72 Upper High Street in the densely populated Himmelpfortgrund (Gate of Heaven) suburb of Vienna, his father by now a headmaster in his own right. No. 72 was a substantial building but it was made up of sixteen apartments, each with a kitchen and a single multi-purpose room. The Schuberts rented two of these apartments, but by day they had a further 200 occupants as two shifts of 100 boys crowded in for lessons at Franz Theodor's obviously thriving school. The house was later renumbered 54 Nussdorferstrasse. Either way it is less prosaically known as the Red Crayfish (Zum roten Krebsen). By the turn of the century demand for places at the school was such that bigger premises were sought and in 1801 the school and family moved to the nearby Säulengasse. It was here that young Franz Peter was given his own early education.

Remarkably, Schubert was the only notable composer of the so-called Viennese School to have been born in Vienna: Beethoven came from Bonn, Haydn from

Rohrau in Lower Austria and Mozart from Salzburg. (For the record, all three principal protagonists of the *second* Viennese School, Schoenberg, Berg and Webern,
were born in Vienna roughly a century later.) In the twentieth century the Viennese
musical audience has earned the reputation of being one of the most consistently
demanding – some would say discerning, others fickle. It is questionable whether
it was any different in Schubert's day.

At the time of Schubert's birth, Austria – along with most of Europe – was at
war with revolutionary France, fighting the armies of Napoleon Bonaparte both on
the Rhine and in Italy. Early in the year Napoleon crossed the Alps from Italy, took
Graz and appeared to be on the point of attacking Vienna itself. On Easter Monday
1797 the Austrian volunteer corps assembled in Vienna, drew strength and courage
from a mass celebrated on the parade ground, and marched, accompanied by military music, towards the enemy. Deutsch tells us that their route took them past
Schubert's birthplace and so, at the age of seventy-six days, Schubert experienced
his first public musical performance. As it happens there was no battle this time
and Napoleon signed the first of several peace treaties a few days later. He gained
the upper hand, however, twice during the following decade and the young Schubert
grew up in a city frequently at war, constantly changing hands, and yet indefatigably
Viennese.

One reason for this was the cosmopolitan make-up of the population: Germans,
Italians, Hungarians, Bohemians, Poles, Slovaks, Slovenes, Serbs, Croats and more,
a cross-section of the Habsburg empire. In general they mixed freely and happily,
and where you lived was determined more by your financial or social status than
your ethnic origin. The substantial Jewish population, living inevitably close to the
synagogues in the Leopoldstadt area, do not figure greatly in the artistic world into
which Schubert entered, though their influence on Viennese culture later in the
century was very much more significant.

Dangerous though it may be to generalize about national traits, the Viennese
have long had the reputation for a love of food and wine, or plain gluttony as a
Berliner, Christoph Friedrich Nicolai, visiting Vienna in 1781, described it. As a
patriotic Prussian he attributed this deplorable propensity to the Austrian mon-
archy, and to Catholicism, a religion 'all in show, lacking high culture and preoccu-
pied with sordid material matters with results that are worse than the paganism of
old'.[1] He further declared his Protestant fundamentalism by recording the general
stoutness of the citizens and the likelihood of their early death from apoplexy. Perhaps he was hardly the best person to recognize the extraordinary gastronomic
diversity available to a population made up from such promising origins: Viennese
cooking was as miraculously varied as it was profligate. The coffee-houses and inns
were places of both physical and intellectual succour and they were affordable not

only by the wealthy but also by the traditionally impoverished artistic aspirants. We know a good deal about Beethoven from his café life, rather less about Schubert, though for much of his adult life his evenings ended with a drink or coffee with friends.

The Viennese were easy-going in ways which contrasted greatly with many other societies at the end of the eighteenth century. Certainly they had little interest in disturbing the *status quo* or, more pertinently, in revolution. God was in place, not to be disturbed. The Catholic faith did nothing to challenge the existing order, clerical or lay. The empire flourished and could be counted on to run itself without interfering too much in the everyday life of most people. Politics rarely entered the thoughts of the Viennese as long as they were left to eat, drink and multiply. Only a few artistic lunatics sought to defy established mores. For sure, Joseph II had laid open the path to emancipation by embracing the modernity of the Age of Enlightenment, but his successors, Leopold II and Francis I, undid much of the good work and ensured the preservation of the old autocratic system of state.

The Vienna of 1797 was a mixture of twisting, narrow streets, full to the brim with humanity, and wide open spaces, palaces, castles and gardens roughly radiating inside or outside the defensive walls of the ancient city. It boasted eighteen churches and eight convents in the inner city and a further thirty churches and eight convents in the suburbs, the convents divided unequally between thirteen monasteries and three nunneries. Of more relevance to the adult Schubert was the existence of five theatres of which the most important were the Burgtheater (a theatre for spoken plays), the Kärntnerthor (an opera house with Italianate tendencies) and Schikaneder's creation, the Theater an der Wien – where Mozart's *Magic Flute* had been first performed. There were also various concert halls, among them those of the Philharmonic Society, the University and the Redoutensaal. Music and dance thrived both in the aristocratic ballroom and in the café. Domestic music-making was in the ascendancy. Concerts ranged from the monumental spectaculars for huge, popular audiences at the Hofberg to the intimate salons where musical amateurs (in the best sense) enjoyed an abundance of high-quality chamber music. Church music, particularly in the court chapel, maintained a degree of excellence and originality remarkable in an essentially complacent society. Literature, at least German literature, was only of moderate importance to most educated people; though Goethe's works were known to many at all social levels, poetry readings were confined to small groups of enthusiasts – and were often the focus of unwanted attention from the police, who (perhaps not entirely without foundation) regarded such gatherings as a source of mischief if not downright sedition.

It sounds like the kind of world in which the young Schubert might reasonably be expected to thrive, and be encouraged to develop the talent he showed in his early years. But such an assumption would fail to take into account the tyranny of Viennese etiquette and fashion. While the aristocracy could walk through the streets, join in popular festivities and mix daily with the general public, they nevertheless remained a closed elite, their privileged position as yet unopposed. Beethoven they were prepared to welcome into their midst because he stimulated them musically and, at one remove, romantically (possibly even intellectually), but there was no question of their embracing him as one of themselves. Schubert sought to be part neither of the aristocracy nor of fashionable society, but he dearly wished to gain the patronage of a wider artistic world than his own specialist circle. His mistake was in expecting to be accepted on his own terms.

To return to the infant Franz Peter: the family had by now moved round the corner to a house called the Black Horse in the Säulengasse, and here he both lived and studied, his father giving him a thorough grounding in the fundamentals of mathematics and literature, Latin and music. The position of headmaster offered little in the way of social standing or remuneration and Franz Theodor's sons were readily pressed into service in the school. Franz Peter's oldest brother, Ignaz, taught him the piano (or fortepiano as we now tend to call the early successor to the harpsichord); his father gave him his first violin lessons, while Michael Holzer, choirmaster at the Liechtental church, introduced him to the organ and gave instruction in singing, harmony and counterpoint, and general musicianship. At the age of ten he was first soprano in the choir, played the violin in the organ-loft and composed songs, string quartets and keyboard works. According to Ferdinand Schubert (another brother, older by two and a half years), Holzer is reputed to have said, 'If ever I tried to teach him something new he already seemed to know it. Frequently I just looked at him in amazement.'

Then in May 1808 an announcement appeared, advertising entrance examinations to fill two choristers' vacancies at the Imperial and Royal Court Chapel. Successful candidates would also receive a free education at the seminary attached to the chapel. This education might be continued free of charge if the boy demonstrated the right moral and intellectual fibre after his voice had broken, subject (of course) to imperial decree. The school was popularly known as the Konvikt, a far from sinister title coming from the Latin *convictorium* meaning a communal house, and was run by teachers in a holy order, the Pii Fratres or Piarists. It had the reputation of offering the finest education in Vienna. The opportunity was too good to miss and the eleven-year-old Schubert was presented for audition (for it seems only the musical part of the boy's potential was tested, certificates of progress in academic subjects and bodily health being deemed sufficient otherwise). His examiners included the seminary director Innocenz Lang and court musical director Antonio Salieri. (Whatever Salieri's achievements – and they include teaching Beethoven as

The seminary (Konvikt) attached to the Imperial and Royal Court Chapel, at which Schubert received his secondary education. Watercolour by Franz Gerasch.

well, in time, as Schubert – his popular copybook has always been blotted by his unfortunate rivalry with Mozart.) In the end three boys were admitted: an alto, Maximilian Weisse (who in adult life became a notable astronomer); and two sopranos, Franz Müllner and Franz Schubert. Most of the 130 boarders at the school came from army and civil service families and in comparison Schubert's background was pretty humble. He started badly by arriving for audition in a pale, almost white, coat which earned him the nickname of 'the miller'. However, there does not seem to have been any lasting animosity towards him, for there are no records of his being the victim of bullying or class distinction once he had started at the school.

Music flourished at the Konvikt and Schubert found himself in a world of church

Antonio Salieri, who did much to further Schubert's musical development both at the seminary and after he had left. Oil painting by an unknown artist.

services, regular practices, and daily performances by the orchestra which could be heard outside in the University Square where they attracted a large audience each evening. His early academic reports show good progress in all subjects: Religious Instruction, Latin, Greek, Mathematics, Natural History and Physics, Geography and History. He also gained good marks for application and morals and in his very first report (17 April 1809) Lang describes him as 'a musical talent'. Significant among his teachers was Wenzel Ruzicka, a viola player at the Burgtheater and court organist. He had established the seminary orchestra, which he conducted (later allowing Schubert to direct it as his deputy), and soon had Schubert among the first violins. He also taught him piano and organ and said of him, simply, 'He has learned it from God.' In fact Ruzicka had no obligation to do more than teach the piano at the seminary but a number of letters survive testifying to his zeal and enthusiasm in organizing extra-curricular activities. For this posterity must be thankful, because it was at this time that Schubert's musical development suddenly shot forward. There are the first real compositions including a song, 'Hagar's Lament', which not only shows that Schubert had been studying the works of Zum-steeg (one of the most influential and innovative song composers of the late eight-eenth century) but also gives a number of pointers to what might be described as Schubert's vocal trademarks over the next seventeen years.

Amongst the violinists in the seminary orchestra was Josef von Spaun, a law student nine years Schubert's senior, whose writings about him are of great biographical value. He would in due course introduce the young composer to many of those who were to play a significant role in both his personal and creative life, including Franz von Schober, the poet Mayrhofer and the singer Vogl. Another fellow violinist was Anton Holzapfel, who half a century later described the schoolboy Schubert as a 'short, stocky boy with a friendly, round face'. More pertinently, he recalled his friend's marked intellectual superiority, citing how Schubert presented him with a long ode which he had written in the style of Klopstock – a feat far beyond the capabilities of his classmates. Infuriatingly, Holzapfel confesses to having lost the poem, but what little survives of Schubert's other poetic writings does not suggest a potential Goethe. Holzapfel's memories of the orchestra include frequent performances of symphonies by Haydn and Mozart and the first two symphonies of Beethoven. It was an ambitious repertoire. Neither was chamber music neglected, for the quartets of Haydn and Mozart were also played. The young Schubert was getting an exemplary grounding.

It is almost impossible to give watertight dates for his early works, though it is surely more important to academics than to the general reader that they should be placed precisely in the catalogue. It is just as hard to date many of the events in Schubert's life. There is, for instance, some doubt as to exactly when he experienced his first opera. Most sources suggest that it was Spaun who introduced him to the medium, taking him at the age of fourteen to *Die Schweizerfamilie* (The Swiss Family), an opera by Joseph Weigl, at the Kärntnerthor in July 1811. Certainly Schubert was, around this time, smitten with the concept of opera, which became a major composing objective for the rest of his life and was the one in which he failed most miserably. Spaun had been struck immediately by Schubert's sense of commitment and exceptional musical talent. One day he came across the boy playing Mozart quietly by himself, and Schubert improvised a minuet for him on the spot: 'He blushed, but he liked my approval of his work. He confided in me that he often wrote down his musical ideas, but he was afraid his father might find out, so I was not to tell anyone.' From that time Spaun slipped Schubert the odd piece of manuscript paper and another debt of gratitude must be recorded.

The year 1812 found Napoleon overstretching himself in Russia and losing out to Wellington in Spain, so for the moment Vienna was able to drink its coffee, stroll in its woods and enjoy its music and drama with only the slightest wary glance over its shoulder. Schubert continued to do well at school and to dabble in composition. Suddenly disaster struck. On 28 May 1812 his mother died at the age of fifty-five, the cause of death being given as nervous fever. Scholars seem to agree that this was a euphemism for typhus abdominalis, the disease to which Schubert's own death is often attributed. Oddly enough, this is one of the very few facts we know about Schubert's mother. There are no pointers in extant letters (or even in the reminiscences of Schubert's schoolfriends later in life) to her character or personality, or indeed to what family traits she may have passed on to her son.

The death of his mother coincided with a watershed in Schubert's musical life. Within a month he began lessons in counterpoint with Antonio Salieri, something of an honour, for Salieri did not habitually take pupils so young. One or two of Schubert's exercises have survived and demonstrate the boy's diligence and ability in formal studies, and an understanding of the Italian style is evident from some early settings of Metastasio. Then on 26 July 1812 the words, 'Schubert, Franz, crowed for the last time', were written in Schubert's own hand at the end of an alto part of a mass composed by Peter Winter. The boy's voice had broken. This could have meant his immediate withdrawal from the seminary, but Schubert's grades in all subjects were good or very good and his place in the school was secure for as long as he maintained this standard of work.

We get a glimpse of what life was like for the young Schubert in a letter he wrote to one of his older brothers on 24 November of that year. It is his earliest surviving letter.

Straight out with what troubles me, and so I shall come to my purpose the sooner, and you will not be detained by any precious beating about the bush. I have long been thinking about my situation and found that, although it is satisfactory on the whole, it is not beyond some improvement here and there. You know from experience that we all like to eat a roll or a few apples sometimes, the more so if after a middling lunch one may not look for a miserable evening meal for eight and a half hours. This wish, which has often become insistent, is now becoming more and more frequent, and I had willy-nilly to make a change. The few groats I receive from Father go to the deuce the very first days, and what am I to do for the rest of the time? 'Whosoever believeth on Him shall not be put to shame.' Matthew, iii. 4. I thought so too.– How if you were to let me have a few Kreuzer a month? You would not so much as know it, while I in my cell should think myself lucky, and be content. I repeat, I lean upon the words of the Apostle Matthew, where he says: 'He that hath two coats, let him give one to the poor', &c. Meanwhile I hope that you will give ear to the voice that calls unceasingly to you to remember

Your

loving, poor, hopeful

and again poor brother

Franz.

It is probably no different from hundreds of begging letters sent from young lads away at boarding-school to older brothers who had found employment and apparent wealth. Nor does the letter suggest that the Konvikt was more unpleasant than any other institution of its day. True, back in 1809, Schubert is reported to have referred to it as a prison, but there is no doubt that the seminary provided him with considerable opportunities to further his musical ambitions, which would not have been the case had he remained at home. Franz Theodor had only one ambition for his son, that he should become an assistant schoolmaster in his own school.

But the diligence and devotion which Schubert had been lavishing on all his scholastic activities began to wane (and whether incorrect identification of the Biblical quotations in the letter was a genuine slip or a deliberate ploy to gain greater sympathy is open to conjecture). Something had to go. How else can he have found the time to write so many musical works, and of such diversity? From 1811 and 1812 there survive orchestral overtures, the first movement of a symphony, parts of a *Singspiel* (an opera with spoken dialogue), church music, part-songs, chamber music including string quartets, a little music for the keyboard, and (prophetically) songs.

Hearing for the first time, say, an early quartet or songs such as 'Der Vatermörder' (The Parricide) or either setting of 'Der Geistertanz' (The Ghost's Dance) it would be easy to dismiss them as nothing more than the promising attempts of a gifted teenager, and compare them unfavourably with the more accomplished youthful works of Mozart or the astonishingly mature and wholly inspired creations of the adolescent Mendelssohn. Perhaps that is fair in the case of the early quartets, for Schubert may well have been daunted by the works of Haydn and Mozart in this genre, which were certainly formidable models to emulate. There is promise in the evocative brooding quality to the opening movement of the Quartet D18, which hints at the pent-up energy of the A minor Quartet of 1824, but it is unfulfilled in the succeeding movements (and, indeed, in the next few quartets, despite their abundantly experimental nature and glimpses of genuine Schubertian melody). Schubert had not yet reached the point where he could be judged on equal terms with Haydn or Mozart and he plainly had a long way to go to catch up with Beethoven who had by then completed eleven quartets (the six of op. 18, the three 'Razumovsky' Quartets, op. 59, plus opp. 74 and 95). In some ways he never did catch up with him.

Compared with the chamber music scene, song-writing before 1812 was a far less advanced art. Essentially there were two kinds of song: simple repetitive (strophic) songs which used the same music for each verse in the manner of folk-songs or hymns; and the more extended ballad type which resembled an opera scene or cantata in miniature, the music changing to illustrate the words as the tale unfolds.

Folk-song, for the most part, fell into the former category and so did a high proportion of the hundreds of songs influenced by the giant of German literature, Johann Wolfgang von Goethe. He approved of music, encouraged the marriage of words and music, but held very strong views about how this was to be achieved. His ideal was that the composer should find a tune which would fit each verse of the poem, match the general mood and tone, but leave it to the performer to add expression or nuance. The most obvious parallel is with the singing of hymns where the tune is repeated, unaltered verse after verse, save perhaps for an occasional change in the dynamics, one verse louder, another softer.

For example, the first musical version of Goethe's famous poem 'The Erl-King' (Erlkönig) was made by the actress, singer and composer Corona Schröter. She created the title role in Goethe's Singspiel *Die Fischerin* in 1782 and composed this setting to open the play. It is a charming little tune of which Goethe heartily approved, but one has to say its lilting melody would be no less appropriate to a song about skipping lambs or daffodils in spring than it is to Goethe's blood-curdling tale of infanticide.

The narrative or dramatic ballad was the province, mainly, of Johann Rudolf Zumsteeg, Johann Friedrich Reichardt and a host of others whose work the young Schubert either aped or at least used as a model. Until recently these composers have been very much confined to the university library and lecture theatre, some of Haydn's canzonets and a few of Mozart's *Lieder* being the only late eighteenth-century songs heard frequently in the concert hall. With the burgeoning of authentic

Anna Kleyenböck, Schubert's stepmother, who married Franz Theodor in April 1813 when the composer was 16. Drawing by Moritz von Schwind.

Franz Theodor Florian Schubert, the composer's father: oil painting by Karl Schubert.

performance, however, and the restoration of the fortepiano to popular acceptance, singers (at least those with enquiring minds) are exploring this repertoire, giving us a welcome opportunity to put German song as a whole into a wider context, and thus helping us to reassess the early Schubert songs and perhaps to realize that even his first efforts were the equal of any but the very best of Zumsteeg. Many of them are bloodthirsty, some of them ramble a bit, several are incomplete, but they display a directness and ready identification with the drama of the poetry and already demand that essential quality in the singer of Schubert songs: an understanding that it is absolutely necessary to approach the song through the words, and that it is not enough merely to get round the notes. Above all, we see emerging a quality of keyboard writing which requires the player to be as sensitive to the meaning of the text as the singer.

On the eve of his sixteenth birthday, 30 January 1813, we find Schubert the seminarist awarded a 'Meerfeld Endowment for impecunious youths of good family', enabling him to remain at the Konvikt. This endowment (originally established for orphans) required the holder to recite a rosary for the founder and his family once a month and to confess and take communion on the anniversary of Meerfeld's death. There is no record of how seriously Schubert took his obligations.

The other important event in the early part of that year occurred on 25 April when Schubert's father, now aged forty-nine, remarried. His twenty-nine-year-old bride, Anna Kleyenböck, was one of four daughters of a silk manufacturer; she was clearly fond of her step-family, and in years to come she would be prepared to raid her housekeeping money more than once to provide a loan for Franz Peter when he was in need of help. A few days after the wedding Schubert composed a poem:

TIME

Unrelenting does she fly,
Once departed, never tarrying.
Thee, O fair companion of our days,
To our resting place we shall be carrying.

But a breath! – for such is Time.
Let this breath sing worthy measures.
To the throne of justice go thou forth,
Voicing songs of virtue's heav'nly treasures!

But a sound! – for such is Time.
Let this sound be music's treasure.
To the seat of mercy go thou forth,
Pouring out repentance without measure.

Unrelenting does she fly,
Once departed, never tarrying.
Thee, O fair companion of our days,
To our resting-place we shall be carrying.

The mature Schubert is already discernible in several of the songs of this period, one of which is 'Verklärung' (Transfiguration). The words are from Alexander Pope's *The Dying Christian to his Soul* translated into German by J. G. Herder, and though the poem dates from 1730 the sentiment is very much in keeping with one of the great romantic ideals, that death is infinitely preferable to the vicissitudes of life, physical or artistic. Schubert, with the eagerness of youth, plunges straight in with a forceful instruction to death to take over the soul. Then in a passage of extraordinary repose, belying the composer's sixteen years, angels whisper to the spirit, 'Come to your rest'. I find it impossible to agree with commentators who have suggested that Schubert at this age had no emotional identification with death. How many composers of any age would have the boldness and confidence to dismiss the Grave and its Victory, Death and its Sting, in a mere twelve notes for the singer punctuated by five brief chords in the accompaniment?

The concentration and conciseness of 'Verklärung' is in complete contrast to another song begun in September 1813, 'Der Taucher' (The Diver). It is a huge ballad in the Zumsteeg tradition, rarely heard even today because it takes over twenty minutes to sing and requires the vocal artistry and stamina of an accomplished opera singer. Several versions of the song exist, which is interestingly the case with a good many songs throughout Schubert's brief composing life – early evidence to refute the idea that he simply dashed off music as it came into his head and then abandoned it if he got stuck. 'Der Taucher' is a poem by Friedrich von Schiller, a poet whom Schubert was to set more than forty times. Schiller frequently presented Schubert with the problem of finding music for an abstract idea, and later on it was to take him several attempts to arrive at the definitive versions of such great Schiller songs as 'Gruppe aus dem Tartarus' and 'Das Geheimnis'. In 'Der Taucher', however, the story is straightforward enough and Schubert's revisions were made more to pace the drama than for any intellectual subtlety. The diver is a noble youth who risks plunging into a whirlpool to retrieve a golden goblet hurled by the king. There are ferocious musical descriptions of the action and vivid portrayals of submarine horrors until the last time when the youth fails to return. Opera has been condensed for the drawing-room, and in the ballad tradition 'Der Taucher' must be accorded an honourable place.

As 1813 progressed there was for the first time a deterioration in one or two of the scholastic grades achieved by Schubert. It had been proposed that he should be awarded another endowment, but correspondence during September and October between the seminary authorities and the emperor, no less, states that a further year's tenure would only be granted on condition that Schubert rose above the second rank after the vacation and did not relapse at the next examination, 'since singing and music are but a subsidiary matter, while good morals and diligence in study are of prime importance and an indispensable duty for all those who wish to enjoy the advantages of an Endowment'.

The surviving documentation is unfortunately patchy, but it would appear that Schubert was, indeed, offered a further endowment. Then a government decree to the directorate of the seminary on 23 November 1813 includes the words, 'Franz Schubert having renounced the Meerfeld Endowment', confirming that Schubert himself had turned it down. Under quite what circumstances he did this is not clear, nor is it known precisely when he left. Schubert's friend Spaun reported that Schubert used all his school preparation time for composition and that his father disapproved strongly. Salieri, on the other hand, was willing to testify on Schubert's behalf in the debate about whether or not to offer him a further year's funding. We can only assume that the young man had decided for himself that further residence at the seminary would simply get in the way of his composition and that he would stand a better chance if he threw in his lot with the schoolmastering career on which his father insisted. He remained on cordial terms with Salieri and continued to take lessons with him for a further three years. But for the academic year 1813–14 Franz Peter Schubert attended the teacher training college (Normal-Hauptschule) in the Annagasse, living at home with his father and new stepmother.

Yet 1813 should not be allowed to disappear without mention of 28 October, the date on which Schubert wrote '*Finis et fine*' at the end of his first completed symphony, in D major (D82). It has never been part of the standard orchestral repertoire, but it is worth seeking out in its own right and not merely as an exercise in preparation for the 'Unfinished' and 'Great' C major Symphonies. Schubert had learned his orchestral music from practical experience as a player. The students in the Konvikt orchestra had tackled not only works by the great masters, but also those of many lesser figures as well. The players were no doubt talented youngsters, but not so able technically that they could make light of badly written or inappropriate scoring, and Schubert quickly came to assess from the music he found before him, what would work and what would not. It is interesting to note that the manuscript of the symphony contains a number of detailed alterations of a kind which suggest that Schubert actually heard the work performed (very probably by his Konvikt companions) and that he was then able to obtain more readily the effect he heard in his head.

If the chamber music of the period is less successful than this symphony it is no less innovative, and we see Schubert prepared to experiment, unafraid to make mistakes at a time when he could safely learn from them. The one complaint which might reasonably be levelled at some of these early instrumental works could also be applied to one or two later pieces: Dvořák summed it up many years afterwards as 'Prolixity; he does not know when to stop.'

CHAPTER 2

1813–15

It might be thought that by leaving the seminary Schubert would have lost touch with the friends he had made there and with the artistic world to which it offered an opening. This was not the case. In particular, Spaun remained a close friend and frequent companion, in spite of the difference in their ages. They went to the opera together and saw, amongst other things, Mozart's *Magic Flute*, Cherubini's *Medea*, and Gluck's *Iphigénie en Tauride*. Inevitably, in our tabloid age, the exact nature of Schubert's relationship with the older Spaun is questioned, and an early opportunity may as well be taken to dispose of the matter of Schubert's sexuality.

The plain fact is that we do not have enough safe evidence to make an outright judgement. We will soon encounter the only woman apparently seriously to have won Schubert's heart, Therese Grob, and there was at least one other female infatuation about which we can be reasonably sure. Spaun eventually married, as did a number of Schubert's close friends, even Schober and Schwind, though that in itself proves nothing. Nor can any conclusions be drawn from the fact that Schubert often shared a room with his male companions. His friends wrote or spoke about him, clearly with affection, but also (during his lifetime) with utter discretion. Much seems to hinge on the interpretation of words such as 'intimate' used long after Schubert's death. For instance, Anton Holzapfel writes in 1858:

In the same way I think I must draw your attention to Schubert's intimate relation-

Josef von Spaun, the most loyal of Schubert's friends: a caricature by Moritz von Schwind.

ships with the singer, Vogl, and with the poet and censorship official, Mayrhofer, because both of them, especially Vogl, exercised a great influence on Schubert, though it would be difficult for anyone except Herr von Spaun to supply information about this.

Yet this is after he has discoursed quite freely on Schubert's love for Therese Grob. And there is ambivalence in another of Holzapfel's statements: 'Schober's equivocal moral behaviour was not entirely unknown to me, though I know nothing about his influence on Schubert.'

Anselm Hüttenbrenner in a letter, also of 1858, comments, 'Towards the fair sex he was boorish and, consequently, anything but gallant.' He goes on to relate what he knows of Schubert's affection for Therese and its failure, summing it up with the remark, 'From that time, when he saw his dearest one lost for ever, he had a dominating aversion for the daughters of Eve.' But with so many of these post-humous accounts there are fundamental errors of detail that seriously undermine their reliability. Hüttenbrenner, for instance, described Schubert's love as 'a teacher's daughter from the country' who 'is said to have submitted to her father's wishes and married someone else'. If this was Therese Grob, and all other evidence points to her, then her father was already dead at the time she knew Schubert and her mother was the prosperous owner of a Viennese silk-weaving business. Most of these comments were collected by Ferdinand Luib in the late 1850s with a view to publishing a biography of Schubert. In the end this never appeared, but much of his somewhat suspect material was used by Heinrich Kreissle in a large volume published in 1865, and his interpretation of the 'facts' encouraged others to fantasize even further. This source apart, we are still left with a few titillating fragments from which much has been extrapolated: a letter from Schober to Bauernfeld in 1869, for example, discloses – or rather, fails to disclose:

There is a sort of love-story of Schubert's which I believe not a soul knows, as I am the only one in the secret and I have told it to nobody; I would willingly have passed it on to you and left you to decide how much of it was suitable for publication and in what way, but of course it is too late now.

There are reports, again dating from after Schubert's death, of an amorous fling with a maidservant on the Esterházy estate in 1818 which gave way to 'a more poetic flame which sprang up in his heart for the younger daughter of the house, Countess Karoline. This flame continued to burn until his death. Karoline had the greatest

Therese Grob, Schubert's first (and possibly, only) love, in later life: oil painting by Heinrich Hollpein.

Contemporary illustration of a scene from the final version of Beethoven's opera Fidelio: *Schubert attended the first performance in 1814 at the Kärntnerthor theatre.*

regard for him and for his talent but she did not return his love.'[2] Spaun, who was the most faithful of Schubert's friends and who knew him longest, gives nothing away, and criticizes Kreissle's book for suggesting that while Schubert was 'eaten up with love for the young Countess Esterházy he was secretly interested in someone else on the side'. 'I ask, what is the point of such gossip?' wrote Spaun, and it is difficult not to agree with him. Until more contemporary documentary evidence is produced we can only speculate. The music itself certainly gives no clue.

Schubert's visits to the opera inspired him to attempt one of his own. He started it in October 1813 while he was still at school, obviously with the approval of Salieri, and completed its three acts by May of the following year. Salieri suggested improvements and the revised version of *Des Teufels Lustschloss* (The Devil's Pleasure-House) was ready on 22 October 1814. It set a pattern for almost all Schubert's theatrical works in that, so far as we know, it was never performed in his lifetime. In May 1814 Schubert visited the Kärntnerthor theatre for the first performance of the final version of Beethoven's *Fidelio*, one of the very few operas in the German language to gain lasting acceptance in German-speaking countries. Though Schubert tried several times to add a German opera of his own to the standard repertoire he failed hopelessly, often falling foul of theatrical politics, though what survives does not suggest that he ever found a suitable plot nor that he acquired the stagecraft to handle it. It was said (after Schubert's death) by Moritz von Schwind that Schubert had to sell his school books in order to attend that performance of *Fidelio*. As Schwind did not meet Schubert until the 1820s his story cannot be wholly relied upon, though it might possibly have some relevance to the training college report of Schubert's examination in August 1814 which shows a smattering of 'moderates' among the 'goods' and one 'bad' – for religion!

May also saw the start of composition of a Mass in F major (D105), not the first in this key but the first to be completed. It was the first of Schubert's works to be performed in public. In October 1814 Schubert's parish church of Liechtental celebrated its centenary. It was at the mass on Friday 16 October that the seventeen-year-old composer directed the new work; his brother Ferdinand played the organ and the soprano solo was sung by Therese Grob. A second performance was given ten days later in another church and it is thought Therese was again the soloist.

What is equally likely is that the congregation contained a number of foreigners visiting the city for the Congress of Vienna. Over the next nine months diplomats from the allied states were engaged in redrawing the map of Europe for the post-Napoleonic era (though, as it happens, Napoleon made an unexpected comeback halfway through, and the battle of Waterloo was yet to be fought). By the final settlement in 1815, Austria built up considerable territory in northern Italy. That the removal of the French threat afforded Francis I and his chief minister, Prince Metternich, the opportunity to consolidate their repressive regime at home – and indeed to become champions of reaction in Europe – was not yet of significance to the youthful Schubert. Rather more important to him was the esteem in which his father now held him following the success of this mass. So proud was he that he obtained a five-octave fortepiano from the Viennese maker, Konrad Graf, an instrument which was to play a significant role in influencing his son's taste in piano sound and writing for the piano, both in terms of sheer volume and the subtleties of tone quality. Later in life Schubert wrote of the deplorable 'chopping' action of contemporary pianists: several accounts of Schubert's own delicacy of touch at the keyboard survive, and the piano works themselves reflect this refinement.

Before coming to the two other particularly important events of 1814 we should allow ourselves a moment with one of the earliest of the Schubert string quartets which finds a place in today's repertoire, and is frequently performed at that, the one in B flat (D112). It was Schubert's habit to date many of his manuscripts as he

Mälzels Metronom ♩· = 72.

Gretchen am Spinnrade.

Aus Göthe's Faust.

wrote works or even individual movements, and this quartet was apparently begun on 5 September 1814 and completed on the 13th; at the end of the first movement he added the words, 'Finished in $4\frac{1}{2}$ hours'. You may believe that if you wish, though it seems likely that that was how long it took to write down the final version from a sketch or ideas that had been floating about for rather longer. Certainly Schubert could compose with amazing speed, apparently untroubled by the noise and activity around him. For there was little peace and quiet to be had in a crowded schoolhouse by day and – after the birth of Schubert's half-sister, Josefa Theresia in April 1815 – presumably very little at night either.

The B flat Quartet is a work of charm and beauty from the very outset with its singing violin solo, which Alfred Einstein calls 'genuine Schubert'. And his phrase, 'bucolic in a melancholy kind of way', so perfectly summing up much of Schubert's jollier music at this time, is certainly appropriate to the Minuet. But suddenly, as Westrup says, 'the Finale of this quartet is unlike any other composer's work and unlike anything that Schubert himself had written earlier ... We begin to suspect that we are hearing a ghostly premonition of the Scherzo of the C major Symphony.'[3] The boy has become a man.

Opening page of the first edition of 'Gretchen am Spinnrade', the first great art-song. The repetitive, 'spinning' nature of the piano-writing is apparent even from its look on the page.

The Devil's Pleasure-House, the mass and quartet had taken up a good deal of Schubert's available free time during 1814. He completed his teacher's course at the training college and began, reluctantly, to teach in his father's school. It is hardly surprising therefore that few other works were attempted. There are, however, thirteen song settings of poems by Friedrich von Matthisson, the first contemporary poet to inspire the young composer, which are significant in showing how far Schubert had come in developing an independent role for the piano accompaniment in conveying the meaning of the text.

So by this time the groundwork was already done for Schubert's first Goethe setting, 'Gretchen am Spinnrade' (Gretchen at the Spinning-Wheel) [CD1]. This

Johann Baptist Mayrhofer, arguably the best of the poets amongst Schubert's artistic circle, and a great influence on Schubert's development. Detail from 'A Schubert Evening at Josef von Spaun's' by Moritz von Schwind, 1868.

great song has had all manner of epoch-making claims made for it, and there is no denying its genius or vividly unsettling imagery. Nevertheless, in the history of music, the song's importance lies in the nature of the piano part, which John Reed aptly describes as 'a musical metaphor'.[4] The piano part *is* the song. Gretchen sits in her room spinning and bewailing her fate, having given herself to Faust only to become the abandoned mother of his child. The piano literally spins a repetitive, circular figure which gives an instant impression of the scene and mood before a note is sung. It gives impetus to the song, an inevitability that drives towards the moment at which Gretchen remembers 'Ah, sein Küss!' (Ah, his kiss!). Her pain is such that she stops spinning. The piano stops for that moment, too. In doing nothing it has conveyed more meaning than any positive action could have done. She sinks back into her spinning, her heart heavy, her peace gone. It is the first modern German song.

Goethe would have disapproved strongly of Schubert's song (and did so when it was sent to him with other settings of his poems in 1816) for many reasons. For a start it was 'through composed': that is, not a succession of identical verses but with a melody and accompaniment which develop in a linear fashion as the song progresses. Then Schubert had taken the liberty of repeating Goethe's opening words at the end of the song, thus rewriting the poem. The effect is to complete the circle, emphasizing the ceaseless and remorseless grip of Gretchen's situation. Finally, Goethe would not have condoned the independence of that piano part and, in particular, the manner in which it adds to the substance of the text. It is more than merely interpreting the text, it is lifting it on to another plane. Schubert went on to write seventy-four songs to Goethe texts, many of them among his greatest. 'Gretchen am Spinnrade' is, then, more than just a remarkable song in its own right, it marks the beginning of an important part of Schubert's *oeuvre*.

The other important event of 1814 took place in December when Spaun introduced Schubert to Johann Mayrhofer. Schubert had recently set Mayrhofer's poem 'Am See' (By the Lake); this was the first of forty-seven Mayrhofer settings made over the next ten years, among which are a great many wonderful songs. Mayrhofer and Spaun had been childhood acquaintances at Steyr in Upper Austria and in 1810, after four years of clerking at the monastery of St Florian, Mayrhofer moved to Vienna to study law. He took his law seriously and in 1820 became a censor at the central book censorship office, which must have caused a good deal of consternation within Schubert's liberal-minded artistic fraternity. Mayrhofer was a gloomy individual and much of his poetry reflected his saturnine character (though he also delighted in practical jokes – clearly a man of opposites). He saw the real world as depressingly dark and forbidding, and believed that only death could free the true artist from it, or the prospect of death make it bearable. This longing for an ideal world, *Sehnsucht*, features in much German romantic writing, not only Mayrhofer's, but when Schubert first left home he spent many hours in Mayrhofer's company and came very much under his influence. Later Schubert lodged with him and, though the cordiality of their friendship waned in 1824, Mayrhofer's encapsulation of the conflict between spiritual idealism and the mundane remained with Schubert until his death. For the record, 'Am See' is not wholly successful, a long and rather uneven song commemorating the drowning of the Duke of Brunswick.

It was also in December 1814 that Schubert began work on his Second Symphony, and it took him only sixteen days (or, rather, *nights* for Schubert's day was occupied with instructing the young) to complete the first movement. After a slow introduction, this movement enjoys a gloriously carefree violin melody contrasted with a more sustained theme which reappears some years later in the so-called 'Quartettsatz' (Quartet Movement) in C minor (D703), a classic of the string quartet repertoire. This was not the first time Schubert re-used his melodies, nor was it to be the last.

The symphony was not finished until March 1815 but this was not through idleness. For a start there was the complication of love. Holzapfel admits to having lost a letter from Schubert written at the beginning of the year in which he professed his love for Therese Grob. Neither does Holzapfel's reply survive but he claims to have tried to put his friend off, though we do not know why. He later described Therese as 'not by any means a beauty, but well shaped, fairly buxom, with a fresh, childlike little round face and a fine soprano voice'. Schubert in love was writing songs at a phenomenal rate, at least 145 in the year. Add to that yet another symphony, four dramatic works, two full-scale masses and a number of smaller sacred pieces, many part-songs, a string quartet in G minor, two piano sonatas (neither complete) and a few keyboard dances and his total output during 1815 is over 200 works, more than one every two days! He also found time to visit Salieri for tuition twice a week. The symphony, no. 3 in D major, was mostly dashed off in a couple of weeks in July, yet for all that there is nothing casual or careless about its joyful vigour and sheer verve.

Some of the smaller church pieces were written for Therese and there are soprano solo parts in both masses, in G major and B flat, which were undoubtedly intended for her. Hüttenbrenner's not altogether reliable memoirs give an account of her singing, along with a further view of Schubert's love for her:

During a walk which I took with Schubert into the country, I asked him if he had never been in love. As he was so cold and unforthcoming towards the fair sex at parties, I was almost inclined to think he had a complete aversion for them. 'Oh no!' he said, 'I loved someone very dearly and she loved me too. She was a schoolmaster's daughter, somewhat younger than myself and in a Mass, which I composed, she sang the soprano solos most beautifully and with deep feeling. She was not exactly pretty and her face had pock-marks; but she had a heart of gold. For three years she hoped I would marry her; but I could not find a position which would have provided for us both. She then bowed to her parents' wishes and married someone else, which hurt me very much. I still love her and there has been no one else since who has appealed to me as much or more than she. She was just not meant for me.'[5]

In all this welter of emotional and creative activity there is one musical category that appears for the first time in the list of Schubert's works. Given the significance of the piano sonata in the output of Haydn, Mozart and Beethoven, it is perhaps surprising that Schubert did not attempt a work in the form earlier than 1815. Unfortunately his first two sonatas set a trend: they were unfinished. For at least a century after his death Schubert's piano sonatas were largely ignored by concert pianists.

They were not regarded as 'pianistic' and they suffered from comparison with Beethoven's; they were too difficult for too little show. Happily this view has not prevailed and Schubert sonata cycles are now an accepted part of the recital repertoire. The problem for the pianist is in deciding exactly how many of the unfinished sonatas to include. Some, the so-called 'Reliquie' (D840) for example, stand as they are as successfully as the 'Unfinished' Symphony or Quartettsatz. A number of editors and players have made plausible completions of movements started and then abandoned in full flow, but even this process cannot provide us with complete sonatas in the case of the E major (D157), or the C major (D279), as neither has a Finale – though that is not to say that what does exist is not well worth hearing.

It is a fact of late twentieth-century life that few people make music domestically for entertainment. The satisfaction to be obtained by a group of friends singing madrigals or part-songs can be immense but, with notable exceptions, they are rarely audience pieces. For that reason few of the Schubert part-songs (and there are well over 100) are known to any but *aficionados*. From 1815 alone there is a huge variety, from predictably rowdy drinking songs to unusual settings of the poets Hölty and Körner for two voices and two horns. Both poets were prominent amongst Schubert's 1815 solo song settings as well.

As John Reed remarks, 'There is an emotional ambiguity in Hölty's poetry, a bitter-sweet quality which in many ways resembles Schubert's own attitude to nature and love.' The best-known Hölty setting is 'Seligkeit' (Bliss) of 1816, but the 1815 songs are worth the attention of the serious singer, not least 'An die Nachtigall' (To the Nightingale), D196, and 'Seufzer' (Sigh). The other poets he set in 1815 were Kosegarten (rather ordinary songs to rather ordinary texts, with the exception of 'Die Mondnacht' [The Moonlit Night], which is intimately rapturous), Gabriele von Baumberg (a poetess, with 'An die Sonne' [To the Sun], perhaps the pick of a small crop), Klopstock (particularly the powerful and operatic 'Dem Unendlichen' [To the Infinite One], with its imposing recitative and long-breathed main melody over a rippling accompaniment – a song only for strong voices!), Schiller, Ossian and Goethe.

Friedrich von Schiller was, in Schubert's day, compulsory study for all German speakers with the slightest interest in literature. 'That he was a great man is clear, or he would not have been so taken up by Goethe,' wrote Richard Capell, who goes on to sum up Schubert's identification with his verse: 'And again and again we see the musician returning to the charge – only to be put off by something in Schiller that was prosaic and frigid. What indeed is a Schubertian to say if not that Schiller seems, on the strength of the song-books, to miss the lyrical note?'[6] None of the 1815 Schiller settings does anything to contradict Capell, though the dramatic element is fully present in several songs. The curious are directed to 'An die Freude', Schiller's

'Ode to Joy', a poem made rather more famous in the Finale of Beethoven's 'Choral Symphony of 1822–4. That the melody of Schubert's song with chorus is not unlike parts of Beethoven's chorus is not entirely coincidental. Schubert, as we know, was familiar with, and greatly admired, a number of Beethoven's works. Beethoven's attempts to set the ode had been around in his sketchbooks for thirty years before they reached final form in the Ninth Symphony, and Reed suggests that Schubert may have taken part in performances of Beethoven's Choral Fantasy, op. 80, where an early version of the Ninth Symphony tune makes a first tentative appearance.

Ossian provides a pleasant diversion. In 1759 the first 'Ossianic' fragment, 'The Death of Oscar', had appeared and was followed the year after by further *Ancient Poetry, Collected in the Highlands of Scotland, and Translated from the Galic or Erse Language*. Their 'translator' was James Macpherson, son of a farmer from near Kingussie, and he was encouraged to tour widely in Scotland in search of more material, rumours abounding that a Gaelic epic existed. Sure enough, in 1762 *Fingal, an Ancient Epic Poem, in Six Books* was produced, Macpherson having 'faithfully' translated an epic by Ossian, son of Finn (or Fingal). Home interest was enormous, while on the continent the praise of Klopstock, Schiller and Goethe gave Ossian considerable standing. Goethe quoted Ossian in *The Sorrows of Young Werther* and Napoleon added his weight to the supporters. The works remained popular for at least the first part of the nineteenth century, even after 1805 when an investigative committee appointed after Macpherson's death found them to be an elaborate, if very well constructed, fraud. Schubert, always eager for tales of ruined castles, blasted heaths and treacherous cliffs, embraced Ossian as he did Klopstock and Schiller, and ten songs or fragments survive from 1815–17.

It is a song of September 1815, 'Cronnan', which stands out for me amongst the Ossian songs. Schubert sets this long *scena* in music that is coldly atmospheric, with a slowly swirling accompaniment representing the threatening waves of mist rolling over the heath. What follows is a lengthy dialogue between a returning soldier and his loved one's ghost, at the end of which the opening music returns with chilling effect, the more disturbing for the use of the moderator* on the fortepiano.

So to Goethe. It is difficult to date all the songs but there are at least twenty Goethe settings from 1815, some of them mediocre, many workmanlike or better, while two are gems, 'Heidenröslein' (The Hedge-Rose) and 'Erlkönig' (The Erl-King). The poem about the wild rose may be Goethe's but it is based on an older folk-song, the boy threatening to pick the rose, the rose replying that it would prick

---

*A mechanical device not only for producing a quieter sound, but a thinner, sometimes more bell-like tone. The *una corda* (left pedal) of a modern grand piano does not produce the same effect.

the boy. The boy picks the rose, the rose pricks the boy. Simple, moralistic and loaded with sexual overtones. Schubert's genius was in composing an art-song which sounds for all the world like a folk-song. You could whistle the tune, and many who do will genuinely believe it is a folk-song, and you could hum it, but it requires considerable vocal artistry and technique to put it over as a simple song under concert conditions. All too often it is coy and coquettish and the audience is made to feel distinctly uncomfortable.

On the other hand the audience *should* feel distinctly uncomfortable in 'Erlkönig'. As in 'Heidenröslein', the story is old, Danish in origin. The Danish *eller-konge* is king of the elves. In translation to *Erlkönig* he has become king of the alders, but he is no less malignant, haunting the Black Forest and luring people, especially children, to their deaths.

After Corona Schröter's setting of the poem in 1782 (Goethe's own favourite), little progress in its musical elaboration had been made by later composers: the forty or so versions that have survived only serve to emphasize the gulf that lies between these very ordinary settings and Schubert's most *extraordinary* one. It is not known precisely when Schubert wrote 'Erlkönig', but the autumn of 1815 is pretty certain and October likely. Albert Stadler in 1858 says that it was written 'in his parents' house in the second half of 1815'. The song derives its energy and its terror from an insistent beating accompaniment in the right hand. This usually consists of rapid triplets in octaves, which very few pianists, even today, can play reliably and evenly, and many have had to find ways of giving the illusion of playing them. In fact a fair copy was made in 1816 to be sent to Goethe. It has *duplet* quavers in the right hand and is the version Schubert himself is thought to have used. It is just as powerful because of the extra tension created between these duplets and the triplet figure in the bass. The other unusual feature of the song is that almost the whole poem is written in direct speech, only the opening scene – father and son riding through the stormy night – and the very end, when the father, reaching home, discovers that the boy is dead, are plain narrative. So three voices have to be conjured up. The singer has to be able clearly to define all three or the song fails to communicate with the audience, but Schubert does a great deal to help. For instance, as the father first speaks, asking his son why he hides his face, the accompaniment, though riding on through the night at the same furious pace, is reduced just to a single note in octaves. When the boy replies, 'Do you not see the Erl-King there?' the restlessness recurs in the piano writing with a suitably diminished chord on the word 'Erlkönig'. The father tries to reassure him that it is only the mist, and the accompaniment returns to the simplicity of single notes. Then the demon speaks, enticing the child with games, and the accompaniment becomes naive in the manner of a popular song. Each time the child cries out thereafter it is a semitone above the piano

(right) Johann Wolfgang von Goethe: oil painting by Josef Stieler, 1828. As a major poet Goethe was unusual in approving the setting of his words to music. However, he had very strict views on how this was to be done, and Schubert never gained his approval during his own lifetime.

accompaniment, creating tremendous tension. The Erl-King next tempts the boy with his daughters and their dancing to rocking triplets in the right hand. Only when the monster says that he will take the boy by force does he get powerful repeated chords to reinforce his will. The child having been taken, to the most anguished accompaniment, the father rides on, the pace of the music increasing as he races home. As he finds the boy dead in his arms the music subsides, the father's utter dismay symbolized by the device of unaccompanied recitative. The song, composed by a young man of eighteen, has lost none of its power to disturb an audience in nearly 200 years.

CHAPTER 3

1816–18

If Schubert's brothers could afford to marry, it seems strange that Franz could not. Like his brothers, he was earning a teacher's salary even if it was at a very low grade, and in April 1816 he attempted to improve his circumstances by applying for a music master's post at the German Normal School in Laibach, capital of the Austrian crown land of Carniola (now Ljubljana). His application was supported by a testimonial from Salieri which carried much weight: 'Since it is Salieri himself who also examined the remaining applicants for this post, his judgement greatly honours Schubert.'[7] Despite such distinguished sponsorship he did not succeed.

Perhaps if he had been appointed, with a salary considerably in excess of his pittance as an assistant in his father's school, Therese might have married him. Maybe he would have settled to teaching the one subject he enjoyed. Following his rejection for the post, however, he seems to have made up his mind to abandon teaching and attempt to earn his living as a composer, a very brave decision – or a very foolish one, for in early nineteenth-century Vienna it was hardly possible to survive solely on composition. Schubert had not yet had a work published; there was no immediate prospect of that happening; there was no system of royalties paid on performances; he was not a solo performer in his own right (as Mozart and Beethoven had been), and he did not have the financial advantage of a moneyed family, or employment in a church or opera house.

In the autumn of 1815, however, came one of the most significant encounters of

Franz von Schober, dilettante poet, actor, lithographer and publisher, the closest of Schubert's friends. Schober's birthplace, Torup Castle near Malmö in Sweden, can be seen in the background. Oil painting by Leopold Kupelwieser, 1823.

Schubert's life, when Josef von Spaun introduced him to Franz von Schober – 'a felicitous poet and artistically extremely impressionable', noted Spaun in 1858, 'with whom Schubert later contracted a close friendship, which was not without influence on him'. In May 1816 Spaun himself was lodging with Josef Witteczek at the house of Professor Watteroth, where there was much lively domestic music-making. It was here that the artistic circle that later gave rise to the *Schubertiade* began to form itself. A wealthy dilettante, Schober came from a rather different background to the other members of that circle, but that was no doubt part of his attractiveness. He was born in Sweden of a German father and Austrian mother and came to Vienna to study law. Shortly after Schubert had learned of his own failure at Laibach, Schober returned to Vienna from a four-month break in Sweden, and by December 1816 Schubert was installed in rooms in the house of Schober's affluent mother. It seems unlikely that he merely walked out on his father's school and more probable that the break took place gradually, but for the first time Schubert was on his own in the world doing exactly what he wanted to do.

As Schober's name crops up frequently during Schubert's life (though not always in the most complimentary terms), perhaps it is simplest to wrap up his biography at one sitting, beginning at the end. Schober died in 1882 in Dresden where he had been living a bachelor's life after a brief and stormy marriage in the 1850s to Thekla von Gumpert, begetter of an annual for flappers, *Töchter-Album* (Daughter's Album). Before that he had been chamberlain and councillor of legation in Weimar, Liszt's secretary, and household manager and assistant to various Hungarian noble families. He was forced to seek these positions because his family's lithographic business folded in 1829, and after his mother died in 1833 he lost a lawsuit against an uncle in an attempt to get hold of a family property in Lower Austria. In Schubert's lifetime, however, he lived the life of a gentleman, dabbling in lithography, acting, writing and publishing. He was kind to Schubert and provided him with a roof over his head at four different times. As a poet he was undistinguished, though Schubert more than once made wonderful songs out of his verse. Schober introduced Schubert to the baritone Johann Michael Vogl, another of the great influences on the composer's life. Some of Schubert's less frivolous friends blamed Schober for bringing venereal disease into Schubert's life, and, indeed, he was lodging with Schober in 1822 when he almost certainly contracted it. Schober probably knew more about Schubert's private life than anyone but he never wrote his stories down, occasionally hinting that there were sensations to be revealed but never actually revealing them. Stories attributed to Schober, such as Ludwig Frankl's 1868 account of Schober trying to persuade Schubert to marry Gusti Grünwedel, are so riddled with inaccuracies that none is credible, however entertaining.

Returning to the early part of 1816, and to the music, fair copies were made of at least sixteen Goethe songs and sent by Josef von Spaun to the poet himself in Weimar. With them he sent an explanatory letter which suggests that this was but the first of eight books, the second also to be of Goethe settings, and that other poets (Schiller, Klopstock, Ossian, etc.) would be accorded later volumes, which would in turn be followed by sizeable instrumental works. The specimen songs were returned without remark. Goethe made no comment on Schubert's work until after the composer's death, when he heard a performance of 'Erlkönig' in 1830 and is reported to have said that he had heard it before and it had not appealed, but that sung as it now was (by Wilhelmine Schröder-Devrient) its merits became more apparent.

Schubert was not put off Goethe's poems by this rejection and made a further eleven Goethe settings in 1816, including 'An Schwager Kronos' (To Coachman Time), a song with the energy and forward drive of 'Erlkönig', admirably capturing the impetuosity of youth. Of the other Goethe songs that year, 'An die Türen will ich schleichen' (I shall steal from door to door), the second of three *Harfenspieler* songs, has particular significance as a forerunner of 'Gute Nacht', the first song in *Winterreise*. 'The image of the dispossessed, the alienated man, which was to haunt Schubert's imagination all his life, finds its first clear realization in the Harper's songs, and particularly in this one.'[8]

Though Schubert was still in love in 1816 – and he wrote almost as many love-songs as he did in 1815 – there are major works in other forms, not least the symphony. Two appeared during the year, one in the spring, the other in the autumn. No. 4 in C minor bears the title 'Tragic', which was added to the manuscript by Schubert himself some time after completion and, while it may be one of his little jokes, it may also have been an attempt to suggest that the composer hoped the symphony would be considered alongside those of Beethoven. The title has certainly led to some adipose and overdramatized performances. Had Schubert really intended this symphony to be tragic he would have given the slow movement deeper emotional weight. Very probably the symphony was written for a private orchestra conducted by Otto Hatwig, a player in the Burgtheater orchestra and a prominent instrumental teacher. Hatwig's orchestra had developed from the family string quartet in which Schubert played the viola, his brothers (Ferdinand and Ignaz) the violin, and his father the cello. (Given Franz Theodor's insistence on the young Schubert becoming a schoolmaster, it would be easy – but wrong – to assume that he disapproved of music as a whole. His misgivings were, quite understandably, those of a father seeking what he thought best for his son.)

The next symphony, no. 5 in B flat major, was definitely written for and performed by this band, and its scoring reflects this [CD1]. There were presumably vacancies at the time for clarinets, trumpets and drums, for there are no parts for them and the wind is confined to just one flute and pairs of oboes, bassoons and horns, giving the symphony a chamber feel. This intimacy adds to the unalloyed joy and happiness which so infect the outer movements, while the second movement is a delicate pastoral aria in which the interplay between wind and strings is the more telling for economy of numbers. The third movement contrasts a vigorous, ardent Minuet in G minor with a G major Trio of great simplicity (and what a charming song Schubert could have made out of its tender melody!). The listener may easily be beguiled into believing that the music simply flowed from the composer's pen, but once again the popular myth must be qualified: this is a piece in which much hard work has gone into producing a beautiful and apparently spontaneous result. Hatwig conducted the first performance at his house in the Schottenhof in the autumn of 1816, but the first *public* performance was not given for another quarter of a century, well after the composer's death.

In 1816 Schubert got as near to writing a piano concerto as he ever got, completing in October the rather unsatisfying Adagio and Rondo concertante in F. The piano writing demands the abilities of a concerto soloist but the 'orchestra' is merely a string trio (violin, viola and cello) and the language and style are more those of the eighteenth century than the nineteenth. The other chamber works of 1816 also reveal the composer either missing the target or as curiously uninspired. They are the

String Quartet in E major, three violin sonatas and parts of a string trio (D471), of which only the first movement is complete. Possibly Schubert himself was less than happy with these essays for he attempted very little more chamber music until 1824 – though it has to be said that two of the works produced in the interim are among the greatest of all, the 'Trout' Quintet and the Quartettsatz. The violin sonatas were published in 1836 after Schubert's death and called 'sonatinas', a title which has stuck to this day, not inappropriately, perhaps, as they are undemanding and fairly unmemorable, however pleasant to hear. It may be no accident that so much of this music is eighteenth-century in feeling, as one of the few pages surviving from Schubert's diary at this period, dated 13 June 1816, reveals:

A light, bright, fine day this will remain throughout my whole life. As from afar the magic notes of Mozart's music still gently haunt me. How unbelievably vigorously, and yet again how gently, was it impressed deep, deep into the heart by Schlesinger's masterly playing. Thus does our soul retain these fair impressions, which no time, no circumstances can efface, and they lighten our existence. They show us in the darkness of this life a bright, clear, lovely distance, for which we hope with confidence. O Mozart, immortal Mozart, how many, oh how endlessly many such comforting perceptions of a brighter and better life hast thou brought to our souls!

Martin Schlesinger was a violinist. Schubert went on to describe the music played in the concert which included a Mozart quintet ('one of the greatest of his lesser works'!) and:

I played variations by Beethoven, sang Goethe's 'Restless Love' and Schiller's 'Amalia'. Unanimous applause for the former, less for the latter. Although I myself think my 'Restless Love' better than 'Amalia', I cannot deny that Goethe's musical poet's genius contributed much to the success.*

Diary entries over the next few days describe walks, disappointment with an exhibition of Austrian painting, and the words of Schubert's contribution to the celebrations for the fiftieth anniversary of Salieri's arrival in Vienna, together with an account of the event. On the following day, 17 June, the diary entry reads:

Today I composed for money for the first time, namely, a cantata for the name-day of Professor Watteroth, words by Dräxler. The fee is 100 florins.

This piece was the cantata *Prometheus*, and it attracted much praise from those who heard it, making it all the more frustrating that the score and parts were lost

---

* 'Rastlose Liebe' (D138) remains in the repertoire despite a certain squareness. 'Amalia' (D195) deserves more frequent airings, in the hands of a soprano with operatic gifts.

in Schubert's lifetime and we have no idea just how good it may have been. We know that the event was organized by an energetic bunch of law students and that Schubert conducted the soloists, chorus and orchestra involved. It seems that there were substantial chorus numbers separated not so much by set-piece arias but by accompanied recitatives. The participants included Franz von Schlechta, who became a pupil at the seminary just after Schubert had left it and wrote a poem dedicated to Schubert commemorating his achievement in *Prometheus*. A year later the poem was published in a Viennese theatrical journal, the first time Schubert's name appeared in print in a periodical. Schubert set only seven of Schlechta's poems over the years, but each setting is of interest. A few days after the *Prometheus* performance Schubert wrote a song, 'Illmerine', to words from Schlechta's play, *Diego Manazares*; this seems to have escaped the attention of most Schubert enthusiasts, which is a pity as it is a poignant song of anxious love.

There was a public holiday in Austria on 8 September 1816 and Schubert's diary entry for that day is a lengthy statement of some of his philosophy of life. The tone is set from the start:

Man resembles a ball, to be played with by chance and passion. This sentence seems extraordinarily true to me. I have often read authors to the effect that the world is like a stage on which each human plays a part. Applause and censure follow in the next world.

Later he writes:

Happy he who finds a true man-friend. Happier still he who finds a true friend in his wife. To a free man matrimony is a terrifying thought in these days: he exchanges it either for melancholy or for crude sensuality.

We do not know if these remarks were provoked by any particular event. By the end of the year Schubert was lodging with Schober: with the loathsome schoolmastering and domestic tedium removed, the creative urge seems also to have moderated, but a few songs were written before the close of the year, including one or two gems.

'Der Wanderer' (The Wanderer), D489, is the most famous [CD2]. The poem is by an otherwise totally obscure doctor, Schmidt of Lübeck, and its theme, the romantic desire for that which can never be obtained, appealed immediately to Schubert. He made three similar versions between October 1816 and May 1821 when it was published by Cappi & Diabelli. A threatening triplet introduction sets the mood and the listener soon senses that the composer has identified completely with his subject, and that the wanderer is none other than Schubert himself. Perhaps more than in any other song we appreciate how Schubert's music can transform and elevate very ordinary words. This poetic stranger, who cannot relate to the everyday world about him, finds no heat in the sun, the flowers faded and life itself withered away: the bleak, dactylic,* hymn-like tune of this passage stayed with Schubert and is the germ from which, six years later, the whole of the so-called 'Wanderer' Fantasy for solo piano was derived.

The other memorable songs are settings of poems by Matthias Claudius, again hardly a major poet but one whose simple verses celebrating life and nature inspired Schubert at this time. The greatest of these settings belongs to 1817, but from November 1816 comes the disarming and perpetually lovely 'An die Nachtigall' (To the Nightingale), D497. Slightly less well-known but no less striking are the 'cemetery' songs, 'Am Grabe Anselmos' (By Anselm's Grave) and 'Bei dem Grabe meines Vaters' (At my Father's Grave) – sincere and classically restrained *tombeaux*.

When Otto Erich Deutsch compiled his monumental catalogue of Schubert's output he identified just under 1,000 individual works, putting them in chronological order, and such was the distinction of his scholarship that few amendments have been made since. It is interesting, then, to note that the Deutsch numbers of the songs written in the early months of 1817 lie between 500 and 550, from which it is easy enough to deduce that more than half Schubert's music had been written before his twentieth birthday. Taking stock of what he had achieved so far there are five symphonies of great charm and melodic delight but not of the intellectual weight of the giant of the medium, Beethoven; of less significance there are piano works, but nothing yet of substance, chamber pieces mostly of a fairly inconsequential nature, unsuccessful dramatic works, and endless part-songs. Some impact had been made by the sacred music. But above all there was a body of some 350 solo songs, more already than the entire output of either Schumann or Brahms, and equal to that of Hugo Wolf. It was no mean achievement for a shy, unassuming young man only just leaving his teens.

Moving into Schober's lodgings must have been an immense relief to Schubert. No longer was he surrounded by the noise and commotion of school life by day and the conservatism of a well-intentioned but artistically dull father by night. Schober was undoubtedly a stimulating companion: a wealthy cosmopolitan, high-spirited, if unstable, and a confirmed hedonist, his artistic interests were wide-ranging, and while he never produced a poetic masterpiece he supplied Schubert with the text for a musical one – 'An die Musik' (To Music) [CD1]. Perhaps the greatness of the song lies in its utter simplicity: a melody of lyrical breadth and sweep is exchanged effortlessly between the voice and the bass of the piano. Similar qualities are there in another Schober setting, 'Am Bach im Frühling' (By the Stream

*One long note followed by two short ones: tum-ti-ti.

in Spring), an attractive song for a deep voice. This is one of those songs impossible to date (1816 is sometimes suggested but there is no way of confirming or denying this unless the autograph is discovered), but its *bel canto* line could just as easily have come from the pen of Bellini or Donizetti, Schubert's Italian near contemporaries. Its theme, the conflict between the joy of nature and the blight of unhappy love, is common to a great many Schubert songs, as is the imagery of the stream.

Of the Claudius settings one, *Der Tod und das Mädchen* (Death and the Maiden) is outstanding, not only for having given rise to one of the great string quartets (though that belongs to 1824), but also as a model of communication with the minimum of means. There really could not be a simpler song yet it carries an appalling message tellingly. The maiden is young. She is not ready to die. Death reassures her that he is not to be feared and that she will sleep softly in his arms. The song is occasionally sung as a duet but there is nothing to indicate that that was Schubert's intention. Death is accorded a low D as he lures the girl to her last sleep, which has given the song an unfortunate degree of notoriety among singers, but a singer's inability to reach the note is of no consequence if what has gone before has captivated the audience completely. More significant is the fact that the huge tonal contrast available on the smaller-scaled fortepiano of Schubert's day helps the accompanist to create much greater impact than is possible on the twentieth-century concert grand when changing from the light, fresh music of the maiden to the portentous, dactylic rhythms of Death's music. Before 1817 Schubert might have been tempted to turn to the highly charged and the grotesque for his depiction of Death. Now death is merciful and, though irresistible, the more frightening for this understatement. The sentiments have a similar resonance to those of Mayrhofer, who dominates the catalogue in the early months of the year, with 'Fahrt zum Hades' (Journey to Hades) and 'Memnon' among the really top-flight songs. Both symbolize the plight of the poet in an unhappy world. Memnon, son of Eos, the Dawn, was killed by Achilles while fighting for King Priam. Turned to stone, he became a statue in Thebes, placed at a spot which caught the first light of dawn. Then, and only then, would the statue come to life, making the sound of a plucked chord. Thereafter the statue is returned to darkness and stone. Once again the piano accompaniment is of crucial importance: based on a figure which at once combines elements of that plucked chord with a tolling bell, it provides a funeral march over which the singer describes the poet's thoughts. In the coolness of death alone is the poet triumphant and the song ends in restrained rapture, the vocal line drawn out to the limit of the singer's breath control as liberty and love shine down as a single, pale, silent star.

For the most part until now Schubert had had to sing his own songs if he wanted them to be performed. According to Albert Stadler, a fellow pupil at the seminary, after Schubert's voice broke, 'he was left with only a weak tenor voice and could no

(right) First page of the autograph manuscript of 'An die Musik' (1817), an unimportant poem but a great song when elevated by Schubert's simplest of settings.

An die Musik

*Schubert and Vogl
(few singers perform
seated today).
Engraving after the
original sketch by
Moritz von Schwind.*

longer continue with his singing' and perhaps it was for this reason that his thoughts turned to Johann Michael Vogl, a baritone who had been active at the German Opera since 1794. Vogl was much more than just a singer, being highly educated (he had been intended for the law), fluent in classical and several modern languages, extremely well-read and an imposing figure to boot. He maintained the baroque tradition of ornamenting the tune when it took his fancy but, whatever his singing habits, his diction and declamatory powers were exemplary. Schober, who had connections with the Kärntnerthor theatre, made the first approach, and after several refusals, Vogl reluctantly agreed to meet Schubert. The story is told in Spaun's memoirs:

He made his appearance at Schober's at the appointed hour, quite majestically, and when the small, insignificant Schubert made a somewhat awkward bow and, in his embarrassment, stammered some incoherent words about the honour of the acquaintance, Vogl turned up his nose rather contemptuously and the beginning of the acquaintance seemed to us to portend disaster. Finally Vogl said, 'Let's see what you have got there; accompany me', and thereupon he took up the nearest sheet of *music, containing Mayrhofer's poem, 'Augenlied', a pretty, very melodious, but not important song. Vogl hummed rather than sang, and then said coldly, 'Not bad'. When after that, 'Memnon', 'Ganymed', and other songs were accompanied for him, all of which, however, he only sang mezza-voce,* he became more and more friendly, though he went away without promising to come again. On leaving he clapped Schubert on the shoulders and said to him, 'There is something in you but you are too little a comedian, too little a charlatan; you squander your fine thoughts without making the best of them.' To others Vogl expressed himself considerably more favourably about Schubert than he did to the latter and his closest friends. (When the song 'Die Dioskuren' came to his notice he declared it to be a magnificent song and said it was frankly incomprehensible how such depth and maturity could emanate from the little young man.) The impression the songs made on him was an overwhelming one and he now approached our circle again of his own accord, invited Schubert to his home, rehearsed songs with him and when he realized the tremendous, overwhelming impression his performance made on us, on Schubert himself and on every kind of audience he grew so enthusiastic about the songs that he himself now became Schubert's most ardent admirer, and instead of giving up this music, as he had previously intended, his enthusiasm for it was kindled anew.*

Of the songs mentioned by Spaun, 'Ganymed' is a further example of the intellectual leap forward made in a matter of months by the young song-writer. However frequently it is sung it never seems to lose the freshness of youth. 'Lied eines Schiffers an die Dioskuren' (Song of the Boatman to the Twin Stars) is another Mayrhofer setting, a serene prayer of the boatman to his guardian stars before setting sail on the treacherous sea.

Meanwhile, efforts to make Schubert's name more widely known continued, and early in 1817 either he or Spaun sent a copy of 'Erlkönig' to the Leipzig publishers, Breitkopf & Härtel. But when the publishers returned the manuscript to Franz Schubert they got an unexpected reply:

... I have further to inform you that some ten days ago I received a valued letter from you in which you enclosed the manuscript of Goethe's 'Erl-King' alleged to be set by me. With the greatest astonishment I beg to state that this cantata was never composed by me. I shall retain the same in my possession in order to learn, if possible, who sent you that sort of trash in such an impolite manner and also to discover the fellow who has thus misused my name.

---

*Literally 'half-voice', a technique used by singers to give a disembodied effect in certain situations or, as in this case, when saving the voice by singing gently (often referred to as 'marking').

This Franz Schubert was a Dresden composer, known to the publisher through Freemasonry. The manuscript was eventually returned to the Viennese Schubert, but Breitkopf & Härtel published nothing by the latter during his lifetime. (Curiously they *did* publish a setting of 'Erlkönig' in 1817 by Petersen Grönland from Schleswig.)

The name Christian Friedrich Daniel Schubart is known less for the quality of his poetry than for his many brushes with authority in his uncompromising championing of liberal views during the eighteenth century. One of his poems, however, provided Schubert with the text for a song so well-known that it might be a folksong – 'Die Forelle' (The Trout), D550. The poem itself is simply a tale of a fisherman using trickery to catch his trout, but it is Schubert's irresistible melody, accompanied by a piano part of such immediacy and vitality, which lifts the song out of the ordinary. Surprisingly Schubert did not set Schubart's final verse in which the poet points a moral to all young girls that they should avoid men with rods! A couple of years later he incorporated the same tune and its characteristic accompaniment into the sunniest of all his chamber works, the 'Trout' Quintet. In sharp contrast is the second version of 'Gruppe aus dem Tartarus' (Scene from Hades) with its terrifying capture of the cries of the damned as they suffer in Hades eternally. What is interesting about this second setting of Schiller's text is how far Schubert had progressed as a song-writer in the eighteen months since his first attempt, which stopped after fourteen bars, the composer realizing he did not then have the means at his disposal to do full justice to the words. He demonstrably had them in 1817.

Throughout the year Schubert returned periodically to the piano sonata and, for the first time, managed to finish several. The precise dating of some of the fragments is tricky but the first complete sonata is almost certainly the A minor (D537), of which the autograph is dated March 1817. Schubert has still not quite sorted out the pacing of the formal elements of the sonata, and there are experimental features in all of them. One, in D flat (D567), is a three-movement work in the classical manner which he brought almost to the end of the Finale in June, and then transposed up a tone into E flat, adding a fourth movement and making various alterations of detail here and there, sometimes to make a passage more pianistic, sometimes to add to or improve the music itself. Comparison of the E flat version (D568) with its D flat predecessor gives some indication of just how hard Schubert worked in order to produce pieces which can give the impression of having been dashed off at a single sitting. Vogl, good friend though he became, never realized this and helped to compound the myth that Schubert was some kind of clairvoyant composing in a trance. Schubert may have worked very quickly and sometimes unsystematically but it was never without a strong controlling intelligence.

Of the other piano works that year the Sonatas in A flat and E minor are unfinished. A case is often made for playing the luminous Rondo in E (D506) as the Finale of the E minor, but it is similar in mood and style to the existing second movement and it seems unlikely that Schubert would have included two such movements, however attractive, in a single sonata. It would be a shame, though, to let this prevent our hearing either piece. Particularly frustrating is the loss of a sonata in F sharp minor of which part of the first movement survives in the autograph manuscript of July 1817. Schubert broke off after 143 very promising bars, within sight of the end of the movement but not close enough for a completion to be more than very speculative. The extant music is tantalizing and we are left to mourn what might have been.

Silhouette of
Schubert, 1817.

There is another completed piano sonata in B major from August, the first movement of which collects together a host of typically Schubertian trademarks, and the Scherzo is entrancing with its sideways harmonic slips and 'sewing machine' Trio. The Finale, too, is bound to raise a smile or two with its sophisticated wit incongruously allied to what hints at being a rumpty-tump country tune. It charms, it amuses, but like so much of Schubert's piano music so far, it does not challenge.

Before leaving the early piano music mention should be made of some of the shorter pieces, of which Schubert wrote a large number throughout his life. Familiar to many pianists old and young will be the two Scherzi (D593) which were written towards the end of this year. Encountered less frequently, but no less engaging, are the Variations on a theme by Anselm Hüttenbrenner, written in August. Like Schubert, Hüttenbrenner was a pupil of Salieri, one of a family of brothers from Graz who came into Schubert's life at various times. Anselm went on to become

director of the Styrian Music Society to which Schubert was later to send the manuscript of his 'Unfinished' Symphony.

On 24 August 1817 Schubert wrote a little 'Farewell to a Friend' (Abschied von
einem Freunde). It is nothing much musically but it is important for two reasons:
first, it is the only song in which Schubert set his own words; second, the departing
friend was Franz von Schober, who had been summoned to France to meet his ailing
brother, Axel, an officer in the Austrian army. This meant that Schubert would have
to give up his room to Axel, who was expected to take a period of leave in Vienna.
In fact Axel died near Saarlouis before Schober could reach him, but this made no
difference to Schubert who was forced to return to his father's house, to a less artistic
milieu and to schoolmastering. He must have felt disappointment but it does not
show in the works of the latter part of the year. There is a violin sonata in A major
which, if not vintage Schubert, is more satisfactory than its predecessors, and a
benign string trio in B flat (D581), still somewhat eighteenth-century in flavour
but beautifully crafted for the instruments and particularly rewarding for the viola
(which Schubert himself played in domestic music-making).

We have been concerned with private music for most of the year, but however
magnificent the songs or lovely the piano and chamber works, none was the stuff
of the concert hall or intended for large audiences. This was a period when the
Viennese musical public had become smitten with the music of Rossini. Even in
his lodgings at Schober's, Schubert was not unaware of this fashion and when he
returned home he wrote a pair of Overtures 'in the Italian Style', in D (D590) and
C (D591). He looked on them more as a challenge to his skills than as a tribute to
Rossini but he was pleased with the results for he made piano duet versions of both
more or less immediately and he was to use material from the D major Overture
again. There is a sunny nature, too, to the symphony on which he was working at
the same time. This is not the symphony you would expect of the composer of
'Memnon' and 'Der Tod und das Mädchen' only a few months earlier. Nor was it
written down in quite the haste of its predecessors, for though it was begun in
October 1817 it was not finished until February 1818. Schubert may have realized
that Rossini's music was making money and his was not. What is certain is that the
Sixth Symphony in C major (D589) has divided opinion amongst critics and students more deeply than the other symphonies.

There is good music in it. It does not speak eloquently to me personally and the
reason is probably that the material, however cheerful, is not of a kind to benefit
from the four-square nature of the architecture. Others point to the fact that, though
there is nothing immature in the handling of the music, it has nothing of importance
to say. Arthur Hutchings summed it up as 'a work which, on the whole, would make
pleasant accompaniment to tea in Shallow's orchard'.[9] On the other hand it has

been described as 'a little gem ... those who have heard Beecham conduct it will not take kindly to hearing it abused'.[10] If the symphony were so substandard would so many record companies have invested so much money in so many performances directed by such eminent conductors?

In any case, the Sixth Symphony has taken us into the early part of 1818, by which time Schubert was living in the Rossau suburb, a little nearer the city centre, where his father had recently taken charge of a new school. Schubert was registered at this address for the purposes of military service, and in the conscription admission form for that year he is described as 'Master of Music, 4 ft 11 inches tall'. He was thus one inch too short for military duty, though, so far as is known, he was exempt neither by being an assistant schoolmaster nor by being a musician, both of which have been cited as reasons for his avoiding army service.

Despite the disappointment of losing his independence, things were not all bad for Schubert during this period. In February an advertisement appeared in the *Wiener Zeitung*, announcing the publication of a *Picturesque Pocket Book* (Mahler-isches Taschenbuch) edited by Dr Franz Sartori. In it were, amongst other diverse items, a description of the journey to Lunz on Lake Erlaf, a copperplate illustration, and a setting of Mayrhofer's poem 'At the Erlaf Lake' (Am Erlafsee) by Franz Schubert. Sartori was in fact Mayrhofer's superior at the central book censorship office, and Schubert's setting was of only part of Mayrhofer's poem (rearranged at that). Nevertheless, this was the first Schubert song to be published. It is more usually referred to simply as 'Erlafsee', under which title it appeared when it was published for a second time in 1822. The words, and particularly Schubert's setting of the altered text, sum up the composer perfectly: 'Mir ist so wohl, so weh' (I am so happy, so sad).

And this was not the only Schubert 'first' in 1818. Also in February appeared a notice advertising a concert to be held at the Roman Emperor restaurant on Sunday 1 March 1818 at 5.0 p.m. The programme was to include 'An entirely new Overture by Herr Franz Schubert'. This was, therefore, the first *public* performance of a work by Schubert. A review in the *Allgemeine Theaterzeitung* of 14 March was enthusiastic:

The second part began with a wondrously lovely overture by a young composer, Herr Franz Schubert, a pupil of our much-venerated Salieri, who has learnt already how to touch and convulse all hearts. Although the theme was surprisingly simple, a wealth of the most astonishing and agreeable ideas developed from it, worked out with vigour and skill. It is to be wished that this artist will quite soon delight us with a new gift.

There were other reviews, including one in a Dresden evening paper (Schubert's first notice abroad), and it is thought that the overture in question was the C major Overture 'in the Italian Style' (D591). A few days later, another performance met with the approval of the *Allgemeine Theaterzeitung*:

The beginning was made with an overture for two pianos, eight hands, by Franz Schubert, performed by the Fräulein Therese and Babette Kunz and Herren Schubert and Hüttenbrenner. The reviewer regards it as his duty to draw special attention to the young artist, Herr Schubert, since he has several times had an opportunity of admiring his rich gifts. Profound feeling, disciplined yet spontaneous force and appealing charm mark his every work, large and small, and once practice, that mother of all human perfection, has done her own work with him, they will without a doubt find their favoured place among the productions of the day. The performance too deserved all praise.

The review – by Schubert's loyal friend, Franz von Schlechta – does not further identify the particular overture. None for such forces has come down to us but it is quite likely to have been one of the 'Italian' Overtures which he had already arranged for four hands and which have survived in that form. The concert was a private one this time but it, too, received a mention in a German musical review, the *Allgemeine musikalische Zeitung* of Leipzig. The same paper attended a midday concert given a couple of months later, organized by a cellist, Anton Schmid, commenting 'Better than the leading personage were all the other ingredients: viz. a quite interesting overture by Herr Schubert, Salieri's pupil . . .' It would perhaps be unfair not to point out that the 'leading personage' was in fact an amateur musician, Schmid being an accountant by profession.

Performances and reviews notwithstanding, Schubert was not writing music. There are a few pages of a piano sonata in C major (D613) and twenty-five pages packed with sketches of symphonic music, all in D major, pointing to an attempt at another symphony but one which remained unfulfilled. A flash of the real Schubert can be found in the arresting Rondo in D for piano four hands, which was inspired by Josef von Gahy, a gifted pianist with whom Schubert had only just become acquainted and with whom he was to spend many blissful hours in that most sociable of musical occupations, playing piano duets. Even songs are few and far between during the first half of 1818, though the quality remains excellent. 'Auf der Riesenkoppe' (On the Giant Peak) is a return to the episodic nature of the more youthful songs (and, indeed, the words are by a poet, Theodor Körner, who had particularly appealed to Schubert back in 1815), but its harmonic language is wide-ranging. April 1818 saw Schubert at work on the first of four settings of Alois Schreiber, whose poems had been published the previous year. All are important in the development of Schubert's song-writing technique and the first of them, 'An den Mond in einer Herbstnacht' (To the Moon on an Autumn Night) is as exquisite as it is haunting. The moon's slow progress across the black sky is that of a friendly companion, bringing hope to the lonely traveller by night: but the moon's light cannot penetrate the dark chambers of the tomb. There is a transparent quality to melody and harmony alike, creating an image of the stillness and silence of a moon-lit night. The music changes subtly with the words yet its rhythmic pulse, like a heart-beat, persists until it stops with death.

The other Schreiber songs properly belong later in the year but may best be dealt with here. 'Der Blumenbrief' (The Letter of Flowers) is the archetypal encore, yet it is bitter-sweet Schubert at his best, a melody of delicacy and loveliness, cata-loguing the messages each flower bears to the poet's beloved. In complete contrast, 'Das Abendrot' (Sunset) is a showpiece song for a bass with a solid low C. Finally there is an uncommon foray into the pious with 'Das Marienbild' (The Portrait of the Madonna), which contains some pleasing music but is almost sugary in compar-ison with a tiny sacred song written right at the end of the year, 'Vom Mitleiden Mariä' (Mary's Suffering). While outwardly hostile to the priesthood and its ways, Schubert seems to have retained an inner respect for the human suffering that lies at the root of Christianity. This miniature Stabat Mater, set to a text by Schlegel, is deeply felt, rapturous, yet astonishingly simple. It is as if Schubert wished to pay homage to the sacred music of Bach and to his formative years in the choir-stalls at Liechtental church.

Returning to chronology, in July 1818 Schubert received a passport enabling him to travel to Hungary. He had been introduced (by Johann Karl Unger, father of the singer, Karoline Unger) to Count Johann Karl Esterházy and was engaged to teach music to his daughters, the Countesses Marie and Karoline, at the family's summer residence at Zseliz (present-day Želiezovce in the Slovak Republic). This was just over 100 miles east of Vienna, necessitating a journey by coach of some fourteen stages. In order to accept this engagement Schubert resigned from his father's school and never returned to teaching, though for some years to come he was still officially described as being a school assistant in the Rossau district. Zseliz was a small château surrounded by an extensive park, vineyards and farmland, and Schubert stayed in the bailiff's lodge. Though the village people spoke Hungarian many of the servants also spoke German and he immediately felt at home and happy.

… I live and compose like a god, as though that were as it should be. Mayrhofer's 'Einsamkeit' is ready, and I believe it to be the best I have done, for I was without a care. I hope that you are all merry and in the best of health, as I am. Thank God I live at last, and it was high time, otherwise I should have become nothing but a thwarted musician.

Schubert's letter is interesting not only for its clear reference to the stultification he felt as an assistant schoolmaster but also for the high regard in which he held 'Einsamkeit' (Solitude). It is a song of enormous length which frightens away most singers and not a few audiences but, as John Reed suggests, if 'Einsamkeit' is looked upon not as the last solo cantata but as the first song cycle, it becomes perfectly performable.

Perhaps the most frustrating of all Schubert's unfinished piano works, the F minor Sonata, dates from this time. But the best of the piano music of this period is for piano duet, very likely written to be played by, or with, the young countesses of whom he was in charge. As well as some Variations on a French Song and a set of Polonaises (D599) there is a full-scale sonata in B flat which, while not challenging the Fantasy in F minor for supremacy, is well worth inclusion in the piano duettists' repertoire. It may also have been at Zseliz that Schubert composed the three *Marches militaires* (D733) of which the first, in D major, is exceedingly well-known. The others are worth investigation, too, though the D major, with its magical middle section, is undoubtedly the trump card.

Early in his stay at Zseliz Schubert put the finishing touches to a German Requiem. He wrote it for his brother Ferdinand, who clearly intended to pass it off as his own. Some of the correspondence between the brothers survives and, though the work is not of enormous significance in Schubert's output, and the deceit passed off as a trifle, the letters are almost a holiday snapshot album of the young composer away from home for the first time.

24 August 1818

Dear Brother Ferdinand,

It is half-past eleven at night, and your German Requiem is finished. It made me sad, believe me, for I sang it from the depth of my soul. Add what is missing, i.e. write in the words below the music and the signs above it. If you wish to make a number of repeats, do so, without writing to Zseliz to ask me about it. Things are not well with you: I wish I might change with you, so that you might be happy for once. You would then find all heavy burdens cast off your shoulders. I could wish this for you with all my heart, dear Brother. – My foot is going to sleep, much to my annoyance. If the dolt could write it could not go to sleep … Good morning, dear little Brother: I have now slept together with my foot and continue my letter at 8 a.m. on the 25th. In exchange for your request I have another: love to my dear parents, brothers and sisters, friends and acquaintances, not forgetting Karl in particular. Did he not remember me in his letter? … Kick my city friends mightily, or have them kicked, to make them write to me. Tell Mother [his stepmother] that my laundry is very well looked after, and that her motherly care greatly touches me. (But if I could have more apparel, I should be extremely glad if you were to send me an extra supply of handkerchiefs, scarves and stockings. Also I am much in need of two pairs of – cashmere trousers, for which Hart may take the measure where he will. I should send the money for them at once.) My receipts for the month of July, including the travelling expenses, amounted to 200 florins. – It is beginning to get cold here already, yet we shall not leave for Vienna before the middle of November. I hope next month to go for a few weeks to Freistadtl, which belongs to Count Erdödy, my count's uncle. They say the country there is extraordinarily pretty. I also hope to get to Pest, as we are going for the vintage to Pócs-Megyer, which is not far from it. It would be uncommonly agreeable for me if I were to meet the administrator Daigele there. But altogether I look forward to all the vintages, about which I have been told a lot of such nice things. The harvest too is very fine here. The corn is not put into burns here, as in Austria, but enormous stacks are erected, which they call Tristen. *They are often some 80 to 100 yards long and 100 to 120 feet high. They are stacked with such skill that the rain, which is made to run off, can do no damage. Oats and the like are buried in the earth, too. – Well and happy as I am here, and kind as the people are, I look forward with immense pleasure to the moment at which the word will be 'To Vienna, to Vienna!' Indeed, beloved Vienna, thou holdest all that is most dear and cherished in thy narrow space, and nothing but the sight of this, the heavenly sight, will appease my yearning. Requesting once again the fulfilment of the wishes mentioned above,*

A hearty greeting to my *Aunt Schubert and her* *daughter.*	*I remain, with true affection for you all,* *Your sincerely faithful Franz.* *A thousand greetings to your good wife* *And your dear Resi.*

It is not known if Schubert ever managed to get to any of the places mentioned in his letter. Freistadtl (Bratislava) and Pest (not yet Budapest) are in opposite directions from Zseliz. Hungarian wines were well-known in Vienna and Schubert will have been acquainted with some of them. The wine of Pócs-Megyer was red. The most famous Hungarian wine of the day, though, was Tokay, the wine of the Tsars, capable of infinite ageing and having legendary miraculous powers. Tokay and its properties were celebrated in a poem by Gabriele von Baumberg, a friend of Countess Esterházy, which had been set to music by Schubert in 1815. The music suggests that the eighteen-year-old had not experienced Tokay for himself – the song ('Lob des Tokayers') is a rumbustious march.

A few weeks later, on 8 September 1818, Schubert wrote to several of his friends, including Schober, Spaun and Mayrhofer in a long letter, of which the following might perhaps give the flavour:

How infinitely the letters from you, all and sundry, delighted me is not to be expressed! I was just attending a deal in oxen and cows when your nice, portly letter was handed to me. As I broke it open, loud cries of joy burst from me on beholding the name of Schober. I read it in a neighbouring room, with continual laughter and childish pleasure. It was as though I were laying my hands on my dear friends themselves. But I will answer you in good order:

Dear Schobert,

    I see we shall have to keep to this transformation of the name. Well then, dear Schobert, your letter was very welcome and precious to me from beginning to end, especially the last sheet. Yes, indeed, this last sheet gave me sheer delight. You are a magnificent chap (in Swedish, of course), and believe me, my friend, you will not succumb, for your understanding of art is the purest and truest imaginable ... For at Zseliz I am obliged to rely wholly on myself. I have to be composer, author, audience, and goodness knows what else. Not a soul here has any feeling for true art, or at most the countess now and again (unless I am wrong). So I am alone with my beloved and have to hide her in my room, in my pianoforte and in my bosom. Although this often makes me sad, on the other hand it elevates me the more. Have

Three views of Zseliz, showing (centre) the exterior, (left) Schubert's room during his second visit in 1824, and (right) the music room. Watercolour by A. F. Seligmann, 1818.

no fear, then, that I shall stay away longer than is absolutely necessary. Several songs have materialized these days – very good ones, I hope ...

Now a description for everybody:

Our castle is not one of the largest, but very neatly built. It is surrounded by a most beautiful garden. I live at the inspectorate. It is fairly quiet, save for some forty geese, which at times cackle so lustily together that one cannot hear oneself speak. Good people around me, all of them. It must be rare for a count's retinue to fit so well together as these do. The inspector, a Slavonian, is a good fellow, and has a great opinion of his former musical talents. He still blows two German dances in 3/4 time on the lute, with great virtuosity. His son studies philosophy, is here on holiday just now, and I hope I shall take to him. His wife is a woman like all women who want to be ladies. The steward fits his office perfectly: a man with an extraordinary insight into his pocket and bags. The doctor, who is really accomplished, ails like an old lady at the age of 24. Very unnatural. The surgeon, whom I like best, is a venerable old man of 75, always cheerful and happy. May God give every one so happy an old age! The magistrate is an unassuming, excellent man. A companion of the count, a merry old fellow and a capable musician, often keeps me company. The cook, the lady's maid, the chambermaid, the nurse, the manager, &c. and two grooms are all good folk. The cook rather a rake; the lady's maid 30 years of age; the chambermaid very pretty and often my companion; the nurse a good old thing; the manager my rival. The two grooms are more fit for traffic with horses than with human beings. The count is rather rough, the countess haughty but more sensitive; the little countesses are nice children. So far I have been spared dining with the family. Now I cannot think of any more; I hardly need tell you, who know me, that with my natural candour I hit it off quite well with all these people ...

Dear Mayrhofer, my longing for November will hardly be less than yours. Cease ailing, or at least dabbling in medicines, and the rest will come of itself ...

How serious was Schubert's relationship with the chambermaid we can only speculate (as we might over his rivalry with the manager). She was probably an Austrian for her name was Pepi Pöckelhofer; she became lady's maid in 1818 and later married the new valet, Josef Rössler (probably about 1830). She retired from service in 1845 as a waiting-woman.

Schubert's older brother, Ignaz, wrote to him in Zseliz in October:

You happy creature! How enviable is your lot! You live in sweet, golden freedom, can give free rein to your musical genius, may let your thoughts stray where they will; you are loved, admired and idolized, while the likes of us wretched scholastic beasts of burden are abandoned to all the roughnesses of wild youngsters and exposed to a host of abuses, not to mention that we are further humiliatingly subjected to an ungrateful public and a lot of dunderheaded bigwigs. You will be surprised when I tell you that it has got to such a pitch in our house that they no longer even dare to laugh when I tell them a funny yarn about superstition in the Scripture class. You may thus easily imagine that in these circumstances I am often seized by a secret anger, and that I am acquainted with liberty only by name. You see, you are now free of all these things, you are delivered, you see and hear nothing of all these goings-on, much less of our pundits.

Franz responded:

You, Ignaz, are still quite the old man of iron. Your implacable hatred of the whole tribe of bigwigs does you credit. But you have no conception what a gang the priest-hood is here: bigoted as mucky old cattle, stupid as arch-donkeys and boorish as bisons. You may hear sermons here to which our most venerated Pater Nepomucene *can't hold a candle. They chuck about blackguards, riffraff, &c. from the pulpit, something lovely; they put a death's head on the pulpit and say: 'Look here, you pock-pitted mugs, that's how you will look one day.' Or else: 'There, a fellow takes a slut into the pub, they dance all night, then go they to bed tight, and when they get up there are three of 'em,' &c. &c. – Whether you thought of me while you were guzzling I don't know ...*

While Schubert was away, attempts were made in Baden and Vienna to perform his overture to Goethe's play, *Claudine von Villa Bella*, which was one of the several music-dramas written in that productive year, 1815. Both performances were cancelled, the one in Baden because the orchestra could not play it. There may have been more than a little mischief in the Vienna cancellation. Schubert, for all the freedom from drudgery afforded by the break at Zseliz, could not wait to return to Vienna and in November he went to lodge with Mayrhofer. It was the renewal of an alliance of like minds and though Schubert had already made most of his finest Mayrhofer settings the poet was, nevertheless, a considerable influence on Schubert's artistic development over the next couple of years.

CHAPTER 4

1819–20

In view of his state of emotional exaltation, with its contrasting periods of melancholy and depression, which drove him to suicide about 1830, it was not to be wondered at that [Mayrhofer] attached himself to the highly gifted Schubert and that they shared lodgings together; no more is it to be wondered at if their continued living together foundered on their day-to-day relations, perhaps on small differences of opinion regarding money matters, in which Schubert may well have often been to blame. Certainly the cleavage between Mayrhofer's inclination and his position in life, for he was compelled to act as a respectable Imperial book censor whereas he was an enthusiastic admirer of intellectual freedom, gave rise to the malady in his extremely sensitive soul and to the difficulty of living with such a character.[11]

Despite their apparent unsuitability for each other, Schubert and Mayrhofer shared their lodgings on the third floor of a house in the inner city until the end of 1820 'under the care of the excellent widow Sanssouci, who tried to keep things reasonably tidy for the two unpractical gentlemen'.[12] Whatever their domestic relationship, their artistic interaction was extremely fruitful. As Maurice Brown has put it, 'It is moreover an interesting facet of Schubert's work in Lieder to find how the greater Mayrhofer settings often led to even greater Goethe settings – as though Mayrhofer had tapped the springs in Schubert from which Goethe could draw a finer music.'[13] Vogl was pleased to find Schubert back in Vienna and introduced him to the directors of the Kärntnerthor theatre who responded by asking Schubert to compose the music for a one-act Singspiel by Georg von Hofmann, *Die Zwillings-brüder* (The Twin Brothers), in which Vogl would play both brothers. Schubert set about the task immediately and the overture was finished on 19 January 1819. Ten sung numbers followed quickly, although the opera was not given its first perform-ance until June of the following year. Schubert's friends attended the première in large numbers and the enthusiasm of their applause contrasted somewhat with the lukewarm reception of the regulars. Schubert sat in the gallery with Anselm Hüttenbrenner but refused to dress for the occasion, so Vogl had to appear on stage to receive the applause for the composer and to thank the audience on Schubert's behalf. This was typical of Schubert, according to Hüttenbrenner.

Schubert's outward appearance was anything but striking or prepossessing. He was short of stature, with a full, round face and was rather stout. His forehead was very beautifully domed. Because of his short sight he always wore spectacles, which he did not take off even during sleep. Dress was a thing in which he took no interest whatever; consequently he disliked going into smart society, for which he had to take more trouble with his clothes. As a result many a party anxiously awaited his appearance and would have been only too glad to overlook any negligence in his dress; sometimes, however, he simply could not bring himself to change his everyday coat for a black frock coat; he disliked bowing and scraping, and listening to flattering talk about himself he found downright nauseating.

Also in January 1819 there was another performance of the cantata *Prometheus* at Ignaz Sonnleithner's house. Sonnleithner was a Viennese lawyer who held regular concerts in his third-floor apartment, and it was his son Leopold who introduced Schubert to these events. Leopold wrote a short biography of Schubert shortly after the composer's death but it is his (not wholly accurate) 1857 memoirs which are most frequently quoted, shedding, as they do, some light on Schubert's daily routine:

Schubert was extraordinarily fertile and industrious in composing. For everything else that goes by the name of work he had no use. Seldom going to the theatre or into fashionable society, he loved to spend the evening at an inn, in the company of gay friends, and on such occasions midnight often passed unnoticed and pleasure was indulged to excess. As a result of this he acquired the habit of staying in bed in the morning until 10 or 11 o'clock; and as this was the time when he felt the greatest urge to compose, the morning hours passed in this way, and the best time for earning money by teaching was thus lost.

Later on Sonnleithner writes again about Schubert's night-life:

What Schindler* says about his propensity for drink is probably rather exaggerated; under no circumstances should too much attention be paid to this matter in his biography. But unfortunately I must confess that I saw him in a drunken state several times. On one occasion I was with him at a party, in one of the suburbs, where there was a great deal of music-making and feasting. I went home at about 2 o'clock in the morning; Schubert remained still longer and the next day I learnt that he had to sleep there as he was incapable of going home. This happened in a house where he had not long been known and where he had only been introduced a short time previously. This note, by the way, is only for the biographer, not for the biography.

What was important was that Schubert's music was being performed, talked about, and noticed beyond Vienna. 'Schäfers Klagelied' (Shepherd's Complaint), a Goethe setting from 1814 which Schubert revised for the tenor Franz Jäger to sing at a public concert at the Roman Emperor on 28 February 1819, even received a review in the Berlin *Gesellschafter*:

A vocal piece, 'Shepherd's Complaint', composed by young Schubert and sung by our valiant tenor Jäger, proved the most enjoyable. We look forward, indeed, to a larger work by this hopeful artist which he is now preparing for our delectation.

The 'larger work' was presumably *Die Zwillingsbrüder*.

But in Vienna itself progress was still slow. From this period there are two letters to Anselm Hüttenbrenner, who had left Vienna (much to Schubert's annoyance) to work as a lawyer in Graz. In May 1819 the composer wrote:

Dear Friend,

You are a rogue, and no mistake!!! It will be a decade before you see Vienna again. Now one girl, now another turns your head: well then, may the deuce take all girls, if you allow them to bewitch you in this manner. For heaven's sake, get married, and there's an end of it! – Of course you may say, like Caesar, you'd rather take first rank at Graz than second in Vienna … There is little news here; if one hears anything good, it is always the same old things … In spite of Vogl it is difficult to outwit such canaille *as Weigl, Treitschke, &c. – That is why instead of my operetta they give other rot, enough to make your hair stand on end.*

Weigl and Treitschke were, respectively, conductor and producer at the Kärntnerthor and the 'same old things' were Rossini's operas.

A couple of months later Schubert was himself writing from the country to his brother Ferdinand:

---

*Anton Schindler was leader of the Josefstadt theatre orchestra and confidant of Beethoven.

So far I am pretty well, only the weather refuses to be favourable. We had a very violent thunderstorm here yesterday the 12th, which struck Steyr, killed a girl and paralysed the arms of two men. At the house where I lodge there are eight girls, nearly all pretty. Plenty to do, you see. The daughter of Herr v. K[oller], where Vogl and I eat daily, is very pretty, plays the pianoforte well and is going to sing several of my songs.

Please forward the enclosed letter. As you see, I am not quite so faithless as you may imagine ... The country round Steyr is inconceivably lovely.

Steyr, Vogl's birthplace, where Schubert was commissioned to compose the 'Trout' Quintet: coloured lithograph by Jakob Alt.

Schubert was on holiday in the company of (and at the expense of) Vogl. There is simply no means of knowing what the 'enclosed letter' may have been nor to what Schubert was referring in using the word 'faithless'. It has been suggested that he was still in love with Therese Grob and that his brother was expected to act as a go-between, but there are no grounds for this supposition. Steyr was Vogl's birthplace, a town of beauty and antiquity, prosperous and musical. It had been important since the Middle Ages for the manufacture of arms, and there was a substantial mining industry round about. Herr von Koller was an iron merchant and his daughter, Josefine, sang in a performance of 'Erlkönig' in which she took the part of the child. Schubert was the father, Vogl the Erl-King, and the piano was played by Albert Stadler with whom they were staying, evidence (in this determinedly authentic age) that Schubert quite happily allowed his solo songs to be performed by more than one singer. Josefine also sang in the first performance of a cantata composed for Vogl's birthday on 10 August, 'Der Frühlingsmorgen' (Spring Morning). Stadler was again the pianist and, moreover, he acted as librettist, lacing the text with numerous references to the many operatic parts in which Vogl had starred over the years. Music-making in Steyr was clearly fun and Schubert entered into the spirit of it wholeheartedly. This is nowhere better exemplified than in the famous 'Trout' Quintet, which was commissioned by the town's leading amateur musician, the cellist Sylvester Paumgartner. He it was who, happily, suggested that the work should incorporate the music of the song 'Die Forelle'.

It was a felicitous choice of melody, for its bubbling gaiety and irrepressible joy sum up Schubert's own happiness and the beauty of the countryside around Steyr. The tune is used as the basis for a delightful set of variations, the fourth of five movements, each of which is infused with a quality of carefree innocence. The work is also unusual in being, still, the only repertoire piece written for violin, viola, cello, double bass and piano. With this scoring the quintet could easily sound lugubrious, but it must be remembered that the instruments of Schubert's day had a much clearer tone and far less weight and volume than modern instruments. This is particularly so of the fortepiano which, with its much lighter bass, often benefits from the reinforcement given by the double bass. Occasionally, too, the double bass is given its own turn with the melody, Schubert revelling in the fun, yet there is no sense of the ridiculous or grotesque about it. Schubert's song owed much of its geniality to the dancing triplet rhythm of the piano accompaniment, and as early as the slow introduction to the quintet's first movement, triplet figures hint at the merriment and vivacity to come, reappearing in the second movement and as an adornment to the onward thrust of the Finale. Intriguingly, though the song employs the simplest of harmonies, the quintet is packed with those delicious harmonic twists and turns so characteristic of Schubert, which never fail to delight audience and performers alike. Surely this is the work to take to your desert island to be played when you need to be cheered up.

There is another work in A major which shares much of the amiability of the 'Trout', and that is the Piano Sonata D664 [CD1]. The autograph manuscript is lost and there is no definitive evidence to show that it was composed during this holiday, but there is every chance it was written for Josefine von Koller. It is the shortest of all the complete sonatas, and certainly one of the most endearing. Concise and restrained, this is essential Schubert, both lyrical and personal.

Schubert and Vogl also visited Linz, where Schubert met members of the Spaun family and renewed his acquaintance with Josef Kenner whom he had known at the seminary. Kenner was a poet of sorts and Schubert had already set three of his ballads back in 1815. Kenner's greater significance to Schubertian understanding and myth, however, lies in the strength of feeling running through his correspondence when the possibility of a Schubert biography was mooted in the 1850s.

The holidaymakers went back to Steyr before returning to Vienna, and an album leaf written for Katharina Stadler is dated 14 September 1819, very probably the day on which they left:

> *Ever enjoy the present wisely: thus will the past be a fair*
> *remembrance for thee and the future hold no terrors. [Schubert]*

> *On earth naught can such pleasure give*
> *As in the hearts of friends to live. [Vogl]*

On reaching Vienna Schubert resumed lodging with Mayrhofer and settings of several of his poems followed shortly. It was Mayrhofer who brought to Schubert the deepest meaning in the word 'Consolation' (Trost), and the song with that title, D671, plays on the horn calls evoked in the first line of the poetry. 'Nachtstück' (Nocturne) is better known, and is yet another example of poet and composer in one mind welcoming death as the solution to their earthly problems. 'Die Sternennächte' (Starry Nights), a serenade, and 'Beim Winde' (In the Wind) are unjustly overlooked. However, the autumn of 1819 also produced two songs, by other poets, which claim the attention of most commentators. First is 'Prometheus' (D674), a setting of Goethe for bass voice which drew from Dietrich Fischer-Dieskau the enthusiastic comment:

Grandeur and dignity speak out of this music, and nowhere is this clarity or its transparency sacrificed for the sake of expressiveness ... Prometheus points to the future and blazes a new trail ... Not until Wagner's Tristan do we meet another composition with such daring harmonies and fascinating progressions.[14]

The other song of significance is a setting of Schiller, a single verse from 'Die Götter Griechenlands' (The Greek Gods) [CD2] which drew from Schubert a characteristic response that is never quite sure whether it is in A minor or A major. It is, if you like, an unanswered question, one that Schubert continually seems to be asking with his obsessive recourse to this haunting tonal device and the ambivalent harmonic chiaroscuro to which it gives rise. Schubert returned to this melody, its harmonic ambiguity and the key in 1824 when he wrote his A minor String Quartet. The song is perhaps less remarkable than the quartet to which it gave rise but it was not the first time Schubert used A minor in this way. The study of particular keys and their significance to Schubert is beyond the scope of this book, but it is not immaterial and quite clearly Schubert's responses to certain emotional stimuli were consciously associated with certain keys, harmonic patterns or melodic shapes. However, as John Reed warns, 'Schubert thought nothing of transposing his songs to suit individual singers, or the convenience of publishers. Moreover, the autograph, where it exists, and the first edition often differ in the key used. Not too much weight, therefore, should be attached to individual examples.' Perhaps all that should be added at this point, then, is the rider that pitch in Schubert's Vienna was, in general, a little below that of modern concert pitch, though there will have been considerable variation with nothing like the standardization that prevails in Europe today.

Although the music of *Die Zwillingsbrüder* belonged largely to 1819, the first performance took place on 14 June 1820 and was in many ways the most important event of the composer's year. Mozart's youngest son, Franz Xaver (now styling himself 'Wolfgang Amadeus' after his father) was amongst the first-night audience and he described Schubert as 'a beginner'. He suggested that the 'little operetta' contained some pretty things but was rather too serious. He had put his finger on one of the main problems for Schubert: he wanted to write serious German opera but his language and vocabulary were not compatible with his objective at this stage of his career.

The reviews were disappointing to Schubert though, on the whole, they were fair. The Vienna *Sammler*, for example, concluded:

The music is the neat minor product of a young composer. It must have been preceded by very fair studies in composition, for the style of this opera is pretty pure and shows that its author is no novice at harmony. Many of the melodies, however, are a little old-fashioned, and some even tuneless.

The Dresden *Abendzeitung* remarked sourly:

This gifted young man too might be reminded of the age-old saw, 'Excess is unhealthy', for the public acclaimed the operetta like a great masterpiece, which it is not.

The Vienna *Conversationsblat* was a little more generous:

The general verdict on Schubert can only be favourable, although not to the point to which his numerous friends endeavour to force it. He will do great and beautiful things, and it is in this hope that we welcome the modest artist very cordially.

The Leipzig *Allgemeine musikalische Zeitung* was more forceful:

In this first dramatic essay he seems to attempt to fly as high as Beethoven and not to heed the warning example of Icarus. Little true songfulness is to be found, whereas hardly any repose is to be met with in confused and surcharged instrumentation, anxious striving after originality and continual modulation.

In case so many quotations from the reviews of the day might be considered excessive it should perhaps be pointed out that these were the first detailed criticism Schubert had received. None was more detailed than the Vienna *Allgemeine musikalische Zeitung* whose critic (possibly Josef von Seyfried, the incumbent editor) penned an essay of some length comparing Schubert's operetta with those of two composers of French opera, Méhul and Cherubini, a kinder exercise than comparing Schubert's effort with the legacy of Mozart, though Mozart could hardly be kept out for ever:

Herr Schubert is too much wedded to details of the text, and this chases him and his hearer restlessly through modulations and allows of no point of repose; he tries to express words in music instead of painting the nature of a whole speech by means of the character of a whole piece, which, as Mozart proves, is the only way of attaining to the highest aims of art and of conquering its greatest difficulties, by producing regular, rounded-off pieces and yet by making the whole call forth the required feeling. For this Herr Schubert has allowed himself to be led too far astray by his laudable

The Theater an der Wien as it was seen in 1830, shortly after Schubert's death.

endeavour to go his own way, and he has done away too drastically with the conclud-
ing formulas of musical numbers. Is a letter to be regarded as unoriginal because it
is subscribed 'Your obedient servant'? To this habit, which makes suddenly ending
pieces appear hacked off to us, the greatest of living composers, Beethoven, has per-
haps succumbed most thoroughly; but is he a less original mind for that? Generally
speaking one should even avoid the appearance of wanting to be original: one must
simply be so.

Despite the lack of enthusiasm among reviewers, the management of the Theater
an der Wien commissioned Schubert to write the music for a three-act play by the
same author, Georg von Hofmann. It is said that it took him only a fortnight to
complete the music and *Die Zauberharfe* (The Magic Harp) was presented to the
public for the first time on 19 August 1820. Again the reviews tended to
condemnation:

The score shows talent here and there; but on the whole it lacks technical resource
and wants the grasp which only experience can give; most of it much too long, inef-
fective and fatiguing, the harmonic progressions are too harsh, the orchestration
redundant, the choruses dull and feeble. (Leipzig *Allgemeine musikalische Zeitung*)

Much might be said of the score if The Magic Harp, *being a magic play, also had*
magic music . . . But the Magic Harp *music is often thin, insipid and stale in taste . . .*
(Vienna *Sammler*)

Whatever the real merit of the music, and Maurice Brown is prominent amongst
those who feel that the conservative critics were simply incapable of understanding
Schubert's idiom, the overture is justifiably popular with concert audiences and the
record-buying public today, though few will know its provenance, for it is usually
referred to as the Overture to *Rosamunde* [CD2]. There is no justification for the
title. True, the *Rosamunde* incidental music lacked an overture but when the music
was first performed Schubert used the overture to his opera *Alfonso und Estrella*
for that purpose. (This is not to say that one should not perform the *Zauberharfe*
overture alongside the *Rosamunde* incidental music: it makes a most delightful
assemblage.)

If the summer of 1820 was the most eventful part of the year musically, the most
dramatic moment occurred in March when the police raided the rooms of Johann
Senn, 'a splendid, warm-hearted young man, of restrained power, a stubborn philo-
sopher, candid with his friends, reserved with others, frank, passionate, a hater of
all imposed constraint'.[15] He had been at the seminary with Schubert but had been
stripped of his scholarship in 1814 for standing up against the authorities when they
imprisoned a fellow student. Student life had again come under official suspicion

following the murder of the dramatist August von Kotzebue by the student Karl Ludwig Sand in 1819, and Senn, who came from the Tyrol and supported the cause of its independence, had attracted police attention by joining student gatherings at an inn. On the night of the raid on his rooms, Senn was in the company of several fellow students including Franz von Bruchmann. Schubert, who was also present, escaped with no more than a black eye. Senn's principal sin, according to the report of the Police High Commissioner, was to say that 'he did not care a hang about the police' and that 'the Government was too stupid to be able to penetrate into his secrets'. It earned him fourteen months in prison without a trial followed by deportation to the Tyrol. Senn never saw Schubert again, but Schubert set a couple of his poems in 1822.

At about the same time he composed five songs to texts by Bruchmann. These can be discussed at their proper time, but meanwhile Bruchmann was already playing a considerable part in Schubert's artistic life. As the son of a wealthy wholesale merchant he had the means to act as host to many of the leading figures in Viennese progressive culture. In particular, the scholar and writer Friedrich von Schlegel visited regularly. Schlegel was at the centre of a group of writers and thinkers who warmly embraced the romantic view of nature as the interface between God and man, a view upheld by Schubert. While it is not known whether Schubert and Schlegel ever actually met at Bruchmann's, the artistic link was evidently formed. Schubert had made his first Schlegel settings in 1818 (including the lovely 'Vom Mitleiden Mariä') and amongst those of 1820 perhaps 'Die Vögel' (The Birds) could be singled out as a perennial favourite for the light soprano, and no less worthy because of its frequent use as an encore.

Early in the year Schubert made a start on a work in a form that he otherwise sadly neglected, the oratorio or sacred drama. He began *Lazarus* in February but soon abandoned it. The fragments that remain demonstrate the composer's usual problems in turning his essentially gentle song style into something more substantial. More frustratingly, they also show a use of what we now call the 'leitmotif', a particular melody or figure which becomes associated with a certain character or event, giving immediately recognizable identity each time the theme is heard. It was a device of which Wagner was to make notorious use some years later.

It must be said, however, that in most musical respects the year 1820 is unremarkable, even though there *are* interesting diversions such as the enchanting setting for female voices and piano of the 23rd Psalm [CD3] or the early versions of a male-voice part-song, 'Gesang der Geister über den Wassern' (Song of the Spirits over the Waters), which began its life with a piano accompaniment but ended up requiring the services of two violas, two cellos and a double bass. There are songs, of course, and one might point to the eternal fame of 'Frühlingsglaube' (Trust in

Schubert listening to a string quartet in the music room of Johann Steiger von Arnstein: pencil sketch by Friedrich Gauermann.

Spring) and 'Freiwilliges Versinken' (somewhat mundanely translated as 'Free Fall' or 'Voluntary Oblivion') [CD1]. The former needs no introduction to concert audiences, a tune of the utmost simplicity but exquisite beauty expressing the optimistic romantic ideal that nature will, in the end, overcome man's tribulations. 'Freiwilliges Versinken', on the other hand, may not date from 1820 at all, but whenever it was written the song demands prominence somewhere in this book, for it is one of Schubert's greatest. It tells of Helios the sun-god, who must, like the poet, die daily to give life to those who seek a happier land. Hardly surprisingly, the words are by Mayrhofer. It is a song of extraordinary strength and repose, and as Fischer-Dieskau says, 'It is doubtful whether the disappearing sun and the rising moon have ever been more beautifully depicted.'

But from 1820 there is no orchestral music, no piano music (apart from the Six Ecossaises, D697) and no chamber music, with the single exception of what is arguably the greatest of all his string quartet offerings, the Quartettsatz, written in

December [CD3]. The title gives a misleading impression that this movement was all Schubert intended to write, though in fact a significant part (forty-one bars) of the following Andante exists in manuscript. Nevertheless, as with the 'Unfinished' Symphony, this part-work is quite able to support itself, accomplishing in some eight minutes what many quartets fail to do in twenty-eight. Before contemplating the surviving movement it is worth giving a moment's thought to the Andante. Schubert must have felt dissatisfied with his sketch for the opening of this movement. For sure he had other distractions in the social life of his artistic circle and in his continuing attempts to write a serious opera, but it is strange that he never summoned the resolve to complete the quartet. Did he perhaps realize, or at least fear, that he did not have the resources within his invention and technique to follow the first brilliant movement? It is also conceivable, if less plausible, that he was deeply wounded when the only real love of his live, Therese Grob, at last forsook him, marrying the baker Johann Bergmann on 21 November 1820. The miracle of the surviving movement is its ingenuity, the whole piece being derived from a seemingly innocent little phrase, no more than a tremulous version of the descending fourth, from which emerges the essence of Schubert, angry, wistful, passionate and nostalgic.

CHAPTER 5

1821–2

The year 1821 was no more productive in musical terms than the previous one had been, but the biographer can learn a little more about Schubert from the slightly more plentiful documentary evidence that has survived. From early in the year there are three testimonials including a joint one from Josef Weigl (director of the court opera) and Antonio Salieri (court musical director). There is also one from Ignaz Franz von Mosel (court secretary) and another from the court music chamberlain, Moritz, Count Dietrichstein. It seems that Schubert sought a position at the court opera either as composer or conductor, but the new management which took over the running of the theatre later in the year was Italian and so his application came to nothing. Schubert had been introduced to Mosel and Dietrichstein through the poet Matthäus von Collin, a cousin of Spaun, and another link with the Viennese romantics. Collin, in due course, furnished Schubert with the texts for several fine songs and also introduced him to Ladislaus Pyrker, a Hungarian-born priest, poet and dramatist who became Patriarch of Venice in 1820. In May 1821 Pyrker wrote to Schubert from Venice:

Your kind proposal to dedicate to me the fourth book of your incomparable songs I accept with the greater pleasure, since it will now frequently recall to my memory that evening when I was so much moved by the depths of your being – particularly through the sounds of your 'Wanderer'! I am proud to belong to the same country as you . . .

*Pencil drawing of
Schubert by Leopold
Kupelwieser, 1821.*

Perhaps it was inevitable that some publisher would eventually take notice of Schubert, but it was the performance of his songs by Vogl and August von Gymnich which provided the catalyst. Schubert did indeed accompany his songs on many occasions but he was not known to the musical public at large as a soloist. Those who were known in this way found little difficulty in getting their compositions published, however mediocre in comparison with Schubert's. It was Leopold Sonnleithner and his friends, fired by Vogl's performance, who had the desire and determination to see Schubert's music in print, and when they set to they encountered no problem in raising the funds through private subscription to have 'Erlkönig' engraved by the firm of Cappi & Diabelli. And so 'Erlkönig' became Schubert's opus 1. A notice in the official *Wiener Zeitung* on 2 April 1821 announced its publication, price two florins, the song 'reverentially dedicated to Moritz, Count von Dietrichstein'. Sufficient money was raised for 'Gretchen am Spinnrade' to follow on 30 April. Further Goethe songs (including 'Heidenröslein') appeared as opus 3 on

29 May, the same day as opus 4, the collection dedicated to Pyrker. With these well-placed dedications Schubert actually earned a little money for once. In November 1821 he wrote to Spaun:

Your letter gave me much pleasure, and I hope that you continue keeping well. – But now I must tell you that my dedications have done their work: that is to say, the Patriarch has forked out 12 ducats and, through Vogl's intervention, Fries 20, which is a very good thing for me. Will you be good enough, therefore, to close your correspondence with the Patriarch by a message of thanks suited both to him and to me?

Fries was Moritz von Fries, 'Count of the Realm, Knight of the Austrian Imperial Order of Leopold', as more respectfully referred to in the dedication of opus 2. After Schubert's death, Sonnleithner recounted how the proceeds of sales of these pieces paid off the composer's debts with his shoemaker and tailor, settled his outstanding rent, and dealt with his account at the coffee-house and inn. A further eleven songs appeared after opus 4, making a total of twenty in print by the end of 1821. By the time of his death, seven years later, 169 had been published with opus numbers. When one includes the few others which had appeared as supplements or in journals, this comes to 185 or twenty-nine per cent of Schubert's total output of songs.

There were good reviews for the new publications, particularly 'Erlkönig'. The Dresden *Abendzeitung* enthused:

This splendid composition cannot fail to seize; it has now appeared in print here, at Cappi & Diabelli's, and I am convinced that I shall earn the gratitude of any reader who wishes to procure this masterpiece for having drawn his attention to it.

Title page of 'Der Erlkönig', Schubert's opus 1, published on 2 April 1821 by Cappi & Diabelli.

Josef Hüttenbrenner, writing for the Vienna *Sammler*, was equally positive:

This ballad, sung on 7 March by the renowned Court Opera singer, Herr Vogl, at the concert organized by the Society of Ladies of the Nobility for the benefit of its charities, pleased so much by its music that it had to be repeated by general request. The same piece had already been performed at the foremost houses where music is cultivated, and everywhere Herr Schubert's composition earned the merited – that is to say the most resounding – success. The favour with which music-lovers have received it appears to be justified by the judgement of the most excellent local connoisseurs of art, according to which Goethe's words have been most justly conceived by the young composer and their characteristic features have been reproduced with an arresting truthfulness in this thoroughly original composition. Musical Vienna, on its executive side, can thus but ardently welcome the fact that the setting of the above ballad is now to enjoy a larger publicity, and it is the less doubtful that the editor will be favoured with success because the subscribers already amount to a sufficient number to cover the costs of publication.

Other reviews and notices testify to the increasing number of performances of Schubert's songs. Things did not always go as well as might have been hoped: one diarist tartly records '3 musical pieces by Schubert – of which the last, "The Spirits above the Waters", went under completely'.[16]

Meanwhile Schubert was enjoying life, if a letter of 30 January 1821 sent by Josef Huber to his fiancée is to be believed:

Last Friday I had excellent entertainment: as [Fräulein] Schober was at St Pölten, Franz invited Schubert in the evening and fourteen of his close acquaintances. So a lot of splendid songs by Schubert were sung and played by himself, which lasted until after 10 o'clock in the evening. After that punch was drunk, offered by one of the party, and as it was very good and plentiful the party, in a happy mood anyhow, became even merrier; so it was 3 o'clock in the morning before we parted. You may imagine how agreeable the enjoyment of so many cultivated men, which I missed for so many years, must be for me, and that it is further enhanced by the recollection of my student years. For this I would gladly leave all that is called entertainment.

It is possible that it was to this very evening that Schubert referred in a letter to his brother Ferdinand:

As I was seedy today on account of yesterday's dissipations, I did no work on the Offertory, and it is therefore not ready. What is more, Anselm Hüttenbrenner is here, with whom I have made an appointment for 6 o'clock tonight. If you should feel inclined to be with us, come to Frau von Sanssouci's in the Wipplingerstrasse, where

Schubert's room at 21 Wipplingerstrasse, where he lodged alone for the first time in 1821. The relative lack of clutter in Schwind's pen-and-ink drawing suggests it was early in Schubert's tenure!

I used to live, and perhaps enquire below in the tobacco vaults, about 6 o'clock. If not, we shall meet tomorrow at the Cross Inn.

These letters provide us with a written record of one of the first of what have come to be called the 'Schubertiads', those informal (and often bibulous) evening gatherings of friends and acquaintances at which only music by Schubert was played or sung, frequently with improvised dances or charades for which the composer played the piano. This one happened to be all-male, but this was by no means always the case. Schubert's letter is undated but it is likely to have been written in January or February 1821 as it was about then that he left the lodgings he shared with Mayrhofer above Frau Sanssouci's tobacco shop to live alone, for the first time, in rooms nearby. He had recently made the acquaintance of a young man, still only sixteen, who was to become an artist of some distinction – Moritz von Schwind. His pen-and-ink drawing of Schubert's room in his new lodgings is contemporary. It shows a piano on which is piled music in some abandon, while underneath a box contains further volumes. Later, after Schubert's death, Schwind made his famous sepia drawing of one of the Schubertiads, *Schubert-Abend bei Josef von Spaun*. It depicts an attractive scene – Schubert playing the piano studiously, Vogl seated alongside him singing, the ladies grouped round them on chairs, the men standing, listening intently, behind – and perfectly captures the spirit and atmosphere of these happy evenings (see front and back endpapers).

In the summer of 1821 Schubert composed an aria and a duet to be inserted into *La Clochette* by the French composer Hérold, which was performed at the Kärntnerthor under the German title *Das Zauberglöckchen* (The Magic Bell). The duet fared reasonably well at the hands of the critics, but the aria received the following savaging from the Vienna *Allgemeine musikalische Zeitung*:

For one thing, the voice-part continually lies high, even in forte, and what is even more damaging is the frequent repetition of one and the same high note. It is clear that Herr Rosner is incapable of singing it properly to the end. Drastic changes of tempo, by the way, disturb its unity ...

Schubert took refuge in a visit to Atzenbrugg, an estate some twenty miles north-west of Vienna managed by Schober's uncle. Here there was a great deal of convivial singing, feasting and dancing. Schubert had been before and, as in the previous year, one of his fellow guests was the painter Leopold Kupelwieser whose portraits of Schubert and Schober are a valuable record. His watercolours depicting excursions, charades and other group activities, capture what seems to have been a particularly relaxed and carefree atmosphere.

Schubert returned to Vienna in August and began work on a symphony in E major often referred to as the Seventh Symphony. The D major sketches of 1818 bear witness to his previous unsuccessful efforts to write a symphony. Composition

Kupelwieser's watercolour representing a charade at Atzenbrugg in 1821. Schubert has finished improvising his accompaniment while the artist leans on the instrument, his dog, Drago, sheltering beneath it.

Excursion of the Schubertians from Atzenbrugg, 1820: watercolour by Kupelwieser who is standing on the extreme left with Schubert.

had not come easily; there were, for example, seven attempts to compose a finale, none of them very promising – though the scholar is glad of an opportunity to study Schubert's working methods from the scraps remaining. The E major work is fascinating for similar reasons, though on this occasion Schubert worked in a completely different way. All 147 pages of the orchestral score are ruled out and the slow introduction and first seventy-five bars of the Allegro first movement written out in full. Thereafter the symphony is 'whispered in', with very often no more than violin or flute music indicating the general nature and direction of the melody. At other times, a passage may be more fully worked out with accompanying material and bass, almost as if the composer was improvising with the orchestra. There is enough here for the expert to have a crack at completing the score, and it has been done in several ways, but surely the reason Schubert abandoned the work was that what he had written failed to inspire him to continue. It marked a return to the eighteenth-century classical style, with pretty but unremarkable tunes incapable of carrying the emotional weight and structural development he had found possible in that one C minor quartet movement written in the previous December.

Another reason for giving up the symphony was that Schubert had embarked on yet another operatic project, *Alfonso und Estrella*. The libretto was by Schober, written, he said, 'in a state of very happy enthusiasm, but with great innocence of heart and mind'. The two of them decided to leave the bustle of Vienna behind in order to concentrate on their work and in September set off, via Atzenbrugg, for St Pölten where one of Schober's relations was bishop. They stayed at Ochsenburg Castle and between 20 September and 16 October the first act was completed. To

finish the opera the men returned to Vienna, from where on 4 November Schober
sent an account of their activities to Josef von Spaun:

*Schubert and I have now returned from our half country and half town holiday, and
we have brought back recollections of a lovely month. At Ochsenburg we were much
taken up with the truly beautiful surroundings, and at St Pölten with balls and concerts; in spite of which we worked hard, especially Schubert, who has done nearly
two acts, while I am on the last. I only wished you had been there to hear the glorious
tunes as they arose: it is wonderful how once again he poured forth rich and teeming
ideas. Our room at St P. was particularly snug: the twin beds, a sofa next to the warm
stove, and a fortepiano made it all very domestic and cosy. In the evenings we always
compared notes on what we had done during the day, then sent for beer, smoked our
pipes and read, or else Sophie and Nettel came across and there was singing. There
were a couple of Schubertiads at the Bishop's and one at the Baroness Münk's, of
whom I am quite fond, where a princess, two countesses and three baronesses were
present, all most generously ecstatic. Now we have come here with my mother. At
Heiligen-Eich we were entertained to dinner, and for a travelling present Heaven
sent us the first of the glorious days that have gladdened us till now, i.e. for a matter
of a week. The Bishop too has now followed us, so that St P. has been transferred to
Vienna. He and Mother are well. They are more than usually cheerful and send you
their greetings. That we have sadly missed Kuppel, who had promised to follow us
but did not, and you too, you can imagine; for we should have been particularly glad
to make you two judges of our work. Altogether, I feel like one who has looked into
the sun and now sees everywhere those confounded black spots – so disturbing is
your departure for me. The Crown we found utterly desolate.*

The letter goes on to catalogue incidents in the daily life of many of their friends:
playing whist in the coffee-house, gambling, Kupelwieser's painting, a performance
of Weber's *Der Freischütz* which did not please much, and so on. The whole gives
a sense of a closely bonded group of artistic people of differing talents and background who shared the same interests, enjoyed each other's companionship, and
provided mutual sympathy and support. Within this group Schubert felt comfort-
able, but outside it he became increasingly ill at ease.

Alfonso und Estrella progressed steadily and the score was completed by the end
of February 1822. It was an act of faith to write it, for neither Schober nor Schubert
had been commissioned. When they began it they still had friends at the
Kärntnerthor but by the close of 1821 the new management was in place, headed
by Domenico Barbaja. This most famous of contemporary impresarios already
managed all the opera houses in Naples and was later to run La Scala, Milan, as
well. Italian opera was central to his thinking, and it was not long before Vogl and

other Viennese singers left the company. They took with them Schubert's chances of performance – and the opera in fact lay unperformed until 1854, when it was heard in Weimar. Schober's libretto promised more than those of Hofmann had done, with hero and heroine meeting in unlikely circumstances, falling in love but being kept apart until the end of three acts by intrigues both political and amorous. It gave Schubert the opportunity to compose a sequence of arias, duets and larger ensembles which were, in effect, songs (of his best kind) on a larger canvas. Indeed, though *Alfonso und Estrella* is unique among Schubert's dramatic works in having no spoken dialogue, the overall effect does remain one of a succession of set pieces rather than an emotional experience building up inevitably. Nevertheless, there is some quite glorious music; Alfred Einstein was moved to liken part of the score to 'Verdi and mature Verdi at that', and Maurice Brown considers it 'first-rate, full of Schubert's most endearing lyricism and dramatic genius'. Having once played the role of King Troila in one of the very rare stagings of this opera, I am bound to agree with Brown's view of the lyricism, but have to say that it was not an easy opera in which to convey a sense of dramatic continuity and progression.

There were very few songs in 1821, but among them are seven settings of Goethe. 'Geheimes' (The Secret) is a wonderful little song, its short, tiptoeing vocal phrases and whispering piano accompaniment gently confiding to us the secret of the beloved's meaningful glances. 'Grenzen der Menschheit' (Man's Limitations) requires a bass voice of exceptional quality for its successful execution, as if Schubert expected to demonstrate man's insignificance in comparison with the gods.

At the beginning of 1822 – when they were still at work on their opera – Schubert moved into Schober's lodgings in the Spiegelgasse. This was the second time that Schubert had shared an apartment with Schober, and it was not to be the last. The relationship between the two young men was obviously close, but it was not regarded with unqualified favour by some of the composer's friends. Josef Kenner, writing in the 1850s, remembered:

Schubert liked to visit us in Upper Austria and for me too he retained, to the end of his life, the kindly interest of the old Seminary days; but his body, strong as it was, succumbed to the cleavage in his – souls – as I would put it, of which one pressed heavenwards and the other bathed in slime.

And later:

Schubert's genius subsequently attracted, among other friends, the heart of a seductively amiable and brilliant young man, endowed with the noblest talents, whose extraordinary gifts would have been so worthy of a moral foundation and would have richly repaid a stricter schooling than the one he unfortunately had. But shunning so much effort as unworthy of genius and summarily rejecting such fetters as a form of prejudice and restriction, while at the same time arguing with brilliant and ingratiatingly persuasive power, this scintillating individuality, as I was told later, won a lasting and pernicious influence over Schubert's honest susceptibility. If this was not apparent in his work it was all the more so in his life. Anyone who knew Schubert knows how he was made of two natures, foreign to each other, how powerfully the craving for pleasure dragged his soul down to the slough of moral degradation, and how highly he valued the utterances of friends he respected, and so will find his surrender to the false prophet, who embellished sensuality in such a flattering manner, all the more understandable. But more hardened characters than he were seduced, for longer or shorter periods, by the devilish attraction of associating with that apparently warm but inwardly merely vain being into worshipping him as an idol.

This intimation seemed to me indispensable for the biographer's grasp of the subject, for it concerns an episode in Schubert's life which only too probably caused his premature death and certainly hastened it.

But it must, of course, remain a mere intimation and no name may be mentioned, for Schubert's fame should not be misused as a pillory for the purpose of perpetuating the memory of wicked people.

All this sounds rather mysterious, but Kenner makes his meaning clearer in a letter of 22 May 1858:

May I be allowed to preface my reply to your questions, dated 15 to 17 of this month, with the remark that by Schubert's seducer I meant Franz von Schober, whom I had known, and known intimately, since 1808 at the Kremsmünster Seminary ... Later experiences showed that, under the guise of the most amiable sociability, and even of engaging affection, there reigned in this whole family a deep moral depravity, so that it was not to be wondered at that Franz von Schober went the same way. Only he devised a philosophical system for his own reassurance and to justify himself in the eyes of the world as well as to provide a basis for his aesthetic oracle, about which he was probably as hazy as any of his disciples; nevertheless he found the mysticism of sensuality sufficiently elastic for his own freedom of movement; and so did his pupils. The need for love and friendship emerged with such egotism and jealousy that to his adherents he alone was all, not only prophet, but God himself and apart from his oracles he was willing to tolerate no other religion, no morals, no restraint ... as regards women he was completely unscrupulous, for he had learned to recognize only two kinds: those with whom he was successful and were therefore worthy of him and those with whom this was not the case and who were therefore not worthy of him.

Meanwhile, in February, Weber came to Vienna to conduct a couple of performances of his opera, *Der Freischütz*. Schubert was introduced to him, but whatever help Weber might have been able to offer the younger man was effectively nullified by Schubert's ill-timed criticism of one of his other operas, *Euryanthe*, when it was performed in Vienna the following year. Schubert was probably no more than honest in preferring one to the other, but he was clearly not highly skilled in diplomacy.

In January the *Allgemeine musikalische Zeitung* of Vienna published a detailed criticism of a number of Schubert's songs. It was evidently written by someone who knew not only the songs published so far but also many of those existing at that time only in manuscript (possibly the editor, Kanne). It could hardly have been more complimentary:

The new books of songs by Franz Schubert, again published by Cappi & Diabelli and containing 'The Overblown Lime-Tree', 'The Flight of Time' and 'Death and the Maiden'... give us a welcome opportunity thoroughly to recommend to the musical public not only these, but far more particularly the earlier songs published by the same artistic house and written by a young composer with a rich lyrical gift, and openly to express our respect for his excellent talent. Not often has a composer had so large a share of the gift for making the poet's fancy so profoundly impressive for the receptive listener's heart. This is shown with especial felicity by Goethe's song for Gretchen at the spinning-wheel, where the vivid imitation of the sound of a spinning-wheel makes a most characteristic background in a Rembrandtesque chiaroscuro for the description of the profoundest depths of a woman's being, lost now in gloomy visions of the present and the future, now in sweetly melancholy recollections of the past. No feeling heart can follow the changes of the unhappy Gretchen's emotions depicted here without being seized by sadness and by the foreboding of the fearful proximity of the evil powers which ensnare her. Equally excellent, both in the voice-parts and in the characteristic accompaniments, are 'Memnon' and 'Antigone and Oedipus' (both to poems by Mayrhofer)... These beautiful poems Herr Schubert has reproduced by music of stirring truthfulness. The introduction to 'Memnon' conjures up the magic sounds of the famous Egyptian statue. No womanish plaint desecrates the heroic king's mournful words. The pain that burns in his breast blazes up into wild flames which at last die down in rapt anticipation.

At about the same time Schubert was commissioned to compose a hymn or cantata for the birthday of Emperor Francis I, which was performed in February by the pupils of the Theresianum, a school for the children of the nobility founded by Empress Maria Theresa. At the same concert 'Erlkönig' was sung. Schubert's musical star was ascending. His relations with his fellows, however, were not always so stellar, as a letter from Holzapfel to Stadler suggests:

Schubert, as they say, made bruit, *and he will likewise, as they say, make his* sort. *I rarely see him, nor do we hit it off very well, his world being a very different one, as it should be. His somewhat gruff manner stands him in very good stead and will make a strong man and a ripe artist of him; he will be worthy of art ... Schubert is working at an opera, the words of which are by Schober, a work at which they are said to have both laboured together in mutual understanding.*

In particular, Schubert's continuing proximity to Schober led to an estrangement with Michael Vogl. The immediate effect of this was that Vogl refused to use any of his (dwindling) influence to have *Alfonso und Estrella* staged in Vienna. Josef von Spaun's brother, Anton, writing to his wife in July 1822, described the situation:

To me Vogl is extremely pleasing. He told me his whole relationship to Schubert with the utmost frankness, and unfortunately I am quite unable to excuse the latter. Vogl is very much embittered against Schober, for whose sake Schubert behaved most ungratefully towards Vogl and who makes the fullest use of Schubert in order to extricate himself from financial embarrassments and to defray the expenditure which has already exhausted the greater part of his mother's fortune. I wish very much that somebody were here who would defend Schubert at least in the matter of the most glaring reproaches. Vogl also says Schober's opera is bad and a perfect failure, and that altogether Schubert is quite on the wrong road.

Anton suggests that Schober's relationship with Schubert included access to his money (royalties from the publication of songs, perhaps) but it may be that Schubert's name was now of such a standing in musical circles that Schober felt able to use it as a lever in approaching others for a subvention. Josef von Spaun, however, was still on the best of terms with Schober, distance perhaps lending enchantment, for Spaun had left Vienna in September 1821 to take up a civil service post in Linz, his home town. Writing to Schober in March 1822 he said:

Winter has gone by since then, and much that is of interest must have happened among you all, of which you should not deprive your far-off dear one. I am so very anxious to know all that the poetic-musical-painting triumvirate has produced. It cuts me to the soul that Schubert has ceased to sound for me ... Persuade him to send me a few new songs one day ... Where have there been any Schubertiads this winter? How are things at the Crown, to whose people I send greetings? ... On the whole I am well content, only nothing can make me forget the happy, sociable hours I spent with you all, and which Schubert so often beautified; I fear they will never return so happily for me.

The 'painting' member of the triumvirate was Schwind, who had been introduced to the Schubert–Schober set by Spaun, and who adopted the phrase, 'One should take a spoonful of music a day' as his motto. They gave each other nicknames and because of his tubby figure Schubert was known as 'Schwammerl' ('Schwamm' being a mushroom). The extension to that most expensive fungus, the truffle, was also used on occasion and much punning went on in the camaraderie of the inn. Anton Prokesch, then a staff lieutenant, joined Schubert's circle around this time, and his diaries make frequent references to their meetings at the Crown, or over lunch at the influential table of the poet Karoline Pichler. Schubert had set a couple of her poems back in 1816, but their friendship did not develop until 1821 when he wrote 'Der Unglückliche' (The Forlorn One), a sort of concert aria. It was this song of which, according to Vogl's wife Kunigunde, Schubert denied all knowledge when shown the manuscript a few weeks after Vogl had sung it: 'It's not bad. Who wrote it?' This remark is often held as an example of the 'absent-minded' Schubert: more probably it was Schubert's attempt at wit missing the target.

Songs were more or less the only things written in the earlier part of the year and there are several particularly fine ones. There is the first of the Rückert songs, 'Sei mir gegrüsst' (I greet you), a most attractive serenade, setting a *ghazal*, an oriental love-poem, in a sensuous, almost erotic manner. It seems probable that Schubert's attention was drawn to Rückert's collection, *Östliche Rosen* (Eastern Roses), by Franz von Bruchmann. Bruchmann also introduced Schubert to the poetry of August, Count Platen-Hallermünde, whom he had met the previous year at Erlangen. Platen's poetry is perhaps of greater significance to later composers (notably Brahms) but the two settings made by Schubert are both good. 'Die Liebe hat gelogen' (Love has lied) is perhaps the finer, a miniature, little more than an epigram, and the more intense in its feeling. A copy of this song was sent by Bruchmann to Platen who then bought copies of Schubert's published music. Today it would be called 'networking'. Schubert was not so entrepreneurial, but the web of literary people who influenced him was growing all the time, and through them his fame spread.

Bruchmann did us all a good turn in September 1822 when he visited the banished Senn in Innsbruck. He brought back the manuscripts of two poems which Schubert must have set there and then, 'Selige Welt' (Blessed World) and 'Schwanengesang' (Swan Song), D744. 'Schwanengesang' could have been written by no other composer, both the beauty and the finality of the swan's song being magically captured in the characteristically Schubertian juxtaposition of A flat major and minor.

There are further Mayrhofer and Schober settings and appropriately, given his indirect influence on this year's songs, several settings of Bruchmann's poems. The splendid, would-be heroic, 'An die Leier' (To the Lyre) encapsulates perfectly the frustrations of the romantic poet in an unsympathetic world. He would sing of the epic deeds of the warriors of old but his lyre will only play songs of love. He would change the strings (and willingly change the lyre) but these, too, sing only of love. So farewell heroes! From the close of the year comes 'Schwestergruss' (Sister's

Greeting), written by Bruchmann on the death of his sister, Sybilla, in the summer of 1820. It is not a great poem, but Schubert's music lifts it on to a very much higher plane and, when it is set in the context of Senn's 'Schwanengesang', Schober's 'Todesmusik' (Death Music) and 'Schatzgräbers Begehr' (Treasure-seeker's Wish), a common thread emerges – one which is continued in the great masterpiece of this period, the 'Unfinished' Symphony in B minor.

We do not know why it was left unfinished. It used to be claimed that it *was* finished, but that the third and fourth movements had been lost or destroyed. It is known that in 1823 Schubert sent the score of the symphony to Anselm Hüttenbrenner, via his brother Josef, presumably in the hope that Anselm would perform it with the Styrian Music Society of which he was then director. But no performance took place, and it was not until 1865 that Hüttenbrenner passed the score on to Johann Herbeck, who conducted the first performance in Vienna in December of that year. In the manuscript there is a single page of the Scherzo which would have been the third movement of the symphony, and it was not long before the suspicion grew that Anselm Hüttenbrenner had lost or destroyed the two missing movements during the forty-odd years since the score had come into his possession. But the discovery in Vienna in the 1960s of the second page of the Scherzo, only partially orchestrated and evidently removed from the score by Schubert himself, lifted the blame from Hüttenbrenner and proved that the symphony was genuinely unfinished.

But we still do not know why. It cannot be discounted that Schubert felt, instinctively, that he did not have the means at his disposal to write two further movements capable of complementing what he had already committed to paper, though the sketch for the Scherzo which survives in piano score promises more than just a token gesture, if it had been fully worked out. It is also possible that Schubert's enthusiasm for the symphony was superseded by a new preoccupation with another of his perpetual problems, the piano sonata, for at this time he also began work on the so-called 'Wanderer' Fantasy which, happily, he did complete. There is little support for the theory that he utilized the material for the remaining movements elsewhere. In the end, the most likely explanation is simply that Schubert could not bring himself to return to or complete a work during the course of which he found he had contracted syphilis.

Nowhere in the contemporary material available to us, nor in the less reliable memoirs of those who wrote about Schubert only after his death, is there specific reference to this particular disease. Analysis of the timing of Schubert's admission to hospital in 1823, the shaving and regrowth of his hair later that year, and many other little medical details deduced from the existing documentation lead to the conclusion that some time in the autumn of 1822 or early in 1823 Schubert realized

The last page of the manuscript of the second movement of the 'Unfinished' Symphony.

that he had syphilis. From then on he knew that he was bound to endure a miserable future and possibly a lingering and unpleasant death and it is inconceivable that his creative work should not have felt the effect of so great a shock.

The 'Unfinished' Symphony hardly needs comment. In its two completed movements it forms a tone poem a little over twenty minutes long which penetrates to the emotional heart of the listener with the most economical of means. It does not arrest in the manner of a Beethoven symphony. It does not wear its heart on its sleeve as later romantic symphonies do. The first movement uses two themes, not dissimilar, the first of which is stated without preamble right at the start on the cellos and basses. It is lyrical, gentle and yet ominous. The cellos, too, are given the first statement of the other main melody, one of the best-known in all Schubert, both romantic and sad. From the different melodic elements which make up these two themes Schubert constructs the entire movement, using the material to create accompanimental figures, to build climaxes, to shape his orchestration. This is brilliantly worked out from the technical point of view, yet the listener should remain completely unaware of the techniques in use. What is astonishing is that such creative energy should be released from so innocuous a beginning. Remarkably, the Andante which follows maintains this tension, being no less emotional nor less direct in the simplicity of its appeal and its economy of material. Having begun in quiet contemplation the symphony evolves in a great passionate arc until at the end of the second movement it sinks away into the ether. We may bewail the movements which Schubert failed to bequeath to us. Concert audiences are more than delighted he left to us what he did.

In the autumn of 1822 Schubert completed his Mass in A flat which had been started in 1819. It is a good sing for a choral society and probably serves the liturgy as adequately as the greatest mass by Palestrina or Haydn. The craftsmanship is there, certainly, but the inspiration is not, and the lasting effect is of sugary piousness rather than religious zeal. Schubert never served God quite so handsomely as he served the gods. In completing the catalogue for this year one ought to mention at least one of several Goethe songs written in December, 'Der Musensohn' (The Muses' Son), a good example of the carefully composed art-song being made to feel as if it were a folk-song handed down from generation to generation.

Pride of place for the end of this year, though, must go to the 'Wanderer' Fantasy for solo piano [CD2]. This powerful and ebullient work gets its title from a fragment of the song 'Der Wanderer'. Perhaps it is only with hindsight that we are able to attach significance to Schubert's choice of the musical phrase to the words 'The sun seems to me so cold' at what was for him such an unhappy time. Not that the fantasy is in any way morbid. It positively teems with life. Nevertheless, the germ of the work is the dactylic rhythm which is derived from this phrase of the song (common to such great 'death songs' as 'Death and the Maiden') and which is used to unify the whole work in a cyclic manner. Schubert was not the first composer by any means to adopt cyclic construction, but by employing it himself for the first time he solved the structural problems he had hitherto encountered in his piano sonatas. It has been suggested that he may have been directly influenced by Beethoven's Seventh Symphony, where such a device is used in the Allegretto. It is certain that Schubert admired Beethoven, but whether his admiration took this particular form can only remain, like so many other Schubertian conjectures, an open question.

CHAPTER 6

1823

It seems probable that it was the onset of syphilis that caused Schubert to leave Schober's lodgings in the autumn of 1822 and return to the schoolhouse in the Rossau. This move has been seen by some as a sign that a reconciliation had taken place between Schubert and his father after Franz had been expelled from the family. There is no evidence to support or deny this though much has been read into an allegorical tale written down by Schubert in July and usually called 'My Dream'. Clearly this can be interpreted either autobiographically or as fiction – the artistic outpouring of a young man wholly caught up in the ferment of the romantic movement – though the fact that the tale is preserved both in a pencil-written original and in a copy thought to be in Schober's hand suggests it may be the latter. Schubert's brother Ferdinand added the title and signature in ink.

I was the brother of many brothers and sisters. Our father and mother were good people. I was deeply and lovingly devoted to them all. – Once my father took us to a feast. There my brothers became very merry. I, however, was sad. Then my father approached me and bade me enjoy the delicious dishes. But I could not, whereupon my father, becoming angry, banished me from his sight. I turned my footsteps and, my heart full of infinite love for those who disdained it, I wandered into far-off regions. For long years I felt torn between the greatest grief and the greatest love. And so the news of my mother's death reached me. I hastened to see her, and my father, mellowed by sorrow, did not hinder my entrance. Then I saw her corpse. Tears flowed from my eyes. Then I saw her lie there like the old happy past, in which according to the deceased's desire we were to live as she had done herself.

And we followed her body in sorrow, and the coffin sank to earth. – From that time on I again remained at home. Then my father once more took me to his favourite garden. He asked whether I liked it. But the garden wholly repelled me, and I dared not say so. Then, reddening, he asked me a second time: did the garden please me? I denied it, trembling. At that my father struck me, and I fled. And I turned away a second time, and with a heart filled with endless love for those who scorned me, I again wandered far away. For many and many a year I sung songs. Whenever I attempted to sing of love, it turned to pain. And again, when I tried to sing of pain, it turned to love.

Thus were love and pain divided in me.

And one day I had news of a gentle maiden who had just died. And a circle formed around her grave in which many youths and old men walked as though in everlasting bliss. They spoke softly, so as not to wake the maiden.

Heavenly thoughts seemed for ever to be showered on the youths from the maiden's gravestone, like fine sparks producing a gentle rustling. I too longed sorely to walk there. Only a miracle, however, can lead you to that circle, they said. But I went to the gravestone with slow steps and lowered gaze, filled with devotion and firm belief, and before I was aware of it, I found myself in the circle, which uttered a wondrously lovely sound; and I felt as though eternal bliss were gathered together into a single moment. My father too I saw, reconciled and loving. He took me in his arms and wept. But not as much as I.

View of the Rossau, to which Schubert returned to live with his father at the schoolhouse: engraving by Johann Ziegler, 1780.

In any case Schubert was ill enough to write on 28 February 1823 to Ignaz von Mosel, 'Kindly forgive me if I am compelled to incommode you with another letter so soon, the circumstances of my health still forbidding me to leave the house.' He was presumably in the infectious early or secondary stages of his illness and as the spring progressed his condition worsened and he was admitted to hospital. His despair is readily apparent from a poem dated 8 May 1823:

My Prayer

> *With a holy zeal I yearn*
> *Life in fairer worlds to learn;*
> *Would this gloomy earth might seem*
> *Filled with love's almighty dream.*

> *Sorrow's child, almighty Lord,*
> *Grant Thy bounty for reward.*
> *For redemption from above*
> *Send a ray of endless love.*

> *See, abased in dust and mire,*
> *Scorched by agonizing fire,*
> *I in torture go my way,*
> *Nearing doom's destructive day.*

> *Take my life, my flesh and blood,*
> *Plunge it all in Lethe's flood,*
> *To a purer, stronger state*
> *Deign me, Great One, to translate.*

During Schubert's illness Josef Hüttenbrenner looked after his friend's meagre supply of cash. Some of his accounts survive; their inaccuracies would hardly satisfy the auditors of today but none the less they demonstrate Schubert's urgent need for money. Cappi & Diabelli had so far undertaken sixteen publications of Schubert's works, for ten of which Leopold Sonnleithner had negotiated that the composer should retain the rights, thus earning him something like 2,000 florins, or 200 florins per opus and the prospect of more had he been willing to wait. So it must be assumed that it was against Sonnleithner's better judgement that Schubert wrote to Diabelli on 23 February 1823:

Herewith I am sending you the Quartet together with the pianoforte accompaniment.
The appearance of the two books of waltzes, &c., seemed to me somewhat strange,

for it was not carried out quite according to arrangements. An adequate remunera-
tion seems to be only indicated.

   Furthermore I should like to ask you kindly to let me see the account for the last
three books, for I intend to draw my balance and will let you have them, if you wish,
for your own property for 300 florins.

   I should also like to ask you for a few more copies of the Fantasy.

Clearly, in order to obtain ready cash Schubert himself was prepared to part with
his music, including any potential future income from it, for quite modest sums.
He had already sold opp. 1–7 and here he is offering three separate works (opp.
12–14) for only 300 florins. The quartet referred to is not a string quartet, for none
had yet been performed in public, but a vocal quartet, 'Naturgenuss' (The Enjoyment of Nature). These part-songs were performed with considerable frequency
not only at private gatherings but even at the Philharmonic Society; it is a pity that
they are so rarely encountered today.

   On 10 April 1823 three songs were published by Sauer & Leidesdorf, described
as 'Privileged Dealers in Art and Alabaster and Music Publishers in Vienna', and
on the same day Schubert broke with Cappi & Diabelli in a letter in an unusually
strong tone:

Your letter was a surprise indeed, since according to Herr von Cappi's own statement
the account appeared to me to be settled altogether. Having by no means discovered
the most honest intentions in my publishers' earlier transactions on the occasion of
the issue of the waltzes, I was well able to understand this second procedure, from
which, gentlemen, you will easily explain to yourselves my reasons for entering into
a permanent arrangement with another art dealer ... But as I doubt very much
whether you take this all-too-human view, I take the liberty of drawing your atten-
tion to the fact that I am still entitled to demand 20 copies of the later and 12 of the
earlier books, and may even more justifiably ask for the 50 florins of which you man-
aged to deprive me in such a subtle manner. If you will kindly add all this up, you
will find that my demand is not only the greater, but also the more just, although I
should nevertheless have refrained from making it had you not so disagreeably
reminded me of it. The debt having long been settled in this way, as you will please
acknowledge, there can be no question whatever of any publication of songs, which
once again you could not estimate cheaply enough, for I am now in a position to
obtain 200 florins per book, and Herr von Steiner has repeatedly conveyed to me an
offer to publish my works. In conclusion I have still to request you to be good enough
to send me all my manuscripts, of the engraved as well as the unengraved works.

         Respectfully,
            Frz. Schubert
               Composer

N.B. I request an exact account of copies delivered to me since our first agreement of sale, as I find that my statement greatly exceeds yours.

Received MSS of 1 Sonata, 2 books of songs and 2 songs on one sheet, returned.
Jos. Hüttenbrenner

In later life Sonnleithner lamented the lack of wisdom in these business moves, saying that Schubert could have received considerable and enduring profit from his works had he not given them away completely for such pitiful sums:

This really rather ungrateful behaviour on Schubert's part did not estrange him from us in any way; we regretted his weakness but continued to promote the performance and furtherance of his works.

The sonata noted by Hüttenbrenner as having been returned is almost certainly the one in A minor (D784). It is easy to read into the starkness of the opening a musical reflection of Schubert's personal unhappiness in the early part of 1823 when this sonata was composed. It could hardly be in greater contrast to the beginning of the previous piano sonata, in A major (D664), and the difference is a great deal more than the simple opposition of major and minor. In the intervening years there had been little purely instrumental music but in three works, the Quartet Movement in C minor, the 'Wanderer' Fantasy, and the 'Unfinished' Symphony, Schubert had demonstrated a new-found ability to use melodic themes. In the 'Wanderer' Fantasy a single short theme had been the principal source of the whole work, unifying it, giving it strength and cohesion. So in this A minor Sonata there is an organic relationship between the individual cells which make up the various melodic and accompanimental figures from which each movement is constructed. In the central slow movement everything grows from a single theme. Three widely differing elements are brought into play in the Finale: the brooding qualities of the opening movement, the lyrical nature of the second and a new scherzo-like triplet figure which races helter-skelter through the movement, demanding considerable skill and confidence on the part of the pianist and leaving the listener exhilarated when the feat is accomplished successfully.

Little mention has yet been made of the many shorter piano pieces, waltzes, ländler, écossaises, and so on, which Schubert composed throughout his life, and there are several sets of dances contemporary with, yet wholly different from, this sonata. Cappi & Diabelli had published some dances (the op. 9 set, for instance) and they, and more like them, could have provided Schubert with a steady income. Instead they are now providing twentieth-century publishers with excellent short, self-contained pieces for young piano students as they climb upwards through their examination grades. But that is no cause to belittle them: in the hands of a cultivated

artist a group of such pieces can prove remarkably refreshing to the jaded ear too
long exposed to programmes of unrelieved earnestness both on disc and in the
concert hall.

Also from early 1823 come two further theatrical works, *Die Verschworenen* (The
Conspirators) and *Fierabras*, neither staged during his lifetime. The former was a
one-act operetta of some promise, the latter a full three-act opera of little. It took
Schubert until 26 September to complete the dramatic music for *Fierabras* while
the overture was not finished until 2 October. He laboured diligently to set the
libretto by Josef Kupelwieser (brother of Leopold) but there was no prospect of the
Italian management of the Kärntnerthor taking any notice. Performances in recent
years have merely confirmed Barbaja's sound judgement in the matter of commercial viability, however worthy the music. Towards the end of the year Schubert
accepted a commission to write incidental music for a romantic drama, *Rosamunde*.
Only two performances were given, the plot being feeble, but a suite made up from
the ballet music and entr'actes has justifiably endeared itself to concert audiences
for many years. There was no overture, and those for both *Alfonso und Estrella* and
Die Zauberharfe have been attributed 'Rosamunde' titles (see p. 59). While Schubert
may always thereafter have entertained hopes of writing a definitive German opera
he completed no further dramatic works.

However, 1823 was an important year for song. There were further Rückert songs,
not least 'Du bist die Ruh' (You are Peace), of which Fischer-Dieskau said 'Schubert
is not singing to an audience out over the prompter's box, he is singing rather to
the inner soul.' Fischer-Dieskau, the consummate Lieder singer, possessed the sort
of technique to raise the performer above the difficulties of this particular song. In
the hands of such a singer it becomes a symbol of the poet unselfishly seeking an
ideal world. Fischer-Dieskau also brought a very special chill to his performances
of the terrifying song 'Der Zwerg' (The Dwarf) [CD1]. It is one of the few settings
of Matthäus von Collin, Josef von Spaun's cousin. In the cold light of day its text
hardly stands up to examination: why on earth would a king allow his queen to be
out in a boat on a lake at nightfall with only a jealous dwarf as companion? The
queen gazes up to the stars who have never lied to her. They tell her that she will
soon depart from this world. The dwarf blames the queen for her own downfall,
for she chose the king instead of him. He strangles her, kisses her pale cheeks and
she slips from his grasp into the deep. He will never more set foot on any shore.
The bass line of the piano accompaniment uses a recurring figure made up of three
short notes and one long one: it begins on a single note, but as the song develops
it too develops so that when the queen slips into the water and the dwarf looks
down on her lifeless body the figure has become identical to the portentous motif
which opens Beethoven's Fifth Symphony. But this dot-dot-dot-dash rhythm can

be found in many Schubert works, not least the 'Unfinished' Symphony, and very often when there is some erotic allusion. If Schubert was the dwarf we can only speculate who was the queen.

Set alongside this 'Wehmut' (Melancholy) and 'Nacht und Träume' (Night and Dreams), two further great Collin songs, and the scene is set for a new step forward in the history of song, and with it a disquieting reminder of the boy who, fifteen years ago, was sent to school in a white coat and dubbed 'the miller's son'. The new Müller (Wilhelm) came from Dessau but studied and lived in Berlin. He was three years older than Schubert and did not live long enough to find out that Schubert had set a number of his poems in two of the finest song cycles in the entire song repertoire Müller, unusually for a poet, actually expected his verses to be set to music, even to the point of feeling them better sung than spoken, though the poems of Schubert's first cycle in fact had their origins in a party game. In 1816 a group of cultivated men and women met at the house of a Privy Councillor in Berlin to take part in a sort of literary entertainment in which they tried to revive the spirit of 'Old Germany', fashionably embracing a romanticized folk idiom (shades of Marie Antoinette). Each participant was required to assume a particular character, write the part in verse and act it through. Given his surname Müller was, hardly surprisingly, given the role of miller. After the charades he developed his lines into a fully-fledged cycle of poems and published them in 1821 as the first part of a volume entitled *Seventy-seven Poems from the Posthumous Papers of a Travelling Horn-Player*. They bore the instruction 'To be read in winter' and were accompanied by a prologue and epilogue in rhyming couplets gently debagging those who would play the country bumpkin. As the verses were simple in form they suited Schubert's purpose admirably.

Schubert had already written several lengthy songs which could be described as sequences, developing the musical ideas with the story line, you might say. What he had not so far attempted was a set of independent songs which when performed one after the other would narrate the tale and direct the emotional response of the listener as much by what they add to what has gone before as by their intrinsic content. There was a model in Beethoven's *An die ferne Geliebte* (To a far-off Loved one) which is often said to be the first song cycle. But where that was a set of six short songs forming an uninterrupted sequence rounded off with a reappearance of the opening music, Schubert's *Die schöne Müllerin* (The Maid of the Mill) consists of no fewer than twenty songs, each complete in itself yet adding up to a greater whole. Schubert's intentions were not quite those of Müller, for while the poet wished to distance himself from his rustic characters, Schubert read in his words the impending doom that must befall any innocent soul setting forth into the evil world. He discarded Müller's prologue and epilogue, and three poems which he felt

Die schöne Müllerin was an immediate success, and its popularity increased as the years went by. This title page is from an edition published by Hallberger in Stuttgart, 1877–8, with illustrations by Baumann and Schuster. The first publication (by Sauer & Leidesdorf) was in five books which came out during 1824. They were not supervised by Schubert and contained mistakes which have proved difficult to eradicate. As time went by, publications might have become more elaborate but they were no more accurate!

disrupted the flow of his projected cycle. There is a tradition, assured by Spaun and Schober, that Schubert composed some of these songs in hospital. As there is a noticeable lack of documentary material from June and July 1823, and as Schubert left Vienna for a couple of months' holiday in mid-July to recuperate, this might well be the period when *Die schöne Müllerin* began to take shape. The first surviving letter to refer to the songs is not until 30 November when Schubert wrote to Schober:

I have composed nothing since the opera, except a few Maid of the Mill *songs. The* Mill *songs will appear in four books, with vignettes by Schwind. – For the rest, I hope to regain my health, and this recovered treasure will let me forget many a sorrow;*

only you, dear Schober, I shall never forget, for what you meant to me no one else can mean, alas!

This letter had begun with a lament over the condition of their artistic circle and the lack of any hope of getting his operas performed. But at the same time there was Vogl in Vienna, restored to friendship, writing out the voice parts of the songs himself and singing them to the almost complete exclusion of anything else. Whether he took any part in the preparation of *Die schöne Müllerin* for publication we cannot be sure, but the first of the five books – not four – appeared in early 1824, published by Sauer & Leidesdorf. They were dedicated to Karl von Schönstein, who was not only a great admirer of Schubert's songs but also an amateur baritone of some repute. The publishers were sluggish in the preparation of the later volumes and, Schubert having returned to Zseliz and the summer service of the Esterházy family, Franz's brother Ferdinand was left to oversee publication. These later volumes are full of errors. No early manuscripts survive, either autograph or printer's copy, save for three songs in Schubert's hand transposed down to fit Schönstein's voice. Otherwise the only reasonably reliable source is the 1830 edition of Diabelli which is thought to incorporate those little changes and ornaments added by Vogl and Schönstein in their performances in the intervening years. Neither edition reproduced Schwind's vignettes.

Die schöne Müllerin is the first great song cycle ever written and can still be guaranteed to sell out the hall and attract all the critics when any reputable recitalist gives a performance. Müller's verse is straightforward, not in itself burdened with layer upon layer of meaning. It gives Schubert's music the freedom to provide that meaning and depth. It allows Schubert to dictate the pace, to use purely musical means to communicate with the emotions. The vocal lines are not difficult in themselves (though many a student will disagree) and give the singer room to espouse the folk idiom at the root of the poetry and, much more subtly, in the music. Schubert creates the illusion that these are, indeed, folk-songs, whistled by everyman as he walks down the street. This is the simple life, the roving lad. In the early songs we are introduced to the characters, including the mill-stream which provides a linking thread through the narrative and a solution to the tale. By the fourth song it is apparent that the youth's ultimate fate lies not with the miller's daughter with whom he is head over heels in love, but with the stream itself. In order to be with his love he signs up to work for the miller and is now the miller's boy. Love and the psychological drama progress until the eleventh song, 'Mein' (Mine), in which love is fulfilled and the maid of the mill is indeed his. Doubts then creep in, almost imperceptibly until the appearance of a hunter in the fourteenth song, bringing the harshness of a brutal and cruel world into the peace and bliss of the young lovers' existence. Jealousy reigns as the hunter wins the heart of the miller's daughter: green is her favourite colour, and, like the mill-stream, it courses through the sequence of songs, at first benignly but later hatefully. Everything around the white miller's boy is green, for it is the colour of nature, and he cannot escape its ubiquity. But flowers, at least, wither and will die with the poet in his grave, so the climax of *Die schöne Müllerin* comes with the eighteenth song, 'Trockne Blumen' (Withered Flowers) – once again asserting the romantic belief that pure love can never be fulfilled without death. The mill-stream has the final say, for the last song is the cradle-song of the brook itself, where the poet has found truth and fulfilment in a watery grave. For it Schubert created one of his sweetest lullabies, not sugary, not sentimental, but content and confident in the release death brings. *Die schöne Müllerin* could almost be autobiographical.

For Schubert 1823 ended in the not wholly satisfactory first performances of *Rosamunde*. There were favourable comments, however. Schwind might have been expected to support his composer friend, and he did:

The day before yesterday the Theater an der Wien produced a piece by the wretched Frau von Chézy, Rosamund of Cyprus, *with music by Schubert. You may imagine that we all went to it ... Schubert has taken over the overture he wrote for* Estrella, *as he thinks it too 'homespun' for* Estrella, *for which he wants to write a new one. It pleased so much that, to my great joy, it had to be repeated ... A ballet made no impression, nor did the second and third entr'actes. Well, people are accustomed to talking immediately the curtain has dropped, and I do not see how they can be expected to notice such serious and lovely things. In the last act was a chorus of shepherds and huntsmen, so beautiful and so natural that I cannot remember ever hearing the like before. It was applauded and repeated, and I believe it will deal the chorus in Weber's* Euryanthe *the sort of blow it deserves.*

The *Wiener Zeitschrift* and *Theaterzeitung* were favourable in their comment, the *Sammler* guarded:

Herr Schubert showed originality in his composition, but unfortunately also eccentricity. This young man is as yet in a period of development; it is to be hoped that it will proceed happily. For once he received too much applause; may he never have to complain of too little!

Schubert was back in circulation. Bruchmann wrote to Kupelwieser:

On 11 November we had a Schubertiad at home, at which Vogl took over the singing ... Vogl was much pleased with himself and sang gloriously; we others were merry and bright at table, and our first health was drunk in your honour in Moselle.

And Schwind wrote to Schober:

Last night we were at your mother's ... After a small Schubertiad followed a meal and afterwards a little dance till midnight.

There were readings, too, at the house of the painter Ludwig Mohn, but these seemed too pretentious for the Schubert circle. 'The crowd and the mixture of guests is irksome, and I do not feel at home,' Schwind told Schober, on another occasion announcing:

I am on the point of resigning from the readings, for the reading is so stifled by business affairs and pranks that even to gather together undisturbed is impossible. If you or Senn suddenly appeared in our midst, we should be truly ashamed of such company. Schubert will stick to me.

However, his last letter to Schober that year promised better things:

Schubert is better, and it will not be long before he goes about with his own hair again, which had to be shorn owing to the rash. He wears a very cosy wig. He is much with Vogl and Leidesdorf ... He is now thinking of a concert or a public Schubertiad. If it comes off, I'll write to you.

Unfortunately Schwind was not prophetic about the Schubertiad – there was to be no public performance or concert for another four and a half years yet.

CHAPTER 7

1824−5

(left) 'The Extremely
Good Likeness of the
Composer Franz
Schubert painted by
Rieder' (see p. 109):
watercolour, 1825.

In February 1824 Schwind wrote to Schober:

Schubert now looks much better and is very bright, very comically hungry and writes quartets and German dances and variations without number.

About the German dances we can only speculate but the quartets and variations can be identified reasonably safely and they indicate a return to the composition of purely instrumental music. The variations are surely the set for flute and piano based on 'Trockne Blumen' from *Die schöne Müllerin*. It is slightly incongruous that this most personal song, an encapsulation of Schubert's romantic philosophy, should resurface so soon after its composition in a work which is quite uncharacteristically showy by Schubert's standards. It is a vehicle for the display of technical dexterity by both the flautist and, more particularly, the pianist, which remains in the forefront of the flute repertory though it is not to all tastes, as Westrup's verdict makes clear:

… the total effect of this series of escapades is depressing; and when the variations eventually issue into a march of quite remarkable vulgarity one is constrained to cry 'Enough'. The work might conceivably be tolerable if it were particularly well written for the flute; but it is not.

Opinion on the quartets, however, is almost universally favourable, for the A minor and D minor are to be mentioned in the same breath as the finest quartets of Haydn, Mozart and Beethoven. Both were composed in the early months of 1824 and inspired by Schubert's acquaintance with Ignaz Schuppanzigh, a solo violinist of the highest order and leader of a renowned string quartet with Beethovenian connections. In a letter to Schober of 6 March 1824 Schwind wrote:

Schubert is pretty well already. He says that after a few days of the new treatment he felt how his complaint broke up and everything was different. He still lives one day on panada and the next on cutlets, and lavishly drinks tea, goes bathing a good deal besides and is superhumanly industrious. A new Quartet is to be performed at Schuppanzigh's, who is quite enthusiastic and is said to have rehearsed particularly well. He has now long been at work on an Octet, with the greatest zeal. If you go to see him during the day, he says, 'Hullo, how are you? – Good!' and goes on writing, whereupon you depart.

It is hardly surprising that Schubert had so little time for his friends for the two quartets and the octet together add up to well over two hours of the most inspired chamber music. The A minor Quartet [CD2] was the first to be performed, on 14 March 1824 in the hall of the Philharmonic Society. Schwind reported that Schubert felt it had been played too slowly, if purely and tenderly. A Leipzig newspaper described it as 'not to be despised as a first-born'. In fact it was something like the sixteenth quartet Schubert had written but it was the first to be performed in public in this way and therefore became known as 'Quartet no. 1'. What is more, it became one of only two chamber works to be published during Schubert's lifetime when Sauer & Leidesdorf issued it in September of that year (the other being the Rondo brillant in B minor for violin and piano). At last Schubert seems to have found a way of reconciling what he perceived to be the different natures of instrumental melody and song. This quartet sings.

The other quartet, in D minor, is no less impressive. Where the A minor wears its seriousness with charm, the D minor challenges and threatens. It is usually referred to as 'Death and the Maiden', for it uses Death's music (and particularly its dactylic rhythm) from the song of that name as the theme for the set of variations which form the emotional heart of the work. Perhaps earlier in his life Schubert might have felt compelled to include gay or jovial variations within this movement, but what is so affecting about it is its restraint and simplicity, maintaining through-out the level of sobriety and reflection set at the beginning. To what extent the poem's thesis, that death brings release, was in Schubert's mind when he chose this particular theme for his variations is not known, but as it was one of the main tenets of his artistic circle it seems likely that the connection was not merely fortuitous. Taken alone this second movement could seem to lack variety, but when heard after its powerful predecessor it takes on a pervasive strength. The opening movement is indeed as dramatic as anything in the instrumental music of Schubert, at times violent, forceful, sinister, impulsive and intense. The criticism so often made, that the formal construction of Schubert's music lacks tautness, cannot be levelled at this movement, always fully controlled and contributing to its own dynamic strength. Schubert, who so often was unable to find third or fourth movements capable of balancing his potent opening ones, is here well up to the task, the third movement being a violently syncopated Scherzo and the Finale a tarantella,* a breathless affair in which Schubert's dancers are forced at one moment to pause for recovery before launching headlong into the fray once more.

There is no less inspiration in the third chamber work of early 1824, the Octet. It was commissioned by Ferdinand, Count Troyer, chief steward to the Archduke Rudolph, and a fine clarinettist. He was looking for a companion piece to Beethoven's Septet in E flat, op. 20, and, by most reckonings, he acquired something a great deal superior. The Septet was written for clarinet, horn and bassoon with violin, viola, cello and double bass. Schubert took the same combination and added a second violin. He also adopted Beethoven's overall framework, giving the work a six-movement structure including a set of variations and both a Minuet and a Scherzo.† Effectively Schubert was here writing for a small chamber orchestra, with the strings often treated as a string section rather than as individuals. All the players, particularly the wind players, are expected to be masters of their instruments with a number of very testing moments to separate the sheep from the goats. Count Troyer will, no doubt, have revelled in the opportunities given to him in so many virtuoso passages for the clarinet, not to mention the tranquil solo which starts the second movement. Hear the work played on modern instruments and its difficulty is not so immediately apparent, but there were far fewer mechanical aids on the primitive wind instruments of Schubert's day and, as the twentieth century closes, a new generation of instrumentalists capable of formidable dexterity on these temperamental creatures gives us a welcome opportunity to relive some of the excitement a performance in Schubert's time would have aroused. Once again there is a self-quotation in the fourth of the movements, this time a fragment of *Die Freunde von Salamanka* (The Friends from Salamanca), an opera of 1815 which was not performed in Schubert's lifetime. It is perhaps the least memorable of the movements, which only goes to show how good the others are, the third and last in

---

*A vigorous dance of Italian origin, its name coming from the same root as the tarantula spider, sometimes said to resemble the frenzied agonies of one bitten by the spider.

†The relationship between the minuet and scherzo (and its history) is a subject in itself. At its simplest the minuet might be thought of as a gentle triple-time dance movement, the scherzo a quicker version of the same thing. Scherzo actually means joke.

particular standing out for their vigour. Throughout the whole work there is a sense of fun engendered by the uncomplicated themes, folk-like in their directness and vitality.

It is tempting to treat every solemn moment in Schubert's works of this period as a musical revelation of his depressed state of mind. That he was demoralized by the rejection of his dramatic works, and distressed and worried by his illness is certain. Yet in truth, from the time he contracted syphilis until his death there is little in the music to suggest that he was unable to dissociate his creative processes from his physical and mental condition. Nor was he perpetually miserable:

Our New Year's Eve festivity went off happily. We gathered at Mohn's. Bruchmann and Doblhoff returned on the stroke of twelve from the city, where they expected and sought Schubert. You, Senn and Kupelwieser, Bruchmann and everybody's sweethearts all had their health drunk. Soon afterwards Schubert and Dr Bernhardt announced themselves by a small target-shooting match. Schubert hit, and the shattered window-pane set everybody astir. With the doctor I have fraternized, which should suit me well. I got home at 4.30 a.m. It was all a bit crude, but better than we might have expected.

This is Schwind to Schober again. At this time Schwind was acting as intermediary, relaying messages between Schober, away in Breslau auditioning for the stage, and Justina von Bruchmann to whom he had become secretly engaged. For the sudden proliferation of letters this arrangement occasioned the Schubertian can only be grateful. Here is Schwind, writing on 2 February:

Justina read to me from your letter that you [appeared] with success, and what you write about me. That was on Schubert's birthday. We had a feast at the Crown, and though we were all fuddled, I wished you were present, if only for the sake of Schubert's pleasure over your good fortune. In my consummate tipsiness I was able to see them all as they are. They were all more or less idiotic, and Schubert asleep. Bruchmann alone, although [he] remembers nothing of this, was like someone filled with enthusiasm. He embraced me passionately, drank Julie's health with me alone, and with Schubert and me wished you good health with a warm, everlasting handshake.

(Julie was Bruchmann's betrothed.) Although in this particular audition Schober was unsuccessful, it was partly his dubious choice of the acting profession that led Bruchmann to insist that the engagement to his sister be broken off the following year. A few weeks later Schwind was able to relate to Schober that 'Schubert is quite well. He has given up his wig and shows a charming cygnet's down.'

Then in March 1824, with his chamber works completed and a rest taken after *Die schöne Müllerin*, Schubert returned to song-writing and, for the last time, to

Eduard von Bauernfeld, Viennese poet, critic and dramatist, whose reminiscences are an important if qualified source of information about Schubert's last years. Etching by F. Stober after Daffinger.

the poetry of Mayrhofer. Two of the songs are among his greatest, and both tell of the hope held out by the prospect of eternity. 'Der Sieg' (The Victory) is a rarely heard masterpiece for a bass voice longing solemnly for the life after death. 'Auflösung' (Dissolution) is a seraphic affirmation of faith of such lightness that the poet (and composer) might already be numbered among the company of angels. It is astonishing how two such divergent songs – to compare them would be almost like comparing an elephant with a butterfly – can express such convergent sentiments. It has been suggested that 'Im Abendrot' (In the Glow of Sunset) may also come from 1824. It is not possible to be precise, but it would be a pity to exclude this sublime song from the narrative simply because of academic pedantry. It is the greatest of Schubert's many sunset songs, remarkable for the intensity generated from such elementary material and in the orbit only of singers with a very sure control of long-breathed legato lines and subtly shaded dynamics. It is one of only two settings for solo voice of words by the Pomeranian schoolmaster, Karl Lappe. The other Lappe setting, 'Der Einsame' (The Recluse), is also difficult to date, and is a consummate excercise in mood-painting, Schubert with great economy of means describing the scene as the poet watches the embers gradually dying in the hearth.

In January 1822 the poet, critic and dramatist, Eduard von Bauernfeld, met Schubert, possibly through Schwind with whom Bauernfeld had been at school. He did not enter Schubert's circle of close friends until 1825 so it must be with a degree of objectivity that his eventual publication of Schubert's notebook of 1824 is viewed, particularly since the notebook itself has not survived. The entries, if accurate, provide a sharp image of the contrasts between Schubert's outpouring of chamber music, his social life, and the inward thoughts of a sensitive man:

25 March

Pain sharpens the understanding and strengthens the mind; whereas joy seldom troubles about the former and softens the latter or makes it frivolous.

What I hate from the deepest bottom of my heart is that one-sidedness which makes so many wretches believe that only what they happen to be doing is best, everything else being worthless. One kind of beauty should hold man's enthusiasm all through his life, it is true; but the glow of that enthusiasm should light up every-thing else.

27 March

*There is no one who understands the pain or the joy of others! We always imagine we are coming together, and we always merely go side by side. Oh, what torture for those who recognize this!**

What I produce is due to my understanding of music and to my sorrows; that which sorrow alone has produced seems to give least pleasure to the world.

28 March

From the greatest enthusiasm to the utterly ridiculous there is but one step, as from the deepest wisdom to the crassest stupidity.

It is with faith that man first comes into the world, and it long precedes intelligence and knowledge; for in order to understand anything, one must first believe in some-thing; that is the higher basis on which feeble understanding first erects the pillars of proof.

Intelligence is nothing else than analysed faith.

29 March

O imagination! thou greatest treasure of man, thou inexhaustible wellspring from which artists as well as savants drink! O remain with us still, by however few thou art acknowledged and revered, to preserve us from that so-called enlightenment, that hideous skeleton without flesh and blood!

*This remark has been cited as evidence of the final estrangement between Schubert and Mayrhofer. Certainly there are no Mayrhofer songs after this date.

[Undated] 2 o'clock at night.

Enviable Nero! Thou wert strong enough to destroy a loathsome people to the strains of strings and voice!

There is also a pitiful letter of 31 March 1824 from Schubert to Leopold Kupelwieser, then in Rome:

... In a word I feel myself to be the most unhappy and wretched creature in the world. Imagine a man whose health will never be right again, and who in sheer despair over this ever makes things worse and worse, instead of better; imagine a man, I say, whose most brilliant hopes have perished, to whom the felicity of love and friendship have nothing to offer but pain, at best, whom enthusiasm (at least of the stimulating kind) for all things beautiful threatens to forsake, and I ask you, is he not a miserable, unhappy being? 'My peace is gone, my heart is sore, I shall find it never and nevermore,'* I may well sing every day now, for each night, on retiring to bed, I hope I may not wake again, and each morning but recalls yesterday's grief. Thus, joyless and friendless, I should pass my days, did not Schwind visit me now and again and turn on me a ray of those sweet days of the past. – Our society (reading circle), as you probably know already, has done itself to death owing to a reinforcement of that rough chorus of beer-drinkers and sausage-eaters, for its dissolution is due in a couple of days, though I hardly visited it myself since your departure. Leidesdorf, with whom I have become quite well acquainted, is in fact a truly thoughtful and good fellow, but so hugely melancholy that I am almost afraid I owe him more than enough in that respect; besides, my affairs and his do badly, so that we never have any money ... Of songs I have not written many new ones, but I have tried my hand at several instrumental works, for I wrote two Quartets for violins, viola and violoncello and an Octet, and I want to write another quartet, in fact I want to pave my way towards grand symphony in that manner.

The third string quartet did not materialize yet, only emerging in 1826 as the G major Quartet. Schubert's mood may well have been influenced by the gradual disintegration of the reading circle in the spring of 1824, and significantly Schubertiads tend to be mentioned less in the remaining correspondence. Schober had departed (quite possibly to the benefit of Schubert), Kupelwieser was in Rome, Spaun in Linz, Senn in the Tyrol and only Schwind was left of Schubert's soul mates. There was, then, little to deter Schubert from taking up the offer of a second summer residence at Zseliz in the service of the Esterházy family, which he did grudgingly, leaving Vienna on 25 May 1824. While in the country Schubert received a letter from his father who clearly felt his paternal duties had not decreased simply because his son was now in his late twenties:

*A quote from 'Gretchen am Spinnrade'.

We are heartily glad that you are in good health and have been so well received in the count's household. Endeavour, therefore, to care for and maintain your health, the first among all earthly possessions, and make it your business to deserve the love and respect of all who mean well by you.

You know that, as a teacher of youth, I am always apt to moralize; but believe me, it is not from habit, but from a profound conviction that nobody can be truly happy who is not continually in touch with God and keeps steadfastly to His holy will. We may, nay we should even, moderately enjoy the innocent joys of life with hearts grateful to God; but we must not let our spirits sink in gloomy circumstances either, for sorrows too are a blessing of God and lead those who manfully endure to the most glorious goal.

Where in history is to be found a great man who did not attain to triumph through suffering and unflinching perseverance? That is why I should like to persuade those I love best to such a disposition!

Schubert's brother Ferdinand looked after the management of his compositions during the stay in Zseliz, and this necessitated a good deal of correspondence, some of which has survived. There is much detail about who has been sent which manuscript and why, but there is also a touching exchange about a musical clock at the Crown inn. It was worked mechanically from rolls, and amongst these were several waltzes by Schubert, which brought tears to Ferdinand's eyes when he heard them. Schubert responded:

Was it only the pain of my absence which made you shed tears, and could you not trust yourself to write the word? Or did you feel, on thinking of my person, oppressed by an ever incomprehensible longing, that its dismal veil was enfolding you too? Or did all the tears come to your mind which you have seen me weep? Be that as it may, I feel more clearly than ever at this moment that you, and you only, are my truest friend, bound to my soul with every fibre! – Not to let these lines mislead you into believing that I am not well or cheerful, I hasten to assure you of the contrary. True, it is no longer that happy time during which each object seems to us to be surrounded by a youthful gloriole, but a period of fateful recognition of a miserable reality, which I endeavour to beautify as far as possible by my imagination (thank God). We fancy that happiness lies in places where once we were happier, whereas actually it is only in ourselves, and so, although I had an unpleasant disappointment by renewing here an experience already undergone at Steyr, I am better able now to find happiness and peace in myself than I was then. – A grand sonata and variations on a theme of my own, both for 4 hands, which I have already written, shall serve you as proof of this. The variations have met with a special success.

Once again Schubert was writing piano duets: the Grand Sonata now usually referred to as the 'Grand Duo', and the Variations in A flat were published during the next eighteen months, and both enjoy justified popularity today. The *Divertissement à l'hongroise* may well date from this visit, too, another splendid addition to the duet repertoire. In all probability Schubert wrote these pieces to play with Countess Karoline, by now a young woman of nineteen. Much speculation has surrounded the apparent friendship between Schubert and Karoline, but it seems Karoline's mind and body had not progressed together, for she is said to have been sent outside by her mother to play with her hoop at the age of thirty! Be that as it may, she is usually taken to be the 'certain attractive star' referred to by Schubert in a letter to Schwind in August. Certainly Schubert composed the part-song 'Gebet' (Prayer) for her. There is nothing, however, to suggest that Schubert this time renewed his former relationship (if, indeed, there ever was one) with the maid, Pepi Pöckelhofer, and by September he was thoroughly miserable:

Now I sit here in the depth of the Hungarian country, whither I unfortunately let myself be enticed a second time, without having a single person with whom I could speak a sensible word. I have written hardly any songs since the time you went away, but tried my hand at several instrument things. What is to happen to my operas Heaven knows! Notwithstanding that I have now been in good health for five months ...

This was written to Schober, still away in Breslau trying for the stage, and the same letter included a short poem, the second verse of which clearly contained a very personal message (sometimes interpreted as referring to Schubert's continued difficulties with the composition of opera and symphony):

> *Too great my pain, which at my vitals gnaws,*
> *As a last vestige of that power clinging.*
> *Me too these times are fast to ruin bringing,*
> *Wherein all greatness to exhaustion draws.*

When he returned to Vienna Schubert moved into his father's schoolhouse in the Rossau once again, and here he wrote a unique work, the only piece of any merit ever composed for an instrument called the arpeggione. This was a new invention, also known as the bowed guitar, a sort of cello which had the frets, six strings and tuning of the guitar. In its way it was a reincarnation of the obsolete viola da gamba, and it was taken up eagerly by the guitarist Vincenz Schuster, one of those who frequented the musical gatherings at Sonnleithner's. The work commissioned from Schubert, a sonata in A minor, is now universally known as the 'Arpeggione' Sonata. But the life of the instrument was short and the work fell into almost immediate neglect, remaining unpublished until 1871. Oddly enough it was the fact that Schubert realized little of the instrument's potential that led to the work's eventual success, for he wrote hardly anything in the way of what might be described as guitar chords. Effectively he had written an appealing sonata for any melody instrument and it has been taken up with enthusiasm by cellists for whom very few alterations have to be made to the score. It is at least as popular with viola players (who have so few fine works in their repertory), clarinettists, flautists and even exponents of the double bass.

The year 1824 closed, as was customary in Vienna, with the publication of New Year party pieces. This year a Musical Souvenir was produced containing forty new waltzes, and the list of composers includes Franz Clement, for whom Beethoven wrote his Violin Concerto, Beethoven himself, and Schubert. The 1825 parties began with one at the painter Moritz von Schwind's. Bauernfeld recalls:

On Twelfth-night Eve masked procession at Schwind's. Myself as pilgrim. The three kings played dice in full regalia. I distributed poems, Moritz made a drawing for me.

As for Schwind:

For the rest I paint all day and rarely go out. Now and again I go to Schubert on the hop, or to Vogl or the Hönigs ... If only you could see Schubert and me for once, when I go to him in the Rossau early or when we spend a Sunday afternoon together. It's a veritable calamity. But the funniest thing in the world, too. A week ago he came to Hönig's with me, after having already accepted ten times and failed us ten times. We met at six, but did not want to go until 7 o'clock, as the mother was then going out. What was there to be done in the meantime? He would not go to any coffeehouse, so we went to Lenkay, where he had always gone with Senn. Half a bottle of Tokay was served, and when half of that had gone it was not advisable without great danger to go on drinking. The remainder was poured into a little flask and taken with us. As there was nobody about who could have kept it for us, I took it with me to Hönig's, where it was brought out with much laughter and drunk up. Schubert enjoyed himself quite well and wants to go back soon, for he likes Nettl very well. She is a sweet poppet, too.[17]

Nettl (or Netti) was Anna, one of the Hönig family with whom Schwind, in time, fell in love (though he eventually married one Louise Sachs, very happily, it seems). Anna was, according to Bauernfeld, 'not particularly pretty, but graceful, well-educated, domesticated and middle-class rather than artistically gifted'. But at this time Schubert and Schwind were particularly drawn to each other. They sought each other's company often, Schubert referring to Schwind as 'beloved' and Schwind worshipping the composer. On 14 February Schwind informed Schober:

Schubert is well and busy again after a certain stagnation. He has recently come to live next door to us, where the ale-house is, on the second floor, in a very pretty room. We meet daily, and as far as I can I share his whole life with him. In the spring we intend to move to Dornbach, into the house of a good friend of mine. There is a Schubertiad at Enderes's each week – that is to say, Vogl sings . . .

But these were not like the Schubertiads of earlier days. The old artistic circle had broken up and though Vogl and Schubert had re-established their mutual respect there were new jealousies within the entourage that now gathered around the composer:

. . . For when you [Kupelwieser] and Schober had left, the whole circle shaped itself differently, if no better, and had to be dissolved altogether. However, the better ones always find each other again, and then not much is lost . . . Schubert and Schwind are in open feud with Bruchmann. They both seem to me like children, and indeed they give vent to their hatred childishly. They do not meet any more at all, cut each other dead and behave like great enemies.[18]

Unfortunately these jealousies affected relations between two of the great artistic influences in Schubert's life. Bauernfeld's commentary is revealing:

Much with Schwind and Schubert. He sang new songs here. The other day we slept at his place. As we were short of a pipe, Moritz fitted me up something of the kind from Schubert's eye-glass case. Fraternized with Schubert over a glass of sugar-water . . . Visit to the singer Vogl. An odd old bachelor. He reads Epictetus and is a treasury of pleasant dandyism. Moritz behaved with studied rudeness towards him. Schubert is always the same, always natural.

It was about this time that Bauernfeld became more closely acquainted with Schubert and his friends, though they had known each other slightly for several years. His importance to the study of Schubert is immeasurable. Not only was he a tireless correspondent and the keeper of a most informative diary, but the attention to detail which was to mark his later career as a distinguished playwright and man of letters makes his some of the most quoted accounts of events in Schubert's life, even if some of his memories were only published many years after Schubert's death. Of relevance to the later *Schubertiade*, for instance, he writes:

. . . with gay and lively companions, when the wine flowed like water, the excellent Vogl treated us to all the wonderful songs and poor Franz Schubert had to accompany him until his short, stubby fingers would hardly obey him any longer. He had an even worse time at our house parties – only 'Frankfurter' dances in those modest days – at which, however, there was never any lack of charming women and girls.

On these occasions our 'Bertl', as he was sometimes called ingratiatingly, had to play his latest waltzes over and over again, until the whole thing had turned itself into an endless Cotillion, so that the small, corpulent, little fellow, dripping with perspiration, was only able to regain his ease over the modest supper. No wonder that he deserted us occasionally and that, as a matter of fact, many a Schubertiad had to take place without Schubert, if he did not happen to be in a sociable mood or if some guest or other was not particularly congenial to him. It was not uncommon for him to keep a company of invited guests waiting vainly for him, while he sat in comfort with half a dozen assistant schoolmasters, former colleagues of his, drinking wine in a secluded tavern. If we reproached him the next day, he would say with a contented chuckle: 'I was not in the mood!'

In the early part of 1825 the price of a lively social life in the company of Schwind was a falling off in composition: no chamber music, nothing symphonic or dramatic, and only a few songs. However, the composer's recent acquaintance with the noted singer, Sophie Müller, proved a source of inspiration. Her diaries tell of frequent meetings with Schubert, at which she encountered many of his songs for the first time. Often these are referred to as 'new' songs, but for the most part they were simply new to her. One that really was new was 'Die junge Nonne' (The young Nun). Schubert appeared with the song after lunch on 3 March 1825 and when, a few hours later, Vogl turned up, Sophie was able to sing it to him, and also to Mozart's brother-in-law, Josef Lange, who arrived later still. The text, by Jacob

(left) Schubert, Franz Lachner, Schwind and Bauernfeld serenading, and (right) Schubert, Lachner and Bauernfeld drinking. After Schubert's death Lachner became a conductor at the Kärntnerthor theatre and later in Munich. His career was commemorated in a series of humorous illustrations by Schwind, of which these are two. The drawings were made in 1862 on a 12-metre ribbon – the so-called 'Lachner Roll'.

Craigher,* is in the form of a dramatic monologue: a young nun, in the midst of a raging storm, senses the fulfilment of her life in the death which will unite her with her God. Schubert's setting, sparing as ever in its use of material, is immensely powerful. Sophie's comment, 'It is splendidly composed', is a downright under-statement, for it is one of the greatest songs for the female voice in the Schubert *oeuvre*.

Another source of inspiration was the work of Sir Walter Scott whose novels were enjoying a tremendous vogue throughout Europe at this time. Schubert had read some of his verse romances on holiday in 1823, and in a moment of surprising commercial acumen early in 1825 decided to try to cash in on this popularity by setting some of them in both German and English. Unfortunately the German trans-lations he used often departed from the scansion of the original and it was found that the English words could not be fitted adequately to Schubert's music. This meant that Schubert's plan to have the songs published in Vienna and London never materialized, though most of them found their way into print in Vienna within the year. One of them, 'Ellens Gesang III' (Ellen's Third Song), has achieved outstanding fame, though many of those who whistle it walking down the street probably have not the slightest clue that it was written by Schubert. It is the 'Ave Maria' sung at countless weddings during the signing of the register, at school assemblies and even in arrangements for crooner and big band. What is slightly incongruous is that it is not liturgical at all. It comes from *The Lady of the Lake* towards the end of the third canto: the chieftain, Rhoderick Dhu, has exhorted his men to defend their land against the royalists who threaten to overpower it, and Ellen prays to the Virgin. As Schubert wrote:

It seems to touch all hearts, and inspires a feeling of devotion. I believe the reason is that I never force myself to be devout, and never compose hymns or prayers of that sort except when the mood takes me; but then it is usually the right and true devotion.[19]

Can there be a less propitious title to see on a recital programme than 'Grave-digger's Longing' (Totengräbers Heimweh)? But the audience should be no more put off by this title than by Mahler's famous *Kindertotenlieder* (Songs on the Death of Children). There is an unsubstantiated tradition that Schubert was required to return to hospital at the beginning of 1825 (hinted at by Schwind). If his condition

*Jacob Nicolaus de Jachelutta Craigher was a merchant and talented linguist as well as a dilettante poet. He had high hopes of his collaboration with Schubert, but in the event the composer set only three of his poems, the others being 'Totengräbers Heimweh' and 'Der blinde Knabe', though Craigher may also have been responsible for the Italian versions of several songs.

had taken a turn for the worse, in this song at least he stares death in the face with confidence – particularly at the moment where the grave-digger, cross in hand, stands on the very brink of the grave he has dug and gazes yearningly down into the darkness of the tomb. The descending phrase, unharmonized, which Schubert uses at this point, reappears in other songs to represent a similar confrontation with death. It appears also in the A minor Piano Sonata (D845), which was written at the same time.

For many years – indeed probably until after the Second World War – this A minor Sonata and the 'Wanderer' Fantasy were the only Schubert sonatas to find their way into the concert programmes of those few mainstream recital pianists who played Schubert at all. In many respects this is the most Beethovenian of the sonatas, both in terms of its pianistic requirements and its dramatic content. It is a sonata of contrast, opening with a wistful tune which later becomes the 'Toten-gräbers Heimweh' theme, and which is almost immediately countermanded by an insistent martial element with the force of a machine gun's rapid stutter. There is a flavour of Beethoven, too, about the second movement, a set of variations. Very often in Schubert's piano music such movements are little more than harmonized melodies, songs writ large, but here the piano's capacity for playing more than one melody at once (counterpoint) is exploited more fully than usual. Again Beethoven is called to mind in the third movement, a Scherzo which may have been directly influenced by Beethoven's 'Diabelli' Variations. The last movement is straight-forward but has a few tricks in store to tickle the fancy, not least the two sudden chords which bring the piece to an abrupt end.

The spring of 1825 also gave rise to one of those infuriatingly frustrating Schubert sonatas which promise so much yet remain unfulfilled, the one in C major (D840), often called the 'Reliquie'. It is difficult to see why Schubert left it unfinished. The first movement, which begins rather as if it were going to be a C major variant of its A minor companion, is equally fine, and is followed by a splendid and very fully worked out Andante. The Minuet third movement peters out in a scribbled 'etc. etc.' – though he retained enough interest in the work to fill up the page later with a complete Trio section. The Finale admittedly runs out of steam, but that does not detract from the quality of what was completed, and as with the 'Unfinished' Symphony we find ourselves asking: *why* did he lose interest?

Such is the tantalizing nature of so much Schubert! Completions have been made in an attempt to present the whole sonata to concert audiences but, however inspired and scholarly, they are hampered by having to use material with which Schubert himself was dissatisfied. On the other hand, Schubert may simply have left the piece where he did because towards the end of May 1825 he set off for Upper Austria on holiday with Vogl. And unquestionably he appears to have had a new

*'Michael Vogl and
Franz Schubert
setting out to Fight
and to Conquer': a
caricature in pencil,
probably by Schober
c. 1825.*

musical interest. The two men returned to Steyr, visiting Gmunden, Linz and
Gastein, amongst other places, and a letter sent by Schubert's host in Linz, Anton
Ottenwalt, to Josef von Spaun on 19 July 1825 reports that Schubert 'had worked at
a symphony at Gmunden, which is to be performed in Vienna this winter'.

Then on 14 August Schwind wrote to Schubert from Vienna:

*About your symphony we may be quite hopeful. Old Hönig is dean of the faculty of
jurisprudence, and as such is to give a concert. That will afford a better opportunity
of having it performed; indeed we count upon it.*

Bad Gastein, the resort which gives its name to one of Schubert's 'missing' works. Did it ever exist or is it possibly the 'Great' C major Symphony? Drawing by Pezolt.

Hönig's performances were annual events given for the benefit of the widows and orphans of former faculty members, but the next concert, on 30 April 1826, contained no symphony by Schubert and in any case the manuscript of the so-called 'Gastein' or 'Gmunden–Gastein' Symphony was lost – if it ever existed. Otto Erich Deutsch was convinced enough about its existence to allocate it the number 849 in his authoritative catalogue. Some commentators have suggested that this symphony was simply a reworking of the Sonata in C for piano duet (the 'Grand Duo'), which had been written at Zseliz the previous year, but the theory finds little support today.

More possible is the suggestion that the symphony finally became the 'Great' C major. At the head of that manuscript Schubert has written 'March 1828', but this does not negate the proposition, as the date is probably when Schubert began the fair copy, rather than when he began initial sketches (see pages 120–22).

At about this time another letter was sent to Goethe seeking recognition of Schubert's settings of the master's words but, as with the earlier letter, it remained unanswered, though Goethe's diary records that he did receive the songs. Ironically, in that same diary entry, Goethe also mentions the receipt of quartets from the sixteen-year-old Mendelssohn, and a detailed letter of thanks was sent to the young composer. But then Felix Mendelssohn had personal access to Goethe of a kind that was denied to Franz Peter Schubert.

For Schubert the holiday, however, was a great success. Much correspondence survives. Some of it is from the petulant Schwind, some from Schubert himself, missing the companionship of his friends, but one of the most informative letters was written on 25 July 1825 to his father and stepmother:

In Upper Austria I find my compositions everywhere, especially at the monasteries of Florian and Kremsmünster, where with the aid of a gallant pianoforte player I produced my four-handed Variations and marches with notable success. What pleased especially were the variations in my new Sonata for two hands, which I performed alone and not without merit, since several people assured me that the keys become singing voices under my hands, which, if true, pleases me greatly, since I cannot endure the accursed chopping in which even distinguished pianoforte players indulge and which delights neither the ear nor the mind.

Anton Ottenwalt found Schubert in a particularly friendly and communicative mood (remembering that he had been downright rude to many in their Viennese circle shortly before the holiday):

We sat together until not far from midnight, and I have never seen him like this, nor heard: serious, profound and as though inspired. How he talked of art, of poetry, of his youth, of friends and other people who matter, of the relationship of ideals to life, etc.! I was more and more amazed at such a mind, of which it has been said that its artistic achievement is so unconscious, hardly revealed to and understood by himself, and so on. Yet how simple was all this! – I cannot tell you of the extent and the unity of his convictions – but there were glimpses of a world-view that is not merely acquired, and the share which worthy friends may have in it by no means detracts from the individuality shown by all this.

Meanwhile the wanderers were returning to Vienna, bringing with them Leopold Kupelwieser and Schober who lived together for a short time. At home everyone

longed for the return of Schubert to re-create their group, Bauernfeld suggesting
that Schubert and Schwind should take lodgings together with him. But Schubert
did not actually get back until 3 October, by which time he had completed another
piano sonata, in D major (D850). It is both an attractive work and a curious one.
Though full of Schubertian melody and innovative moments, it somehow misses
the mark emotionally. It begins seriously, both heroic and vigorous in mood, but
as it unfolds over some thirty-five minutes there is a relaxation of tension and rather
than evolve into a glorious climax the work moves instead towards amiability and
geniality, typified by the jaunty walking theme of the Finale. None the less this
movement earned from Alfred Einstein the accolade of 'the crown of the sonata'.

While Schubert was at Gastein he met Ladislaus Pyrker, grateful dedicatee of his
opus 4 songs, for the first time since his elevation to the patriarchate of Venice in
1820. Schubert treasured their meeting and immediately set to work on two songs
to poems which Pyrker gave him. He combined the inspiration he found in the
majestic scenery around Gastein with his view of God as seen through the natural
world in the song 'Die Allmacht' (Omnipotence). Because it was published in a high
key it has been sung, traditionally, by high and penetrating sopranos and tenors,
but it is more likely that Schubert wrote it for the lower-voiced Vogl, with whom
(and at whose expense) he was on holiday. Fischer-Dieskau issues a warning to
singers (and audiences) who feel they have to 'belt it out':

*There is good reason for the appeal of this song to powerful voices, but the many
lyrical passages prescribed* pianissimo *should not be overlooked. The song falls victim
all too frequently to the 'Brünnhilde'-type of voice. Of course it demands a big voice
with a wide range, but intensity of expression and meaningful interpretation are
much more important. It is not enough to trumpet forth Jehovah's greatness and his
revelation through Nature.*

Schubert's feelings about nature are clear enough from the letters he sent back from
this holiday, and this song reinforces that wonder in the most poetic way. So, too,
does the other Pyrker song, 'Das Heimweh' (Homesickness), D851. Fischer-Dieskau again:

*While Vogl was trying to soothe his arthritic joints in the thermal baths, Schubert
was enjoying the mountain air of the glaciers in the nearby Hohen Tauern mountains. The tunes of the cowherds and peasants enchanted him, and they reappear in
his music; even the most sophisticated harmonies cannot completely conceal them.*

Yet this is no bucolic romp. As John Reed says, 'it is a locus classicus for Schubertian
images of *Sehnsucht*'.

The signatures of Pyrker and Schubert in the visitors' book at Bad Gastein, August 1825.

Publication of Schubert's music continued, even of the manuscripts held by Diabelli, with whom Schubert had so unfortunately parted company (and who had by now himself parted company with Cappi). In September he issued the Mass in C, which Schubert had composed back in 1816 when he had connections with the Liechtental church. Later, just before his death, Schubert composed a new Benedictus for this mass which Diabelli published with the recommendation that it should be used 'in default of a good soprano singer'. It is not known if Therese Grob was aware of this indirect compliment to her singing. One of the most significant publications of the time, though, was not one of Schubert's musical works but 'The Extremely Good Likeness of the Composer Franz Schubert painted by Rieder. 3 Florins.' Such was Schubert's growing reputation in Vienna that it was deemed worthwhile to issue this engraving. Rieder, according to popular legend, took shelter at Schubert's during a shower and occupied his time with sketching the composer; he later returned to improve the likeness, and the resulting watercolour was signed by Schubert. It is the best-known Schubert portrait and formed the basis of most of those painted after his death.

The year drew to a close as it had begun with the usual round of New Year pieces published for the amusement of party-goers. Schubert was there alongside Beethoven (and over forty others whose names no longer carry any musical significance) and perhaps this is as good a time as any to muse on any personal relationship there may have been between the two.

Schubert knew a good deal of Beethoven's music. That much is clear. He attended performances of Beethoven's works whenever he could and was obviously inspired by Beethoven's example, yet frequently daunted by the prospect of trying to match up to him. The extent to which he knew the great man personally is more difficult to determine. It was said by Spaun (in old age in 1864) that Schubert never met

Beethoven. Ferdinand Schubert, however, said that they met frequently. The reader is at liberty to believe whichever source appeals the more, but as Vienna was not a large city and the different elements of its artistic fraternity known to each other it seems unlikely that the two cannot have had some sort of acquaintance. What is certain is that Beethoven was deaf and not an easy person with whom to make contact, and that Schubert, a shy man outside the safety of his closest friends, would have found it hard to overcome these obstacles in order to speak on anything other than the most superficial terms with the man who was his musical god. There were those among Schubert's friends who were prepared to say 'without exaggeration, we may speak of a second Beethoven'. But did Schubert ever know that the great man himself was reputed to have said of him 'This one will surpass me'?

Schubert, c. 1826: lithograph by Josef Teltscher.

CHAPTER 8

1826–7

If Schubert was in the end likely to be little more than a name to Beethoven, his fame was spreading gently. There were reviews of his music as far afield as Prague, Pest, London, Zürich and Weimar. They are not the sort of notices that composers might hope for today, for the profession of musical journalist hardly existed, but his name was at least being mentioned. All the same, those outside his own small artistic circle still knew him only as a composer of songs and ballads for the voice and waltzes and other short dances for the piano; few knew anything about his more substantial piano music, let alone his symphonic or chamber works, and the one field in which success would have led to wide recognition, opera, had been a downright disaster. The steady stream of his works being published by a variety of houses brought an unsteady income, and when he did have money he spent it freely on his friends – so much so that Bauernfeld described him as the one who played the part of Croesus 'and who, on and off, used to be rolling in money'.

He was still under thirty, but his failure to emulate his idols, Mozart and Beethoven, left him with feelings of both personal inadequacy and frustration with the fickle and decadent tastes of fashionable musical society. And Schubert did little to enhance his appeal to his potential patrons. He disliked bowing and scraping and loathed flattering talk about himself from those he felt unqualified to pass judgement. Schwind, his mercurial and often jealous companion, is said to have described Schubert as looking 'like a drunken cabby'. Franz Xaver von Andlau, who worked in Vienna at the embassy of the grand duchy of Baden, has left an equally unappetizing picture:

His personality was of the most disagreeable kind. He shared with Beethoven his shy withdrawal from the world, his gloomy bearing; one would never have suspected in this wooden appearance, in this unprepossessing exterior, the greatly gifted creator of so many wonderful songs.

The more loyal of the close friends, particularly Spaun, always sought to balance such unpleasant descriptions, if not actually denying Schubert's unsociable behaviour then at least finding an explanation for it. After Schubert's death the misguided opinion that he was an ugly creature often had to be corrected. Spaun, for instance, wrote:

The portrait of Schubert painted by Rieder, and engraved, is extraordinarily like him. Looking at it, one can judge for oneself whether the face is ugly and Negroid. Just as little can one say that Schubert was handsome; but he was well formed and when he spoke pleasantly, or smiled, his features were full of charm, and when he was working, full of enthusiasm and burning with zeal, his features appeared sublimated and almost beautiful. So far as his body is concerned, one might imagine him as a fat lump, from the descriptions in the biography. But that is entirely incorrect. Schubert had a solidly built, thick-set body but there was no question of his being fat or having a paunch. His very youthful friend, Moritz Schwind, exceeded him in girth even in those days.

One of the fullest descriptions of Schubert at this stage of his life comes from Leopold Sonnleithner:

The lithograph portrait of Schubert at Diabelli's is the best likeness, except that the body is much too heavy and broad ... Schubert was below average height, with a round, fat face, short neck, a not very high forehead, and thick, brown, naturally curly hair; back and shoulders rounded, arms and hands fleshy, short fingers, main potelée; *his eyes (if I am not mistaken) grey-blue, eyebrows bushy, nose stubby and broad, lips thick; the face somewhat Negroid. The colour of his skin was fair rather than dark, but it was inclined to break out into pimples and was somewhat darker because of this. His head sat somewhat squeezed between his shoulders, inclining rather forward. – Schubert always wore spectacles. In repose, his expression appeared dull rather than vivacious; sullen rather than cheerful; one could have taken him for an Austrian, or more likely for a Bavarian, peasant. Only if one observed him more closely did his features become slightly animated when there was interesting music or entertaining conversation; the corners of his mouth turned up, his eyes sparkled*

*and his whole bearing grew rather tense. He was only really animated among inti-
mate friends, when there was wine or beer; but even then he never laughed freely
and openly, but only managed a chuckle which sounded toneless rather than bright.
Shy and taciturn, especially in smart society, which he only frequented in order to
accompany his songs, more or less as a favour. Whilst doing this his face wore the
most serious expression, and as soon as it was over he withdrew into a neighbouring
room. Indifferent to praise and applause, he shunned compliments and was content
if his intimate friends gave him evidence of their satisfaction. He sometimes went to
private balls at the houses of families he was intimate with; he never danced, but
was always ready to sit down at the piano, where for hours he improvised the most
beautiful waltzes; those he liked he repeated, in order to remember them and write
them out afterwards. – Mozart and especially* Beethoven *were his ideals; in talking
about the latter's symphonies he became enthusiastic. – There was no trace in him
of a 'musician of the future'.*

Bauernfeld's diaries are frequently enlightening:

*Schober surpasses us all in mind, and much more so in speech! Yet there is much in
him that is artificial, and his best powers threaten to be suffocated in idleness. –
Schwind's is a glorious, pure nature – though always fermenting, as if he were going
to burn himself out. – Schubert has the right mixture of the idealist and the realist.
The world seems fair to him. – Mayrhofer is simple and natural, for all that Schober
asserts that he is a kind of easy-going intriguer. – And I? Ah, if one could know
oneself! Until I have done something worthwhile I am no human being.*

For Schubert the year 1826 should have been seen in at Schober's where there
was a party. For this occasion Bauernfeld wrote a skit based on their artistic circle
in which the members took the parts of Columbine, Pantaloon, Harlequin and so
on, Schubert to be Pierrot. It was a fairly barbed affair and Schubert, apparently ill,
did well to avoid it for his behaviour at parties, even among friends, was not always
predictable. But he was well enough to attend a 'sausage party' at Schober's a couple
of weeks later and to play waltzes, as usual.* At this time, too, Josef Teltscher produced a lithograph of Schubert which was available from Cappi's and it must be seen
as a recognition of Schubert's growing reputation that publishers were prepared
to risk investing in the production of his likeness. Certainly the works issued this
year were both more numerous and more important than those of earlier years. It
was publication of the A minor Piano Sonata (D845) which brought Schubert his

*The sausages in question were Frankfurters, strung in pairs and served hot by the women
to the men. Oddly enough, in Frankfurt am Main, where they came from, they were known
as Vienna sausages!

favourable notices in Leipzig and Frankfurt and caused the Zürich publisher, Hans Nägeli, to commend the work to Karl Czerny, offering Schubert the chance to contribute to a series of piano works by contemporary composers. Though Schubert accepted the commission he somehow managed to let the matter slip. More importantly, the publishing houses of Artaria and Weigl issued works by Schubert during the course of the year and the Leipzig publishers Breitkopf & Härtel and Probst responded courteously to offers of songs, though in fact neither published anything during his lifetime. Schubert's driving need was for ready money and with hindsight it is easy to see how his interests might have been better served had he continued to allow one of his more businesslike friends to handle the publishing aspect of his career for him.

In February the D minor Quartet (D810) was given its première (two years after it was written) in a concert at the house of the singer Josef Barth, with a second performance a month later. On each occasion the quartet was led by Ignaz Schuppanzigh. Whether Schubert hoped to attract enough attention to persuade a publisher to take it on is uncertain, though probable, but in any case the work's technical difficulty is said to have frightened them off. Instead the early months of the year were occupied with a return to Goethe, for the last time, as it turned out. Schubert had made settings of songs from *Wilhelm Meister* before, not least 'Nur wer die Sehnsucht kennt' (Only he who knows Longing) which had occupied his occasional attentions since 1815. This poem, so symbolic of the romantic ethos, had special significance for Schubert, yet it would be fair to say that the only one of the five settings he is known to have made which begins to approach the poem with any degree of success is the one least likely to be heard in the concert hall, the duet version (D877). In the early months there were also settings of Johann Gabriel Seidl, not a distinguished poet but a popular one in his day, who wrote the words of the modern version of Austria's national anthem.

More significant are the two Schlechta songs. 'Fischerweise' (Fisherman's Song) is a delight [CD1]. 'Totengräber-Weise' (Gravedigger's Song) can, when the performer is insensitive or ill-equipped, bore. On the other hand, when singer and pianist combine to bring out the striking integration of melody and harmony the song is suddenly unlocked for the listener, the harmony lurching wildly from key to key. On the right occasion it is one of Schubert's most powerful graveside songs.

Meanwhile Schubert's practical situation remained precarious. On 7 April 1826 he wrote to the Emperor Francis seeking the position of second musical director at the Imperial and Royal Court Chapel, a vacancy caused by Salieri's retirement from his position two years earlier and the promotion of his deputy, Josef Eybler. It was not until the following January that the post was filled, the job going to the court theatre conductor, Josef Weigl, who had not even applied for it. Schubert was disappointed but, according to Spaun, he greatly respected Weigl:

Much as I should have liked to receive this appointment, I shall have to make the best of the matter, since it was given to so worthy a man as Weigl.

And there was another shot at an opera. In May Bauernfeld was in Carinthia on a surveying and map-making project, where he missed the company of his musical friends:

... Thus I thought of the libretto for Schubert and set to work on The Count of Gleichen. *Dramatic and musical contrasts: orient and occident, janissaries and knighthood, romantic wooing and wedded love, &c. – in short, a Turkish-Christian outline. The verses flow pretty easily for me.*

But as Maurice Brown observes:

Once again we are faced with the extraordinary inability of the composer to assess the merit of opera texts: Der Graf von Gleichen *is a lifeless hotch-potch of stock stage situations with, moreover, a bigamous marriage as the central theme. It was prohibited by the censor, but Schubert continued to make sketches, often in considerable detail, for the music.*

Happily Josef von Spaun had returned to Vienna on his appointment as a lottery administrator. His reappearance almost coincided with Vogl's marriage to Kunigunde Rosa. This took Schubert by surprise – at least, to judge from his letter to Bauernfeld of 10 July 1826:

I cannot possibly get to Gmunden or anywhere else, for I have no money at all, and altogether things go very badly with me. I do not trouble about it, and am cheerful ... Schwind is quite in the dumps about Nettel! Schober is privileged business man. Vogl is married!!!

Anna Hönig had criticized Schwind for his lack of religion. His reply, 'Go and fall in love with the Pope!', so impressed Bauernfeld that he incorporated it in one of his comedies. That Vogl had married was not so much an emotional blow to Schubert as it was financial, for the singer had been a considerable support to the struggling composer on many occasions, not least in taking him on several inspiring holidays. Schober was no longer quite the soul mate of old and had taken to living in the village of Währing, though Schwind and Schubert also seem to have lived there from time to time. Certainly it was to Währing that they all repaired for the night when in July Bauernfeld returned to Vienna from Carinthia.

Despite his lack of funds and the changes in his circle of friends, Schubert was composing once again. He rarely failed to respond to the uplifting powers of spring and in March he wrote that most delightful nature song, 'Im Frühling' (In Spring). Spring comes round every year and a bird sings on the bough; it is the same song, but to the hearer who has been through love and rejection it can never sound quite the same again. It epitomizes the many disappointments of Schubert's life, on the face of it the most benign of songs yet with that touch of gentle regret in which Schubert excelled, never shovelling the emotions on when a delicate dusting would do.

Nature, too, is charmingly served in one of the Shakespeare songs written that summer, 'Ständchen' (Hark, hark, the Lark), D889,* while another, 'An Silvia' (Who is Silvia?), belongs to that exalted band of songs known by almost everybody even if they do not know who wrote it. Schubert set both songs in German translations, though in English-speaking countries there is no reason why the original Shakespeare words should not be used as they fit with the music perfectly well. Probably Schubert intended that the songs – there is also a rather less satisfactory 'Trinklied' (Drinking Song), D888 – should be published in both languages in order to maximize their international potential, but only 'Who is Silvia?' appeared in print in Schubert's lifetime. There is a story that 'Hark, hark, the Lark' was written on the back of a pub menu card, but as the manuscript for all three songs survives in a notebook with hand-ruled staves complete with afterthoughts and improvements, this is surely fancy.

Of most consequence, however, among the works of 1826 is Schubert's first chamber work for two years which was, as it turned out, to be his last string quartet, the G major. The key of the work is not insignificant, for G major was not a key to which Schubert often turned. There are no symphonies in it, no other important chamber works and, as yet, no piano sonatas. We do not know what caused Schubert to consider the medium of the quartet once again, though it may have been the public performances of its predecessor, the D minor 'Death and the Maiden'. More likely it was the inspiration of Beethoven, performances of whose late quartets Schubert is known to have attended. In March 1826, for instance, Schubert was at the first performance of Beethoven's op. 130, the Quartet in B flat which in this original version ended with the monumental 'Grosse Fuge'. Schubert's manuscript is dated 20–30 June but, as we know from many other works, these were likely to be merely the dates between which the fair copy was made rather than the outside limits of composition, and in this case certainly do not imply a work dashed off almost at one sitting. Schubert's love of (and skill in handling) the ambiguity of major and minor is at the root of the G major Quartet, unsettling, disturbing and adventurous.

*'Ständchen' is the correct title for this song, not to be confused with the even more famous 'Ständchen' (Serenade) to words by Rellstab (D957).

'Promenade at the City Gate' by Schwind: oil painting, 1827. Schwind is studying the map while his fiancée, Anna Hönig, peeps over the garden wall. In the distance Schubert, Vogl and Bauernfeld are among the walkers.

In many ways the first movement is the most logical, cohesive and taut of all the Schubert quartet first movements, though its appeal is more cerebral and makes greater demands of the listener. The feature which most distinguishes major from minor, the inflection of the third note of the scale, is used as a starting-point for excursions into other keys, and these excursions are carefully signposted and handled in a manner more overtly considered than in any of the earlier quartets. It is as if Schubert had sat down and worked out, mathematically, a route plan before putting pen to paper, and intended the listener to be aware of it. As Reed puts it, 'The G major quartet is an essay on the instability of the third.'

This is in considerable contrast with the piano sonata in the same key, completed a few months later, in October, while Schubert was living, once more with Schober, in rooms in the inner city. Where the quartet questions and provokes, the sonata is full of repose, serenity and relaxation. It lulls the senses and soothes the mind with its long-breathed melodies, the slow pulse of three of the four movements (in the hands of a good pianist these never drag) and its greater harmonic stability – though there are, inevitably, plenty of Schubert's characteristic harmonic side-slips to charm and satisfy. Josef von Spaun visited Schubert during the composition of the sonata and was rewarded by the dedication of the work. It was published the following April by Haslinger, who gave it the bulky title of 'Fantasie, Andante, Menuetto und Allegretto', op. 78, and, while the terms 'fantasy' and 'sonata' were freely interchangeable at this time, the suppression of the title 'Sonata' may have been made to avoid direct comparison with the sonatas of Beethoven.

All the while the Schubert circle was changing, with Vogl taken up with his new bride, Schwind agonizing over his affair with Netti, and Leopold Kupelwieser marrying Johanna Lutz in September. The marriage effectively removed Kupelwieser from the group. Johanna was a remarkable woman. At the wedding Schubert would allow no one else near the piano, improvising dances in his inimitable

Bogner's coffee-house, much frequented by Beethoven and Schubert.

manner. One of these made a deep impression on Johanna and she remembered it, passing it on to her descendants who picked it up by ear. In 1942 Richard Strauss happened to meet one of these descendants and immediately wrote down the tune, subsequently orchestrating it. Over the century which had elapsed since the tune was created it had very probably acquired a few new characteristics, as any melody which is not fixed on paper will, and there is more than a touch of Johann Strauss about it, but it is no less endearing for that.

Towards the end of 1826 Schubert moved yet again, this time to a room on his own near the Karolinentor in the city. His daily life, or rather night-life, at this time is well recorded in the diaries of the brothers Franz and Fritz von Hartmann. Franz reports that Schubert, Spaun, Schober, Bauernfeld and the others met most evenings at the Green Anchor or Bogner's coffee-house, usually staying until midnight and often far longer; they met also at Spaun's or Schober's, and Schubert's songs were sung (despite Vogl's absence). On 15 December a huge gathering took place at Spaun's, which also included Mayrhofer, Gahy (who played duets with Schubert), Schlechta, Witteczek (who, after Schubert's death, amassed a huge collection of his music in first editions or fair copies) and even Vogl (who sang almost thirty songs!). Most importantly for posterity Schwind was there too, and in 1868 he made a sepia drawing based on this evening which has become one of the most familiar of all pictures associated with Schubert. It is not actually a true record of the occasion, but rather a bringing together of many of the people prominent in Schubert's life (see endpapers). Johann Senn, for instance, is represented there, though Schubert did not see him again after his banishment to the Tyrol in 1821. At the end of the year, as was now customary, a collection of new dances was published (by Sauer & Leidesdorf) which included two waltzes by Schubert. On 30 December the friends congregated at the inn, as usual. Franz von Hartmann describes some of their antics:

As we step out of the Anchor all is deeply snowed under. We itch for a game of snowballs, which we carry out immediately ... Spaun is on my side, Fritz and Schober on Schwind's. Schober always hits me hard and without fail, and I him or Schwind in particular. Spaun gloriously protects himself against the shots with his open umbrella. Schubert and Haas take no part in the fight. Home, where the house-steward was rude because we rang so loudly.

The following night there was a New Year party at Schober's. Hartmann again:

On the stroke of 12 glasses were filled with Tokay, and we drank each other's health for the coming year ... Then we drank coffee, smoked again, and at 2 o'clock left at last ... Or rather we waddled off. Parted with Schubert and Bauernfeld in the Singerstrasse.

First page of the manuscript of the 'Great' C major Symphony.

Several excellent songs, the G major String Quartet and the G major Piano Sonata notwithstanding, 1826 had been a marking of time, a lull before the storm. In October, however, Schubert made a presentation to the Philharmonic Society of something he described as 'this, my Symphony, and commend it most politely to their protection'. The society recorded this symphony in its catalogue, yet apparently preserved no such work. There is little likelihood that Schubert donated one of his youthful symphonies to such an august body. He had, long before, parted company with the manuscript of the 'Unfinished'. So it is possible that this was the so-called 'Gmunden–Gastein' Symphony, or (and this theory attracts many eminent Schubertians) that it was the 'Great' C major, traditionally attributed to 1828 but very possibly the same work as the 'Gmunden–Gastein' and therefore written, or at least begun, on that inspirational holiday in 1825. In any case it is as good a time as any to discuss the C major Symphony, for the twelve months following its presentation to the society (if this it was) saw Schubert's output become sparse, however great some individual works may be.

The arguments put forward by John Reed to support the 1825 theory are among the most persuasive in print. He reminds us that one of the binding philosophical elements for the early romantics was the image of nature as a metaphor for human existence, that this is abundantly present in the songs of 1825, that Schubert was then in the midst of glorious scenery and clearly excited by it, and that Schubert's 'grand symphony' was linked in the composer's mind with his apprehension of natural beauty as the vesture of God. He draws a parallel with the painter, Samuel

Palmer, who at this time was also engaged in his most visionary work, and who said of that energetic adherent to the romantic view, William Blake, 'to walk with him in the country was to perceive the soul of beauty through the forms of matter'.

It is not irrelevant that the C major Symphony is approached from this mixed-media angle, for Schubert moved among painters, poets, perfomers, philosophers and political revolutionaries: their thoughts and their works were not conceived in isolation. In 1825 he was on holiday with Vogl, an actor and singer with deep knowledge of many subjects. While symphonies for the most part are abstract creations with no programmatic element or visual drama, they are obviously a great deal more than mere dots on paper. In the case of Schubert's 'Great' C major, many orchestral players have failed to move beyond those dots, seeing it as a tiresome way to fill an hour of their lives and dubbing it Schubert's 'Great Sea Monster'. One musician who immediately saw beyond them, however, was Robert Schumann who, visiting Ferdinand Schubert in Vienna on New Year's Day, 1839, was shown the score and immediately set about the business of arranging a first performance (which took place in a cut version in Leipzig, under Mendelssohn's direction). The audience on that occasion applauded after each movement and the orchestral players warmed to it, but when the same conductor first rehearsed it in London the incessantly repeated string triplets in the last movement reduced the Philharmonic Society's orchestra to helpless laughter. And the work has puzzled many a conductor and untold listeners since. The problem is that it *is* unlike any symphony ever written before, and in all that bounding profusion of energy and huge length it can be difficult to see the wood for the trees. Analysts have had a field-day demonstrating how all the main themes of the symphony derive from the horn melody which opens the work, rising through the interval of a third (the interval which distinguishes major from minor and the device so often used in Schubert's unique treatment of tonality), discussing the manner in which the themes are handled, identifying cross-references to other works, and pointing out how the architecture of each movement can be viewed in purely classical forms and so on. What this analysis cannot explain is summed up by Arthur Hutchings:

Of course the C major sprawls, but its sprawling moves us as profoundly as the most close-knit and apposite orthodox symphonizing . . . no one has yet dared to call its fullness adipose, and no generation has contradicted Schumann's dictum, originally applied to the Andante, concerning its 'heavenly length'.

In contrast with Schubert's earlier symphonies, the C major requires some preparation from its listeners – perhaps even more so than the symphonies of Beethoven. Returning to the concert hall after the lively banter of the bar during the interval only to be thrown straight into that vast introduction demands the capacity to make an enormous mental adjustment in an instant. Concentration will reap its reward. Music, in this age of the CD, is so often used in the background to accompany work, to relieve the tedium of a car journey or even to while away the time on board an aeroplane, and many works, it has to be said, stand up to this treatment perfectly well. But not the Schubert C major Symphony. It can be appreciated best by the listener who has the time and peace of mind to savour that 'heavenly length'; by the listener who can visualize the background of majestic scenery against which it was created, and by the listener who can appreciate that Schubert's intention was not to write 'a Beethoven symphony' but, using the medium of the orchestra, to make a profound statement about his romantic bond with nature on a broader canvas than song.

In January 1827 Schubert composed a number of songs of which 'Alinde' and 'An die Laute' (To the Lute) stand out for their freshness. The former is the charming tale of a poet who is searching for his beloved in the evening. It is an infectious barcarolle and Schubert amuses himself and us with ingenious twists and turns which make each verse subtly different. No less infectious is the strumming serenade accompaniment to the lilting melody of 'An die Laute'. Their obvious happiness is in complete contrast to Schubert's own mood, which by now had become jaded. His illness, his lack of success in several musical fields, his failure to get the court chapel appointment, his poor financial performance, the rejection of several of his works by the publisher Probst, his social diffidence, his unsatisfactory love-life, and his overwhelming belief in the romantic ideal that only death can relieve the suffering of the true artist on earth, made him at best serious and more frequently thoroughly depressed. In February, possibly in Schober's library, he came across *Urania*, a Leipzig almanac of 1823 in which twelve poems by Wilhelm Müller were printed. Müller had been the poet of *Die schöne Müllerin* and Schubert leapt at the new poems with whose content and mood he identified completely. And so the first twelve songs of *Winterreise* (Winter Journey) came into being that month.

The process further exhausted Schubert, though Mayrhofer's assertions that he set these words because of his illness must be treated with caution, and in March he moved into new lodgings with Schober in a building known as the Blue Hedgehog. Meanwhile his idol, Beethoven, was ill and dying. Anton Schindler, Beethoven's companion, relates that a number of Schubert songs were sent to the great man at this time and he is said to have recognized in them a 'divine spark', but Schindler's reminiscences are frequently discredited, as is the story that Schubert was amongst a small group which paid a visit to Beethoven on his death-bed. After Schubert's death Spaun denied the story, though the Hüttenbrenners (who were apparently part of that group) confirmed it. There is no doubt, however, that Schubert was one of thirty-six torch-bearers in Beethoven's funeral procession, 'all in funereal clothes

with white roses and bunches of lilies tied to their arms with crape, and with burning wax torches'. Afterwards they repaired to the inn where until 1.0 a.m. Schubert,
Schober and Schwind talked of 'nothing but Beethoven, his works and the well-
merited honours paid to his memory'. Their social life continued as bibulously as
ever, if the copious diary entries of the Hartmann brothers are any guide. Schubert's
songs were being sung and reviews published as far afield as Leipzig, Berlin and
Munich, for the most part referring to the composer in favourable terms. Schubert
was being noticed. And yet he was not, for if his fame had been more than skin-
deep his music would not have all but disappeared on his death in 1828.

Among those who came to Vienna in March 1827 was Johann Nepomuk Hummel,
a composer whose fame and influence in his day was considerable but whose
standing now is somewhat diminished – one of those composers whose works are
always being rediscovered yet never quite become established in the repertoire. Like
Schubert, Hummel had studied with Salieri, and also with Mozart, Haydn, Clementi
and Albrechtsberger (Beethoven's teacher). Following in Haydn's footsteps he had
held the post of musical director to the family of Prince Esterházy, and had been a
friend and colleague of Beethoven, but unfortunately the two men quarrelled and
this visit to Vienna was intended to repair the damage. While in Vienna Hummel
attended a party given by the singer Frau von Läszny. There he met Schubert, of
whom he had never heard, and Vogl, and during the evening the two of them
performed songs:

*The latter, already elderly, but full of fire and life, had very little voice left – and
Schubert's piano playing, in spite of not inconsiderable fluency, was very far from
being that of a master. And yet I have never again heard the Schubert songs sung as
they were then! Vogl was able to make one forget his lack of voice by means of the
utmost fervour and aptness of expression, and Schubert accompanied – as he could
not help accompanying.*[20]

Hummel was deeply impressed and improvised on one of the Schubert songs there
and then. Schubert, too, was affected by Hummel's playing and would have dedicated his next three piano sonatas to him when they were published had he not
been robbed of the opportunity by death.

In April a subscription concert was given by the violinist Ignaz Schuppanzigh
and at it the first public performance of the Octet (D803) took place. Amongst the
reviews was one in the *Theaterzeitung* which said:

*Herr Schubert's composition is commensurate with the author's acknowledged talent,
luminous, agreeable and interesting; only it is possible that too great a claim may be
made on the hearers' attention by its long duration . . . Schubert has proved himself, in
this species as well, as a gallant and felicitous composer.*

The Hartmann brothers had brought a young civil servant in the Marine Department, Ferdinand Walcher, into the company of the *Schubertiade* and in May he left Vienna on a posting to Venice. Shortly before his departure Schubert dedicated to him the manuscript of a short Allegretto in C minor for solo piano (D915) [CD3]. There could hardly be a gift to treasure more than this exquisite miniature, wandering between minor and major, charming, delicate and utterly assured. Schubert had certainly not abandoned the piano sonata as a vehicle for his profoundest keyboard music but there are hints in this Allegretto that other forms could be at least as fecund, and it is possible that he had already begun to think about the impromptu as an alternative by the early summer. He may have toyed with the first of these while on a short break at Dornbach, not far from Vienna, close enough in fact to be able to meet up with many of the 'in crowd' at the Castle of Eisenstadt, their current favourite for merry evenings. In Dornbach Schubert translated his temporary joy into one of his most engaging spring songs, *Das Lied im Grünen* (Song of the Greenwood), and the opportunity also arose to accompany his friend, Johann Baptist Jenger, to Graz. The visit took place in September and they were the guests of Dr and Frau Pachler: Marie Pachler, a considerable pianist, had been acquainted with Beethoven and delighted in the *Schubertiade* arranged most evenings at her home. By day Schubert explored the local countryside. He composed dances for the piano, a couple of songs, and when he returned home he sent their son, Faust, a *Kindermarsch* (Children's March) for piano duet. These happy days were soon over and Schubert's return to Vienna was not easy. He resumed his lodgings at the Blue Hedgehog in poor health with giddy fits and headaches. Bauernfeld seems to have drifted away from the circle, and Schwind had left, first for Munich, then for Linz. Meanwhile Schubert had been elected a member of the Philharmonic Society of Vienna (as he already was of the societies in Linz and Graz) but the title was purely honorary; it did nothing to further his career, nor did it involve him in the society's activities. In October he received 100 florins for the composition of a German Mass (that is to say, not in Latin) but this is Schubert in sentimental vein, a far cry from the Schubert who discovered more of Müller's *Winterreise* poems and in October began work on the fair copy of Part II of the cycle. With *Die schöne Müllerin* and *Winterreise* Schubert completed what John Reed has described as 'the greatest achievement in the history of song'.

Müller's verses are short lyrics in folk idiom. They are not the outpourings of a literary giant, yet Schubert was able to identify personally with the poet's stance as a receiver of alms from a society hostile to art. He was not only in poor health but also in desperate financial trouble. His music was being published (even once again by Diabelli) but it did not bring him enough to live off, and on one occasion he even sent his friend Lachner off to the publisher Haslinger with a copy of one of

Schubert making music with friends: Josefine Fröhlich beside Schubert at the piano, Vogl behind. Franz Lachner listens on the left; the violinist Ludwig Kraissl and the dramatist Franz Grillparzer are in the foreground. Pencil sketch by F. G. Waldmüller.

the *Winterreise* songs with the instruction that he was to obtain enough money to buy medicine and soup. Because Schubert came across the poems piecemeal he did not quite follow the thread that Müller had intended when the poems are read in the correct order. But it does not matter for there is no narrative in the cycle. It is more in the nature of an epilogue, beginning as the young man leaves after his loved one has already forsaken him (and she is never actually mentioned in the poems). But what a beginning! 'Gute Nacht' (Good Night) portrays perfectly the bleakness of his situation without dwelling on the pain and anguish which he will experience later. It progresses 'in gehender Bewegung' (in a walking movement) which gives an inevitability to what follows. If one song had to be held up as an example of Schubert's breathtaking use of the contrast of major and minor, this would be the song to choose. Essentially it is in the minor but it changes to the major for the last stanza when things seem less desperate. There is nothing exceptional about that – many a piece by many a composer changes from minor to major simply to indicate the triumph of goodness over evil. What is heart-stopping is the sudden switch back to the minor as the young man sings 'Good Night' for the last, pathetic time.

Thereafter the listener is led through a sequence of fluctuations of mood, at times bitter, at others resolute, and for this non-hero there is not even the solace of death. He is condemned to suffer without respite, alone, save for the solitary

Title page of part I of Winterreise, *published by Haslinger in January 1828.*

intervention of the melancholic hurdy-gurdy man encountered in the very last song. Against this background is it not ironic that the one song everybody knows from the cycle is the disarmingly beautiful 'Der Lindenbaum' (The Lime Tree)? True, it is an enchanting song in its own right, a felicitous combination of folk-song and art-song with a magical accompaniment suggesting the rippling of the leaves in the wind. The lime tree has special, almost national, significance for the German-speaking peoples as the centre of village life, a symbol of permanence from early childhood. But within the context of this cycle it takes on a new and deeper meaning relating to the conflict between idealism and painful reality, its beauty the more striking in the changing sequence of moods which the surrounding songs portray.

There are twenty-four songs in all, each demanding (and worthy of) detailed study, far beyond the brief of this book. Those who warm initially only to 'Der Lindenbaum' are in good company for when Schubert, in a voice wrought with emotion, sang through the first set of *Winterreise* songs to his friends, all were dumbfounded by their almost unremitting gloom and Schober confessed to liking only one, 'Der Lindenbaum'. 'I like these songs more than all the others, and you will get to like them too,' said Schubert, and they did, once Vogl had familiarized himself with them and put them across with his usual vocal advocacy. Partly because Vogl sang them first, partly because of one or two transpositions on publication, and to a large extent because of the darkness of the songs, a tradition grew up that they were intended for baritone. Happily that tradition has been broken, though the exact key relationships between one song and the next nearly always cause problems somewhere either for the singer or for the listener, unless the singer is possessed of a remarkable range. However, *Winterreise* is still generally the province of male singers which, when the nature of the poems is realized, may be another tradition worth breaking.

Part I of the cycle was published by Haslinger in January 1828 but he held up publication of the rest until Part I was well established. So it came to pass that Schubert corrected the proofs for Part II on his death-bed, a year after he had written it, and the publication did not take place until a month after his death. Mayrhofer, at that time, suggested that Schubert's own melancholy led him to *Winterreise* – 'The very choice of subject proved an increased seriousness in our musician.' Spaun exchanges chicken for egg:

After he had finished the Winterreise, *Schubert was run down in health, if not to any alarming point. Many believed and perhaps still do that Schubert was a thick-skinned fellow who could stand anything, but we who were near and dear knew how much the creatures of his mind took out of him and in what travail they were born. No one who ever saw him at his morning's work, glowing and his eyes aflame, yes and positively with a changed speech ... will ever forget it ... I hold it beyond question that the excitement in which he composed his finest songs, the* Winterreise *in particular, brought about his untimely death.*

Winterreise certainly perplexes the listener, moving on yet again from the world of the G major String Quartet and C major Symphony, already challenging, to something quite alien. If one needed proof, though, that Schubert had not exhausted his stock of mellifluous melody and that he still recognized the need occasionally to appeal to public taste, the remaining piano pieces and a chamber work from 1827 provide it.

The chamber work is the E flat major Piano Trio (D929). It has been suggested that Schubert composed this expressly for a public concert devoted entirely to his own works. The thought of an event of this kind had been in his mind (and those of his friends) for a number of years but Schubert could not afford the financial risk involved in such a venture himself and, for whatever reason, he had not persuaded any of his wealthier acquaintances to guarantee against loss. The trio is in the repertoire of any self-respecting piano trio today, and despite its undoubted popularity with concert audiences and the record-buying public it does not find universal acclaim from the critics. This is mostly on account of the work's sheer length, lasting around three quarters of an hour, and the repetition of material which is more gesture than substance, held together by Schubert's ubiquitous keyboard triplets, diffuse rather than formally taut. But let a proficient piano trio loose on the second movement and the audience is eating out of its hand. The theme is one of those which has become ideally suited to poignant use in film (as, indeed, it has been used); it was said, after Schubert's death, to be a Swedish folk-tune, 'See the Sun is sinking', and so it may be, but nobody has found the relevant tune in Swedish sources. There is a stroke of genius when Schubert brings this theme back in the last movement, arresting the listener in a most original and affecting manner. The writing for the instruments demands considerable technical proficiency, but Schubert will have been given the best possible first performance in December 1827, with Ignaz Schuppanzigh playing the violin, Josef Linke (also from his quartet) on the cello, and Karl Maria von Bocklet as the pianist. Von Bocklet had been the dedicatee of the D major Piano Sonata and was shortly to be the pianist in the first performance of the Fantasy in C major which Schubert composed in late 1827 for the Czech violinist, Josef Slavík. Schubert had already composed a showpiece for him in the previous autumn, the Rondo brillant in B minor, a vivid and exuberant work. So, too, is the fantasy if you have the patience, for it is long and extravagant, undoubtedly a vehicle for display but musically shallow until the very end. One Viennese critic present at the first performance wrote:

The Fantasy ... occupied rather too much of the time a Viennese is prepared to devote to pleasures of the mind. The hall emptied gradually, and the writer confesses that he too is unable to say anything about the conclusion of this piece of music.

He missed the best bit!

It is often said that the conventions of classical form, and sonata form in particular, restricted Schubert's ability to work with otherwise promising material. The E flat Piano Trio would be cited by many as an example, and they might point to the six *Momens musicals* to show what Schubert could do when relieved of these responsibilities. The title was given by Leidesdorf when these pieces were published in 1828, though whether Schubert's French would have been any better is open to argument. Let us, then, call them *Moments musicaux*, if only to avoid offence, and note that two of them, nos. 3 and 6, had appeared in Leidesdorf's Christmas annuals in 1823 and 1824. Yet Schubert, in the autumn of 1827, matched their style admirably in putting together a suite of six cheering piano pieces as innocent to the ear as they are full of subtlety and surprise to the player. It is probable that both sets of Impromptus for piano (D899 and D935) also date from late 1827, for the first two numbers of D899 were published in December of that year. They are similar to the *Moments musicaux* in their formal and tonal freedom, yet almost every one of them grows from a single idea (a technique recognizable from the 'Wanderer' Fantasy). Essentially they are lyrical pieces in the tradition of the Bohemian pianist–composer Václav Tomášek. Schubert possibly knew Tomášek's work, but he far transcended any model he may have had, his own impromptus being developed on a scale commensurate with the sonatas with which he had had so many formal difficulties. The Impromptus are frequently held up as an example of where Schubert might have taken piano music had he lived longer. As an exercise this is not only irrelevant, but also of little consequence because Schubert's influence on other composers, and on the development of music for that matter, was minimal both in his lifetime and after his death. However, the two sets of Impromptus do succeed in carrying the emotional tension and auditory interest for just under an hour between the pair of them, in a way that Schubert's piano sonatas up to this point often fail to do. Like the *Moments musicaux* the Impromptus are immensely familiar and do not suffer as individual sonata movements do if lifted out of context and played on their own, say as an audition piece or encore. Perhaps Schubert's apparent reconciliation with popular taste and his awareness of commercial qualities was no bad thing.

As a footnote to Schubert's penultimate year, a number of stories persist which suggest that his amorous adventures may not have been quite at an end. Schober is not the most reliable of sources but much later in life at dinner with a journalist he recounted the tale of a young woman, Auguste ('Gusti') Grünwedel, and how he attempted to persuade Schubert to marry her. She is mentioned in Franz Hartmann's diaries for February 1827, 'the loveliest dancer', captivating Spaun and clearly an attractive young woman from a good family. She was, it seems, well disposed to Schubert who, in turn, at least showed her some appreciation. But his painful shyness overcame him and on hearing Schober's suggestion that he might woo her he dashed from the room, sure that no woman could possibly love him. Having run round St Peter's Church telling himself that no earthly happiness could ever be granted to him he returned to his friends, but from that moment *[he] let himself go to pieces; he frequented the city outskirts and roamed around in taverns, at the same time admittedly composing his most beautiful songs in them, just as he did in the hospital too . . . where he found himself as the result of excessively indulgent sensual living and its consequences.*

It is difficult to know what to think – or quite what Heinrich Hoffmann von Fallersleben meant when he noted in his diary:

Schubert with his girl we espied from our seat; he came to join us and did not show himself again.

Pencil sketch of Schubert by his friend Moritz von Schwind.

CHAPTER 9

1828 The Final Year

Whatever the truth may be about Schubert's amorous preoccupations in 1827, there is no doubt that his final year began with a renewal of contact with Countess Karoline Esterházy. We cannot tell if Schubert had any special relationship with the young lady but Bauernfeld in his memoirs left the impression that the composer was head over heels in love with her, describing her as 'the Leonore of this musical Tasso'. She appears as a portrait on the wall of Spaun's room in Schwind's famous portmanteau representation of a Schubertiad, and several others of the circle acknowledged her influence, if nothing else, long after Schubert's death. Spaun, as loyal a friend of Schubert as could be found, points out the Hungarian flavour (relating back to the *Divertissement à l'hongroise* of 1824) in the Fantasy in F minor for piano duet written early in 1828 and dedicated to Karoline. Karoline's sister, Marie, married in December 1827 and it is possible their old music teacher from the Zseliz days was invited to the occasion. But it seems likely they were still in touch on a more familiar basis for not only did Schubert dedicate this great work to Karoline but he also gave her the manuscript of the E flat major Piano Trio, which had just received its first performance, and she kept it for the rest of her short and rather cheerless life (her marriage in 1844 was soon annulled, and she died seven years later). What is certain is that in the fantasy Schubert produced one of the greatest works for piano duet ever written and, arguably, his own greatest keyboard work [CD3]. Here, perhaps more than anywhere else, he managed to reconcile

Karoline Esterházy in 1837, nine years after Schubert's death: watercolour portrait by Hanisch.

freedom with form, to allow himself the luxury of heartfelt inspiration and yet produce a work of powerful direction and purpose. Who has not been moved almost to tears by that most poignant of openings, hovering around the chord of F minor, the phrasing tentative, exploratory, pregnant? It comes back as an introduction to one of Schubert's few successful fugal Finales, its reappearance at least as moving as its first statement. But the moment of greatest pathos comes when it returns for the last time after the fugue has run its course, the hesitant melody enjoying a brief flirtation with the major in its imposing dying moments, before inevitable submission to the minor key which reasserts itself for the conclusion.

Given the quantity of music written in this final year, and its staggering quality, it would be only natural to assume that the notes simply flowed from Schubert's pen. The sketches for the fantasy prove that he worked very hard to achieve his results, sometimes merely adding or subtracting a few notes or a bar here and there, but also discarding whole themes and their working out. The fantasy occupied his attentions from at least January 1828 through to its completion in April and, however much he employed his brain in the process, it is to our joy that his heart, and perhaps the influence of Countess Karoline, was never supplanted.

As the year began, Schubert's circle was still remarkably intact and very much united at the inn (for the chronicles of which posterity must be grateful for the robust nature of Franz von Hartmann's liver), though marriage was intervening again – Josef von Spaun announced his engagement in January. On the 18th of the same month Schubert wrote what is thought to be his last letter to Anselm Hüttenbrenner, asking him to support his brother's application for a post as a drawing master in Graz. In itself the letter is unremarkable, save for Schubert's use of the words, 'Your faithful friend until death', as he signed off. On the whole, however, things were going well, with another special Schubertiad at Spaun's at which Bocklet, Schuppanzigh and Linke again played the E flat major Piano Trio and Schubert and Bocklet played duets. Schubert was pleased to pay tribute to his most faithful friend as he prepared for marriage, and it was probably the last Schubertiad of its kind. Reading parties took place every Saturday at Schober's and it is likely it was here that the *Reisebilder* (Travel Scenes) of Heine were on the agenda. Schubert set six of these poems almost at once. They are among the greatest songs he ever wrote, and among the greatest songs ever written. They did not appear, however, until after his death, when Haslinger published them along with a group of Rellstab songs under the general title *Schwanengesang* (Swansong).

It has become fashionable to dismiss *Schwanengesang* as a cycle and it is perfectly reasonable to do so, for Schubert never intended these songs to be grouped together, nor did he see them as his last word in song, nor is there any reason to sing them in the order in which Haslinger published them, finishing with 'Die Taubenpost' (Pigeon Post), a jewel of a song, but totally unrelated to all that has gone before. It would, none the less, be an unfeeling recipient who failed to be moved by the anthology, which amounts to a distillation of Schubert's various responses to poets and poetry through the years. As there is little to be gained from strict adherence to chronology throughout this final year in which the output is without parallel, it makes sense to deal with *Schwanengesang* as a group, beginning with the Rellstab songs.

Ludwig Rellstab, from Berlin, was a couple of years younger than Schubert. He was one of the very first professional music critics, coming to Vienna in 1825, meeting Beethoven and discussing with him the idea of collaboration in a German opera, for he viewed with abhorrence the Viennese obsession with Rossini. In that respect he shared an opinion with Schubert. Both Rellstab and Schindler say that it was from Beethoven's effects that Schubert acquired his copy of Rellstab's poems, so he may well have begun work on them earlier than the date recorded on the autograph, August 1828. Schubert made seven of his ten settings one after the other, suggesting that he intended them to follow in sequence, and there is a certain unity of purpose to them which ties them to and, equally, dissociates them from the Heine songs in the same published collection. They are old-fashioned, if you like, unquestionably lyrical, beginning with Schubert's last (and possibly greatest) brook song, 'Liebesbotschaft' (Love's Message). It is a marvellous example of mood setting and woe betide any singer who dams the stream by slowing up in the final vocal phrase! Schubert lengthens the notes here in order to achieve the effect without stopping the flow of the brook, yet how few singers seem to have realized this. 'Liebesbotschaft' is followed by 'Kriegers Ahnung' (Warrior's Foreboding), an unusual flashback to earlier years when Schubert divided his songs into distinct sections, but no less powerful for that. 'Frühlingssehnsucht' (Spring Longing) in its eagerness recalls the early songs in *Die schöne Müllerin*, but it is the fourth song, 'Ständchen' (Serenade), which will be familiar to all, perhaps the best-known serenade in song. Against a simple chordal accompaniment (serenades, after all, are sung by amateur musicians under the loved one's balcony, accompanying themselves on the guitar or whatever is to hand) the most sinuous of melodies is woven.

Then comes 'Aufenthalt' (Resting Place), yet another song of the artistic fugitive fleeing the persecution of a hostile world, and again one of Schubert's finest essays in the form. 'In der Ferne' (Far Away), which follows, is a fearsome song of the outcast, its demands on range and breath control effectively denying it to all but a handful of the very finest singers, who must then wrestle with the challenge of conveying the emotional confusion and alienation of the fugitive while outwardly remaining in control of their technical faculties. The group ends, appropriately enough, with 'Abschied' (Farewell), one of the finest of Schubert's *perpetuum mobile* songs, the insistence of the rapidly trotting piano accompaniment reinforcing the determination of the poet to leave everything that is familiar behind.

There are three further Rellstab songs which are not included in the cycle, but the Heine songs in *Schwanengesang* are unique [CD3]. To judge from Schubert's correspondence, he did not intend the Heine songs to form a cycle, but that is how they are most frequently encountered, if only because that is how they were first published. There is some merit, too, in grouping them together for they share a bitterness and sense of tragedy which is more akin to *Winterreise* than

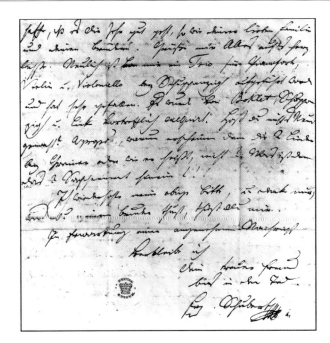

Final page of a letter from Schubert to Anselm Hüttenbrenner, 18 January 1828, requesting his assistance in obtaining a drawing master's post for his brother, Karl. Schubert also mentions the first performance of the Piano Trio in E flat.

Schwanengesang up to this point. I discuss these songs on pp. 162–3.

'Die Taubenpost' [CD3], with which the publisher curiously chose to conclude the cycle, is as charming, cheerful and optimistic a song as you could hope to find. It is probably the composer's last song, dating from October 1828, and it is somehow fitting that Schubert should say farewell to song on such an innocuous note, with a lover sending confidences to his beloved by carrier-pigeon. And the name of this pigeon? 'Sehnsucht' (Longing). Its strutting imparts a delectable syncopation to the piano accompaniment that trips jauntily underneath the fragments of melody, modulated with all the skill and experience of a master.

The contrast between this hopefulness and the real state of affairs for Schubert could not have been greater. His prospects were gloomy. As far back as the previous October he had written to Anna Hönig to cancel an appointment:

I find it very difficult to have to tell you that I cannot give myself the pleasure of being at your party this evening. I am ill, and in such a way which totally unfits me for such a gathering.

As far as publishing was concerned, H. A. Probst wrote to Schubert asking him to send 'anything finished to your satisfaction', but the address of 'Franz Schubert, Esq., Musician and Composer, Vienna' was insufficient for the letter to reach him and it went, instead, to one Josef Schubert, less well-known as a composer, but better known to the post office. Only some time later did the letter reach its intended recipient. But Schott, based in Mainz, wrote to Schubert on the very same day and this letter seems to have reached him direct. That the two publishers should write at the same time is unlikely to be a mere coincidence and it is probable they had both taken notice of one of the favourable reviews which had appeared outside Vienna. Schott apologized for not having responded earlier, but had been engaged in publishing opp. 121–31 by the recently departed Beethoven, no small undertaking! They requested 'Pianoforte works or vocal pieces for one or several voices, with or without pianoforte accompaniment' and they invited Schubert to fix the fee. Almost immediately Schubert replied in unusual detail:

Gentlemen,

I feel much honoured by your letter of 8 February and enter with pleasure into closer relations with so reputable an art establishment, which is so fit to give my works greater currency abroad.

I have the following compositions in stock:

a) Trio for pianoforte, violin and violoncello, which has been produced here with much success.

b) Two string Quartets (G major and D minor).

c) Four Impromptus for pianoforte solo, which might be published separately or all four together.

d) Fantasy for pianoforte duet, dedicated to Countess Karoline Esterházy.

e) Fantasy for pianoforte and violin.

f) Songs for one voice with pianoforte accompaniment, poems by Schiller, Goethe, Klopstock, &c. &c., and Seidl, Schober, Leitner, Schulze, &c. &c.

g) Four-part choruses for male voices as well as for female voices with pianoforte accompaniment, two of them with a solo voice, poems by Grillparzer and Seidl.

h) A five-part song for male voices, poem by Schober.

i) 'Battle Song' by Klopstock, double chorus for eight male voices.

j) Comic Trio, 'The Wedding Roast' [Der Hochzeitsbraten], by Schober, for soprano, tenor and bass, which has been performed with success.

This is the list of my finished compositions, excepting three operas, a Mass and a symphony. These last compositions I mention only in order to make you acquainted with my strivings after the highest in art.

Now, if you should wish anything from the above list for publication, I shall assign
it to you with pleasure against a reasonable fee.
With all respect
Franz Schubert.

My address:
Under the Tuchlauben,
at the Blue Hedgehog,
2nd floor.

We have become so used nowadays to using Deutsch numbers to identify Schubert's compositions that it is easy to overlook the value of the original opus numbers when we are hunting the missing pieces in the jigsaw puzzle of Schubert's chronology. The piano trio to which the composer gives pride of place in his letter to Schott is the recent one in E flat, to which he subsequently assigned the opus number 100. But he had already given opus 99 to another trio, the one in B flat (D898) which implies that he had already disposed of it at the time of this letter – probably to another publisher, though no trace of its having appeared in print at this time has been found. (It was eventually published in 1836.) Detective work of this kind is not the province of this book, but it is recorded here as an example of the imprecise knowledge we still have about some of Schubert's most familiar music. It is, of course, just the same with the patchy biographical details available to us from the incomplete series of letters and diaries that survive today.

Schubert set great store by his E flat trio. He wanted to see this piece in print almost more than any other. He thought he had succeeded when Probst of Leipzig took it on, but in October 1828, only seven weeks before he died, we find him writing impatiently to Probst asking what had become of it. Whether the trio appeared in print before Schubert's death or whether he saw it if it did remains unknown. In many technical respects, however, the B flat is the better trio. Its optimism is conspicuous from the very outset, with a bold opening that gives confidence to the whole of the first movement. Admittedly, it is shorter than its E flat stable-mate by some seven minutes or so and its slow movement, gloriously singing though it is, does not quite have the melodic advantage of the E flat's slow movement. It is in the third movement, the Scherzo, that the B flat scores, with its peal-of-bells theme that lingers in the memory long after it is heard. Perhaps its weak spot is the length of the Finale, as if the composer was determined to include all his design intentions regardless of whether or not the movement could sustain them. It *is* gay and unaffected and it enjoys some striking digressions into remote keys, but there is also a sense in which Schubert keeps going back on his tracks and covering the same

ground again. There are times when his final movements fail to live up to the promise of what has gone before.

Writing for the piano in combination with strings is not as simple as might be
imagined. While there are many advantages in having the different qualities of the
instruments available for contrast, the difficulty is in creating a sustained melody.
The violin or cello can make the longest of phrases sing for ever. Each note on the
piano dies as soon as it is struck, especially on the fortepianos of Schubert's day.
It is not, then, easy to transfer such melodies from instrument to instrument, while
in trying to sustain the harmonies below the strings the pianist is bound to be
employed with a lot of arpeggio figures and repetition. Repetition, however, is a
recurring feature of all Schubert's piano writing and if it is a weakness of the pianist's
technique there will be much spilling of blood in the piano sonatas, in many song
accompaniments and in these two trios. It is another feature of Schubert's piano
writing (possibly developed from his piano duet playing) that he frequently reinforces right-hand melodies by doubling in octaves, which again sorts out one pianist
from another. It is this inherent difficulty in so much of Schubert's piano music
that kept a great deal of it out of the concert repertoire until comparatively recently:
a lot of hard work for not much show.

Returning to early 1828, Schubert was busy working on the Fantasy in F minor for
piano duet and copying out, and making revisions to, the 'Great' C major Symphony.
There is much confusion about this symphony and whether or not it is the lost
Gmunden–Gastein symphony. Assuming it is, and that it was this one Schubert had
already presented to the Philharmonic Society in 1826, he seems to have requested
the return of the score in order to carry out extensive revisions, unique amongst
Schubert's symphonic autographs. He then resubmitted the score to the society, for
he had promised them a symphony. Their orchestra found it too difficult and the
other C major Symphony, no. 6, was substituted. The manuscript must have been
returned to Schubert at this time because it remained in his brother Ferdinand's
keeping after his death. If this is the actual sequence of events it does not, however,
answer the question why the orchestra did not realize it was too difficult before
returning the score to Schubert.

There were public performances of the C major Fantasy for violin and of a con-
certed vocal piece, 'Ständchen' (Serenade), D920 [CD3], a glorious work, all too
rarely performed these days, which was given at a Philharmonic Society concert on
24 January and well received. It had been written in the previous summer at the
request of Anna Fröhlich, one of a family of four musically gifted sisters to whom
Schubert had been introduced at Ignaz Sonnleithner's house in 1820. She had suggested the text by Grillparzer and Schubert hit on the idea of using an alto soloist
with a chorus of tenors and basses plus piano. When he had finished it Anna pointed

out that it was intended for her pupils to sing and that they were female! Schubert reworked it in no time at all and it was first sung under the window of Louise Gosmar, Leopold Sonnleithner's fiancée, on her birthday, the piano being carried there specially for the performance. But Schubert was not there to hear it, and he would not have been there when it was next performed either, if a search party had not been sent out. He was found drinking beer in the Oak Tree, an inn much frequented by musicians, and after hearing it he is reputed to have said to Anna, 'Really, I never thought it was so beautiful.' Anna's sister Josefine was the soloist in all these early performances. Hearing 'Ständchen' today merely underlines the pity that so few choirs sing part-songs any more.

Following 'Ständchen' Schubert was encouraged to write a cantata on an altogether larger scale for Josefine Fröhlich to sing, and *Mirjams Siegesgesang* (Miriam's Song of Triumph) was begun. An opportunity had at last presented itself for the long-mooted concert devoted to Schubert's music to be staged. A room belonging to the Philharmonic Society (just down the road from Schubert's lodgings at the Blue Hedgehog) was reserved for 26 March 1828, but Schubert could not finish the cantata in time. He had taken a renewed interest in the music of Handel, which is apparent enough from the fugues that he incorporated in several works of the period, and *Mirjams Siegesgesang* was certainly Handelian in concept and scale. As a result he did not have time to orchestrate it as he had intended. This was done after his death by Franz Lachner for performance at a memorial concert early in 1829.

But the Franz Schubert invitation concert happened all the same, and an audience of his friends and supporters packed the room. The choice of programme is interesting in that Schubert was clearly out to display his wares to any prospective publisher or critic who happened to attend. It opened with the first movement of a string quartet, possibly the G major, in which case the composer no doubt intended to get its difficulties out of the way before the audience had lost concentration. Vogl and Schubert then gave a group of four songs, presumably meant to demonstrate Schubert's many styles and the breadth of his literary interests for there were two recent settings of Leitner, 'Der Kreuzzug' (The Crusade) – which is rather pedestrian – and 'Die Sterne' (The Stars), D939, an infectious little song in which the dactylic rhythm normally associated in Schubert with death is here the most joyous of 'twinkling' motifs. 'Fischerweise' came next and the group ended with the curious 'Fragment aus dem Aeschylus' (Fragment from Aeschylus), a dramatic scena written in 1816. As *Mirjams Siegesgesang* was not ready, Josefine Fröhlich and Anna's pupils revived 'Ständchen', and then it was time for the centrepiece of the evening. For this Schubert chose the E flat Piano Trio, still the composition in which he placed his greatest hopes.

There was also a new piece written for the concert, 'Auf dem Strom' (On the River). It is another setting of Rellstab and the text may have come to Schubert from Beethoven's collection, adding further substance to the theory that this piece, with its reference to the Funeral March from 'Eroica', was intended as a tribute to Beethoven. (The concert was given on the first anniversary of Beethoven's death.) The poem is about separation and reunion and the journey from life to death. Schubert could have identified with these thoughts at any time of his composing life, so it would be wrong to assume that he saw in them some harbinger of his own forthcoming demise. Indeed, Schubert saw to it that the interest of the potential audience was stimulated by introducing a part for solo horn.

Vogl then returned with Schubert to sing 'Die Allmacht' (Omnipotence), written during their holiday together in 1825. For the finale the Philharmonic Society's male chorus sang the rousing 'Schlachtlied' (Battle-Song). The event was a great success – at least it was for those who were there, for three days later the great violinist Niccolò Paganini gave the first of several Viennese concerts, taking the city by storm, and the newspapers immediately gave over their space to him. There were brief notices about Schubert's concert in Leipzig, Dresden and Berlin, but nothing of consequence in Vienna, where 'the minor stars paled before the radiance of this comet in the musical heavens'.[21]

Franz von Hartmann reported that Schubert's concert was glorious and that afterwards they repaired to the Snail 'where we jubilated until midnight', and Bauernfeld recorded 'enormous applause, good receipts'. Schubert did, indeed, make money from it and, as he was in the process of selling to Schott and Probst several of the works mentioned in his letter (even if both knocked him down to rock-bottom prices), he wrote most positively to them about its success, and of the piano trio in particular, announcing that he had been encouraged to repeat the whole thing. In fact his friends did write to the *Wiener Zeitschrift*, urging the newspaper to support a repeat concert, though it could not and did not. However, Schubert, it seems, was trying to play one publisher off against the other with regard to the E flat Piano Trio, a game at which he was not a star player. Fortunately for the composer, Schott decided to concern themselves with the piano impromptus, deferring the publication of the trio until later – by which time Schubert had already been paid for it by Probst! When Schubert sent Probst the manuscript he made a number of cuts in the Finale, which even he must have realized was simply too long.

Schubert, financially solvent for once, played Croesus once again, Bauernfeld noting in his diary on 9 May: 'Heard Paganini. The admission was paid for me by Schubert . . . Today Schubert (with Lachner) played his new, wonderful four-handed Fantasy to me.' Earlier he had mentioned that Schwind had at last decided to marry Netti, so with Spaun on the verge of marriage, Sonnleithner due to wed the Louise of 'Ständchen', and Bauernfeld increasingly removed from their company, the circle was once again disintegrating of its own accord. Yet throughout the spring and summer reading parties continued at Schober's, and Hartmann's diaries are full of references to the many inn visits he made and the frequency with which he encountered Schubert on these occasions – 'To Grinzing . . . after having ferreted out Schubert too. All four tipsy, more or less, but Schubert especially.' Schubert's health was certainly deteriorating but it seemed to diminish neither his social life nor his creative powers. He made plans to visit the Pachlers in Graz once more and to return to Gmunden, though as it turned out neither trip took place. In June, however, he accompanied Franz Lachner to the Heiligenkreuz Monastery and on the organ there they played the Fugue in E minor (D952), which Schubert had written the previous day. It is his only work for the organ, and as it is composed for two to play it has been heard all too rarely since. Despite the upturn in Schubert's fortunes, his finances were the prime cause of the cancellation of his longer journeys:

> . . . and further the not very brilliant financial circumstances of friend Schubert . . . are the obstacles that prevent us just now from taking advantage of your kind invitation to come to Graz . . . Schubert had in any case planned to spend part of the summer at Gmunden and its environs – whence he has already received several invitations – from accepting which he has however so far been prevented by the above-mentioned financial embarrassments.[22]

The spring and summer, instead, were spent composing and in May he completed the *Drei Klavierstücke* (Three Piano Pieces). They are important pieces, without a doubt, in which Schubert further explores lines of development opened up by the two sets of Impromptus. But they are not as universally inspired, and while there are long passages of fine music (the lovely barcarolle which opens the second piece is taken almost verbatim from a chorus from the ill-fated opera, *Fierabras*), there are equivalent stretches of rather dull note-spinning, making them seem overlengthy to the non-committed listener. In contrast there is more immediate enjoyment to be gleaned from the two early-summer works for piano duet, the Allegro in A minor, published in 1840 under the bogus title *Lebensstürme* (Life's Storms), and the warmly attractive Rondo in A major. There is a case to be made for suspecting that these might have been two movements of a projected sonata for piano duet. Schubert at this time was also completing the Rellstab songs that found their way into *Schwanengesang*, and making several versions of 'Hymnus an den Heiligen Geist' (Hymn to the Holy Spirit) for male-voice chorus, of which the final version also involves wind instruments. There is a mass, too, in E flat, Schubert once again indicating through his music that he served the cause of the gods rather better than God. It has its fine moments but in trying to be liturgical Schubert all too frequently falls back on stock responses, not least in some rather indifferent fugues. Perhaps aware of these shortcomings he decided, almost at the end of his life, to go to Simon Sechter for lessons in counterpoint. There was a purely pragmatic reason why Schubert should do this, for a church position offered the possibility of a stable job with a significant income, and he could not easily compete for such a post without the necessary grounding in those archaic forms that were still so very much a part of church music. He had undoubtedly received encouragement from the church of the Holy Trinity at Alsergrund, where Beethoven's body had been blessed before his funeral, for at least two if not all of the liturgical pieces for soloists, chorus and orchestra which Schubert wrote during the summer were commissioned by this church.

Not only did Schubert spend a great deal of time and energy on these rather insipid pieces but almost everything that he did was now first sketched in detail, maybe left for a while to mature, and only then refined and turned into the finished article. In which case it is all the more miraculous that six magnificent works were still to follow in the last couple of months of his life: three piano sonatas (in C minor, A major and B flat major, D958–60), the string quintet, and two songs at the very top level of inspiration – 'Die Taubenpost' and the glorious 'Der Hirt auf dem Felsen' (The Shepherd on the Rock).

If 'Die Taubenpost' is not Schubert's very last song then 'Der Hirt auf dem Felsen' [CD3] must be. It was commissioned by the singer Anna Milder-Hauptmann, a pupil of Salieri and Vogl who had been principal soprano at the Kärntnerthor from 1808 until 1816 when she moved to Berlin. As a schoolboy Schubert had heard her singing opposite Vogl in Gluck's *Iphégenie en Tauride*. She later became enthusiastic about Schubert's songs, though she predicted that Berlin audiences of the day would find them hard to appreciate, and she may have been right. She did not forget Schubert, however, and wrote to him in 1825 suggesting that he should write an extended scena for her. Schubert did not take up the offer then, but when her next request came he agreed and devoted himself to the brief diligently, adapting the text from Müller, and inserting a middle section usually attributed to the dramatist Wilhelmine von Chézy (who had written the play *Rosamunde* for which Schubert composed incidental music). It is a remarkable song, almost a cantata, in that it is clearly a vehicle for display, a very public piece with the voice complemented by an obbligato clarinet part and soaring bel canto lines of which any self-respecting Italian opera composer might have been proud. The shepherd, represented by the clarinet, longs for the coming of spring and the ending of his winter of darkness and loneliness. Once heard, those comely, graceful lines are etched in the sensitive listener's heart for ever.

No one who has experienced a first-rate performance of the String Quintet will

ever forget it either, particularly if they come across it for the first time unaware of
the reputation it carries. To hear this expansive and supremely poised music in the
knowledge that it was composed at the very end of Schubert's life can all too easily
lead to the deceptive impression that Schubert was at peace with the world and
himself. But this is to miss entirely the disturbing undertones that betray Schubert's
true state of mind. In any case, at a practical level, Schubert was by now almost at
war with Schott and Probst, irritated by their sloth and their constant undervaluing
of his works, and there is a mountain of correspondence surviving to prove the
point. He was unable to go on holiday, but he still entertained hopes of so doing:
'I am now able to tell you, dear lady,' wrote Jenger to Marie Pachler on 6 September,
'that friend Tubby expects an improvement in his finances shortly, and confidently
reckons, as soon as this has happened, to avail himself immediately of your kind
invitation and to arrive at Graz with a new operetta.' Perhaps in his heart Schubert
knew differently, for he wrote to Jenger on 25 September saying, 'Nothing will come
of the journey to Graz this year, as money and weather are wholly unfavourable.'
In the same letter he mentions that he has delivered the second part of *Winterreise*
to Haslinger for publication and he finishes by requesting Jenger to meet him at
Bogner's coffee-house between 4 and 5 o'clock on Saturday afternoon. 'Business as
usual', you might say. But in a postscript he informs Jenger of his new address:
Neue Wieden, Firmiansgasse, no. 496, second floor on the right. Schubert was now
too ill to live alone and had moved in with his brother Ferdinand. Business was far
from 'as usual'. The ravages of his syphilis did not kill him but they contributed
to the strain already put on his body by over-eating and possibly over-drinking.
Nevertheless he could still walk, and did so frequently, and his powers of composition remained undiminished.

One of Schubert's very earliest compositions was an overture in C minor for
string quintet (D8), scored for the usual Viennese quintet of two violins, two violas
and a cello. Schubert did not return to this medium again, probably daunted by
the superb string quintets of Mozart which he knew, and even when he began his
last chamber work he kept away from these forces, employing instead a single viola
but two cellos. In this respect it is not unique, for there are plenty of examples by
Boccherini, though it is highly unlikely Schubert knew these rather flimsy quintets,
written in Spain and published in Paris. Why then did he choose this particular
combination? Though Schubert composed to commission and usually had a specific
event in mind when completing a bigger work such as a symphony, he also composed because he could not stop himself – he simply had to make a statement.
Shortly before he died he met Heinrich Anschütz who had given the oration at
Beethoven's funeral: 'Don't talk to me about music,' Schubert said to him. 'Sometimes it seems to me as though I no longer belong to this world.' Schubert, the artist

unrecognized by uncouth popular culture, believed his solace would come with death. He was confident in death, even if he was afraid of it. He acknowledged the release that was possible only in the cool of the grave. By opting for two cellos Schubert was able to express himself in dark, autumnal colours that would not have been attainable with the conventional quintet.

There is little revolutionary about the construction of the C major Quintet; rather it is the integration of all the elements, melodic, harmonic, architectural and novel which delights the student. What comes over to any listener with half an ear to hear it is a 'distillation of everything that Schubert was on earth to tell us'.[23] It is archetypal Schubert in the opening movement, with a passionate, vigorous main theme emerging almost by sleight of hand from an exploratory, mysterious chordal start. No sooner is that established than the music pivots around the note G to yield to a meltingly beautiful duet which the analysts refer to as the second subject. And so the movement progresses for something like twenty minutes during which time all the emotions are reached, joy, sadness, anger, despair, resignation. To follow that there is no more profound or illuminating slow movement in Schubert than that of the quintet, a movement of astounding repose, dignity and grief-stricken nobility.

But Schubert was not one to leave his listeners in the heavens with no means of returning to earth, and the third movement starts out as a Scherzo of unalloyed rumbustiousness. You might then expect the Trio, which normally provides a contrast in the middle of such movements, to be a bit of light-hearted humour or even an innocent country dance as it sometimes is in Schubert. Not here, however, where the composer pierces right to our hearts with a restrained, sustained and searing interlude that has something movingly valedictory about it: as John Reed has suggested, it is as if Schubert is saying a last farewell to all the formal and harmonic customs and practices which had hitherto ruled his composition. Reed it is, too, who points out that for the sophisticated Schubertian the easy-going Finale is no anticlimax, but rather a recognition of the fact that even the most idealistic romantic cannot survive on vision alone but must take some account of the joys around him here on earth.

There is no knowing exactly when Schubert completed the quintet and almost certainly he must have been working on it at the same time as the last three piano sonatas, from August 1828 into October. It is remarkable how he found so many different moods and characters in these various pieces of music and, in the sonatas particularly, kept them distinct from one another, the C minor turbulent and powerful, the A major more conventional, while the B flat major is thoughtful, solemn and mysterious. That said, there is also a fair amount of borrowing and revision of material from other works, which may have been done quite consciously. Of these sonatas the C minor is the least known, which is a shame. Its opening movement is stormy and dramatic beyond Schubert's normal ambit, and yet there is room in it for a gently lyrical contrasting subject with blatant harmonic side-steps that rarely fail to raise a smile. The slow movement beguiles with its leisurely gait but is nevertheless punctuated by outbursts of passion, and even in the Minuet there are novelties like the sudden empty bars which arrest the attention just when it seems the movement has settled into regularity. Finally there is a vigorous and restless tarantella, which keeps the audience on the edge of its seat but is full of pitfalls for the pianist whose stamina is just beginning to give out – probably a major contributory factor to its relative unfamiliarity. When it is brought off without accident it is an uplifting experience.

The A major Sonata, though longer than the C minor, is less confrontational and perhaps more representative of Schubert's developing thoughts on the sonata as a genre. There is always an experiment going on in the sonatas and here it seems to be a step away from integration of melodies into movements made up of disparate elements. What holds the movements together is not so much a rhythmic or melodic germ as some other common factor, what Philip Radcliffe has described as 'persistent background'. These sonatas are not to everyone's taste because for many people the sonata is something in which the musical argument must unfold with a degree of inevitability, and follow a strict pattern. Schubert turns most of that on its head, not least in the first movement of the A major, full of very lovely music and some master-strokes but in the end in need of a signpost or two from the composer to help direct the mind through the loose structure. Schubert's initial sketches for the Finale show him working on something quite unlike the theme that he eventually used, and if that theme sounds familiar, that is because it is the melody of the central movement of the A minor Sonata (D537) of 1817. It provides an interesting insight into Schubert's maturing response to the same basic material.

Of all the Schubert sonatas, it is the B flat major Sonata which has taken a special place at the head of the table. It opens in a mood of tranquillity, though a sinister little rumbling in the bass gives an early hint of the mysterious and contemplative spirit which intermittently pervades the first movement. A masterpiece of dignified restraint, it broods but never threatens. Schubert set himself up with the problem of having to integrate extended lyrical themes into a substantial movement that would normally be expected to carry greater dramatic weight. But the result is magnificent and, for the Schubertian, one more chance to suspend time and emotions and simply drink in the 'heavenly length'. It might be thought altogether impossible to follow this impressive exposition, but Schubert does so with an equally sublime slow movement, charged with restrained emotion. Its distinguishing feature is a tiny rhythmic fragment in the accompaniment which Schubert had used once before, in the 'Notturno' for piano trio where it was supposed to be based on a pile-drivers' song, marking the united fall of their sledge-hammers. Here it adds a degree of rhythmical tension but also a mystic, disembodied quality. But Schubert reserves his master-stroke for an extraordinary moment towards the end of this second movement when the harmony suddenly shifts down a major third from E major to C major. In the hands of a clumsy pianist this may pass unnoticed, but it should be for any listener a moment of breathtaking rapture.

In this context a Scherzo of a coarse nature would be out of place, and Schubert's is of elfin delicacy, reserving the Trio for a brooding voyage into the minor of the home key – Schubert, as ever, delighting in the ambivalence of minor and major. There is a certain holding back in the Finale, which starts in a similar fashion to that of the 'Trout' Quintet with a held, open octave. The theme seems innocent enough, disappointing perhaps in its light touch, but there is a great deal more vitality to the movement than is at first apparent and it builds up in a way which allows for several outbursts before the crisp and positive last few notes end Schubert's final essay in the piano sonata. All three sonatas were completed by 26 September and Schubert played them on the following day at the house of Dr Ignaz Menz. He had intended them to be dedicated to Hummel, but after Schubert's death the manuscripts lay unpublished until 1838 by which time Hummel, too, had died. So Diabelli rededicated them to Schumann.

Schubert's doctor, Ernst Rinna, had suggested the move to Ferdinand's rooms because the house was nearer the country and he believed Schubert might benefit from the change of conditions. In fact the place was damp and far from hygienic and indeed very probably contributed to Schubert's death, which was now imminent. Early in October 1828 Schubert accompanied Ferdinand and a couple of acquaintances on a three-day walking tour as far as Eisenstadt, where Haydn was buried. It is possible his doctor suggested this, too, but it was by now too late. On the 11th Beethoven's factotum, Anton Schindler, wrote from Pest, inviting him to the première of a new opera by Lachner and suggesting that it might be possible to arrange a concert of Schubert's songs there. He never received a reply, but by then it did not matter, for on 31 October Schubert dined at the Red Cross with friends, tried some fish, and was nauseated by it. His friends were not greatly alarmed as he had suffered with sickness, diarrhoea and nausea in the past. They assumed it was just another stomach illness. He was fit enough to dine with the Fröhlich sisters soon after, to go with his brother to hear his new mass on 2 November and to join him on a three-hour walk afterwards. He began his lessons in counterpoint with Simon Sechter (his exercises were discovered in Vienna as recently as 1969), and outwardly he was happy. He dined with Karl Schönstein, who later recalled that 'He was very cheerful, indeed almost unrestrained in his gaiety, a mood which might well have been induced by the large amount of wine he drank that evening, of which he was no despiser at any time.' Schönstein's account was written many years later and just when the dinner took place cannot be accurately dated, though Schönstein suggests that it was only ten days before Schubert's death. This may be consistent with the standard symptoms of typhoid fever, for during the first week the patient seems fairly normal apart from a degree of depression and lethargy. During the second week a considerable depression sets in, and indeed by then Schubert was too ill to leave his room. He wrote to Schober, who received the letter on 12 November:

Dear Schober,

I am ill. I have eaten nothing for eleven days and drunk nothing, and I totter feebly and shakily from my chair to bed and back again. Rinna is treating me. If ever I take anything, I bring it up again at once.

Be so kind, then, as to assist me in this desperate situation by means of literature. Of Cooper's I have read The Last of the Mohicans, The Spy, The Pilot *and* The Pioneers. *If by any chance you have anything of his, I implore you to deposit it with Frau von Bogner at the coffee-house for me. My brother, who is conscientiousness itself, will most faithfully pass it on to me. Or anything else.*

> *Your friend*
> *Schubert.*

It was the last letter Schubert wrote. Schober did not personally call on Schubert for fear of infection but there remains an unsubstantiated story that a group of musicians including Karl Holz (who had played in the Schubert invitation concert in March) visited him in his rooms and played Beethoven's C sharp minor String Quartet, op. 131. The work had not at that stage been heard in public, but it had been published and we know that Schubert's devotion to Beethoven's music was heightened during his final year. But the story has come down to us second-hand, so we can only hope that Schubert did indeed hear this extraordinary work and gain comfort from it.

During the next week Schubert descended into bouts of delirium. Between these he continued to correct the proofs of *Winterreise*, and he talked with Bauernfeld about *Der Graf von Gleichen* and a new opera project with such enthusiasm that Bauernfeld was quite optimistic about Schubert's prospects. The next day he again emerged from delirium to talk with his brother: 'I implore you to transfer me to my room, not to leave me here, in this corner under the earth; do I then deserve no place above the earth?' His brother assured him that he was indeed in his bed where he had been all along. 'No, it is not true: Beethoven does not lie here.' Even in fever Schubert was unable to rid himself of the overwhelming presence of Beethoven.

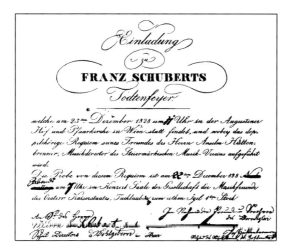

*Invitation to the
memorial service for
Franz Schubert, held
at the church of St
Augustine, Vienna,
23 December 1828.*

The doctor called on 18 November and attempted to reassure the patient but Schubert merely replied, 'Here, here is my end.' Franz Theodor wrote to Ferdinand on 19 November 1828:

My dear son Ferdinand,

Days of gloom and sorrow weigh heavily upon us. The dangerous illness of our beloved Franz acts painfully upon our spirits. Nothing remains for us in these sad days except to seek comfort in God, and to bear any affliction that may still fall on us according to God's wise dispensation with resolute submission to His holy will; and what befalls us shall convince us of God's wisdom and goodness, and give us tranquillity.

Therefore take courage and trust implicitly in God; he will give you strength, that you may not succumb, and will grant you a glad future by His blessing. See to it, to the best of your ability, that our good Franz is forthwith provided with the Holy Sacraments for the dying, and I shall live in the comforting hope that God will fortify and keep him.

Sorrowfully, but strengthened by confidence in God, your father, Franz.

When the priest called to administer the Eucharist, Schubert was no longer able to participate and the church register of St Joseph in the Margareten records that he received extreme unction only. The family chronicle says simply, '[Franz Peter] died Wednesday, 19 November 1828 at 3 o'clock p.m. (of typhus), buried Saturday, 22 November 1828.' Because Schubert died in his brother's house he would normally have been buried in the local church, but at Ferdinand's suggestion the body was taken to Währing, to be laid to rest close to Beethoven.

Bauernfeld wrote in his diary:

Yesterday afternoon Schubert died. On Monday I still spoke with him. On Tuesday he was delirious, on Wednesday dead. To the last he talked to me of our opera. It all seems like a dream to me. The most honest soul and the most faithful friend! I wish I lay there, in his place. For he leaves the world with fame!

Franz von Schober wrote a poem based on the 1817 song 'Pax Vobiscum', which was sung at the funeral. Schwind, who learned of Schubert's death away in Munich, wrote:

I have wept for him as for a brother, but now I am glad for him that he has died in his greatness and has done with his sorrows. The more I realize now what he was like, the more I see what he has suffered ... The recollection of him will be with us, and all the burdens of the world will not prevent us from wholly feeling for a moment now and again what has now utterly vanished.

At the time of his death few of Schubert's compositions were around him, most of them still being at Schober's. His effects were assessed at 63 florins. With his residual debts, plus medical and funeral expenses, he owed something of the order of 1,000 florins, but these were paid off by the following summer, mostly from the proceeds of sales to those publishers who had already committed themselves to specific undertakings. On 23 December a memorial service was held at St Augustine's, the court church, where a similar service had been held for Beethoven, and there was a Schubertiad at Spaun's that evening. A memorial concert was held at the Philharmonic Society on 30 January 1829 and in the autumn of 1830 a monument was erected over his tomb, inscribed with words by Grillparzer: 'The art of music here entombed a rich possession, but even far fairer hopes.'

After the death of Franz Peter, Ferdinand gathered together as many of Schubert's unpublished manuscripts as he could lay his hands on. He made valiant attempts to get them published and offered Diabelli a vast quantity of solo songs, piano music and chamber works. Diabelli issued the songs over the next twenty years as a series of posthumous works (*Nachlass*). He was himself a musician and took his responsibilities seriously, attempting to group the songs together by subject-matter or poet, but he also altered the key of a song if it seemed appropriate to him, changed the piano instructions or even rewrote parts of the text or music. If this now seems thoroughly unprofessional, in Diabelli's day academic truth was less valued than it is now and his alterations were made in the sincere belief that he was making them for the better. He did at least get Schubert's music out into the wider world. Nor were his the last 'improvements', and the first job of the late twentieth-century musician before performing any of this music is to strip away the layers of accretions and get as close to what Schubert intended as is now possible.

The chamber works remained unpublished until a start was made in the 1850s. The scores of the operas, symphonies and masses were not, however, sold to Diabelli and Ferdinand eventually sought Schumann's help in this, resulting in the first performance of the 'Great' C major Symphony in 1839. Ferdinand made a few biographical notes in the months after Schubert's death, but even Spaun felt they were unnecessarily detailed, commenting, 'We shall never make a Mozart or a Haydn out of him.' They clearly viewed their dear friend as a consummate song-writer but were quite unable to assess his place in history.

The admirable Sonnleithner identified the need to attempt a catalogue of the whole of Schubert's output, but the task proved too difficult. By then some of the manuscripts had already been dispersed throughout Europe, many had been lost, others destroyed. It was not until 1951 that Otto Erich Deutsch completed his monumental Thematic Catalogue and though more recent scholarship has refined some of the detail it still remains the fundamental basis for Schubert study. Between 1884 and 1897 Breitkopf & Härtel embarked on a complete, critical edition of Schubert's music. It was a considerable undertaking for its time, and brought to light a great many works that had not appeared before. But inevitably it was overtaken by the advance of musicological research, and as recently as 1967 a new complete edition was begun by a group of scholars in Tübingen. This has been appearing a few volumes at a time over the years since then. It enables the serious student to compare all the known variants of a particular piece for the first time and is now compulsory study for anyone committing their performances to the permanency of disc.

What, in the end, did Schubert leave us? Well, for a start there are no concertos, which is perhaps no bad thing for Schubert was rarely at ease with music for display. Had he been a good enough player himself (like Mozart or Beethoven) he might have been glad of a concerto or two to raise his standing in public, but he was not and he certainly did not move amongst the recognized soloists of the day such as Paganini. By the same token there are very few sonatas or display pieces for solo instruments other than the piano and, their parameters being much the same as concertos, there is little to lament in this. He did leave a number of dramatic works, but however dearly he wished to write a successful opera his essentially lyrical gift, perverse though it may seem, actually stood him in poor stead. The operas and incomplete fragments are full of delightful music, but Schubert seemed utterly incapable of perceiving the catastrophic dramatic failings of the libretti he received. He seems to have lacked the sense of showmanship and theatrical flair instinctive to the composer of opera. There is a fair amount of church music, functional, and sometimes in the rather sugary taste of the day, but not a significant advance on the heritage of Mozart and Haydn.

With the orchestral works we reach an altogether different level of activity, particularly in the eight surviving symphonies. Even here Schubert needed time to grapple with the problems of the form, and the earlier symphonies are probably best seen as modest later classical works written by an incorrigible song-writer – though well worthy of performance alongside the symphonies of Mendelssohn and Schumann for all that. The 'Unfinished' and 'Great' C major Symphonies are, of course, in quite another league, and magnificently deserve their place at the top end of the orchestral repertory. The same is true of the later chamber music and the last piano sonatas, and indeed, now that they are being played regularly and with proper understanding, there are wonderful things to discover in many of the other piano works dotted throughout Schubert's short life.

Ferdinand Schubert, the composer's brother, who did much to further the cause of Schubert's music after his death. Lithograph by Josef Kriehuber.

With such an abundance of great music to Schubert's credit so far, it may seem almost heresy to add that all of it is, in a way, unimportant. Yet the historical truth is that none of these works (with the notable exception of the 'Wanderer' Fantasy) had the slightest influence on the composers who immediately followed him. Partly, of course, this was because he had no pupils, partly it was due to his own difficulties in coming to terms with the formal problems that he set himself, but partly also to the purely practical fact that so few of his compositions were published. By the time his finest orchestral and chamber works were becoming recognized for their true worth, music had moved on apace. Chopin and Liszt (and to a lesser extent Schumann) had taken piano music far away from the classical forms. The Italians still held sway in the opera house, though Wagner's ascendancy had begun to catch the attention in mid-century. As far as symphonies were concerned, Beethoven still ruled the roost from his grave, and church music remained locked in its reliquary. In many of these genres Schubert was an innovator, and often an innovator of heart-stopping genius, but the changes he wrought in the standard classical models were personal to himself and not of a kind to leave a deep or long-lasting impression on the principles of structure and form. What he did with the sonata, symphony and quartet was his own, but it did not change the past and it did not affect the future.

This leaves song. The part-songs, successful in their day, more or less died with Schubert, as did any influence they may have had. The solo songs, however, were an altogether different matter. They were already known throughout Austria and in much of Germany. They were published in large enough numbers to be acquired by a huge number of amateurs and professionals and they became the yardstick against which new compositions were measured. Schumann clearly built on this foundation and Brahms belongs to the same world. Even Hugo Wolf, for many the pinnacle of Lieder composition, could be said to be writing Schubert songs at the other end of the century. Richard Strauss, Reger, Pfitzner, and Schoenberg, too, used the same concept of song as Schubert. In all this great inheritance of the Schubertian *Lied*, it is the composer's understanding and identification with the text that compels the music to be written. In song Schubert was the true romantic, pioneering new forms, dispensing completely with the impedimenta of the past and taking his inspiration from poetry.

As the distinguished pianist Andras Schiff has said, 'It's essential to approach Schubert through the songs. There are endless references to songs in the piano sonatas and string quartets, not just in obvious cases like "Death and the Maiden", but everywhere, and I don't think you can understand Schubert without a very intimate knowledge of the songs.'[24] And it is through the music (and the songs in particular) that we, too, begin to understand Schubert the romantic and Schubert the man. It has taken dedicated Schubertians the best part of a century to scrape away the layers of myth that have been built up about him, partly to fill in the enormous gaps in our knowledge, and partly to protect a rose-tinted image. Only now are those who know Schubert through a lifetime of studying and performing his works really addressing the fundamental truths of his character and those truths are all to be found in his music.

Engraved vignette for the subscribers' copies of the first edition of Schwanengesang, *published by Haslinger in 1829.*

Music Notes

One of the main problems in choosing the works to be included on these discs is the great length of so many of Schubert's best instrumental works. How could one leave out the 'Great' C major Symphony, the String Quintet, the last B flat major Piano Sonata, or the 'Trout' Quintet, to name just four of the most obvious? With a maximum of rather under four hours of disc time available it is easy to see that there would be room for very little else with these alone, so the priority has been to try to balance the familiar with the unfamiliar, orchestral music with song, chamber music with solo piano music, authentic performance with historic performance.

CD1 gives a flavour of the early music – one of the few early piano sontatas which Schubert actually completed; settings of the great German romantic poets, Goethe and Schiller; a group of songs to texts by his friends, and the last-but-one of the early symphonies. CD2 takes as a basis two major works from the middle period, placing them alongside smaller-scale works to which they are related. CD3 brings together late songs and keyboard music prefaced by the slightly earlier Quartettsatz and two of the now somewhat neglected part-songs – in their day among the most popular and frequently performed of Schubert's compositions. The texts of the solo songs, in both German and English, are given at the end of this section.

CD1   Sehnsucht (Longing), D52

An example of an early song (April 1813), not a great one, but admirably demonstrating the accomplishment of the sixteen-year-old Schubert in his last year at school.
The poet is Schiller, to whom he had first turned his attention as early as 1811,
and whose words provided the texts for over forty songs. Schubert returned to this
particular text in 1821, but this first version illustrates the episodic nature of many of
his early songs: short sections of independent melody linked by narrative passages
(*recitative*), almost like a miniature operatic scene. Though Schubert had yet to
encounter the poet Mayrhofer, there is already an affinity with that romantic 'longing' for the unattainable.

*Dietrich
Fischer-Dieskau
(baritone),
Karl Engel
(piano)*

Gretchen am Spinnrade (Gretchen at the Spinning-Wheel), D118

This first Goethe setting dates from October 1814, around the time when Therese
Grob was singing in the F major Mass and Schubert's father had given him a five-
octave Graf fortepiano. We do not know whether Schubert had Therese's voice in
mind when setting these words, but the particular sound of the fortepiano must
have suggested to him the idea for this wholly innovative accompaniment. Arleen
Auger was one of a growing number of singers happy to embrace the performance
of Schubert both with the modern concert grand piano and with the more authentic
period fortepiano. Fewer top-flight pianists yet espouse both worlds, but Lambert
Orkis is one who moves freely between the two. (See pp. 21–2)

*Arleen Auger
(soprano),
Lambert Orkis
(fortepiano)*

Piano Sonata in A major, D664

As the autograph manuscript of this sonata is missing it is not possible to date it
precisely, but most authorities attribute it to the holiday Schubert spent with Johann
Michael Vogl in Vogl's home town of Steyr in the summer of 1819. It may, then, be
no coincidence that it shares the key of A major with that other product of the
holiday, the 'Trout' Quintet. Both are happy, contented works which seem to reflect
Schubert's delight in the countryside around him. In Vienna Beethoven was the
dominant influence and his presence alone may have been sufficient to convince
the sensitive Schubert of his inability to match the intellectual weight of the great
man in such forms as the piano sonata. Here in the country there was no such
shadow over him and he was able to complete a sonata of vernal enchantment. In
this performance Christian Zacharias captures its freshness by always ensuring that
his very considerable artistry, technique and musicality are kept in the service of
the music and do not become vehicles for display in themselves. The sonata's lyrical

*Christian Zacharias
(piano)*

qualities have made it one of the more popular of the early piano works. Yet because of this lyricism there is little drama, and with no minuet or scherzo, the last movement combines a dance-like grace with sonata form. (See p. 55)

Freiwilliges Versinken (Free Fall, or, Voluntary Oblivion), D700

Simon Keenlyside (baritone), Malcolm Martineau (piano)

Johann Mayrhofer, under whose influence so much of Schubert's philosophy was formed, was probably the best poet of those close to Schubert and provided the texts for nearly fifty songs, many among the finest. Behind the bulk of the poems lies a common theme, that the poet is an alien on this earth and true happiness is attainable only through death. In 'Freiwilliges Versinken' the sun-god Helios is the exemplar, for each night the sun dies, plunging his flames into the waters, safe in the knowledge that he can rise again at will to bring life and warmth to the earth. The wide leaps of the vocal line on the words 'scheide, herrlich ... Krone lege' make obvious demands on the singer's technique (and notice how the second syllable of 'Krone' is delayed to create the tension of a marvellous discord with the piano), but the skilled singer must also hide from the listener the vocal difficulties of the phrases on 'die Nacht' and 'weiter Ferne' which rise and yet fade away, calling for breath control of great delicacy and poise. (See p. 61)

An die Musik (To Music), D547

Hans Hotter (baritone), Gerald Moore (piano)

Like Simon Keenlyside, Hans Hotter was described as a baritone when he recorded a number of Schubert songs in the 1940s and 50s for EMI. In truth Hotter was a bass-baritone if not a bass. It was a huge voice with a commanding depth to match his imposing stage presence but, like many great operatic singers, he could scale the voice down yet retain the control necessary to encompass the singing of artsong. 'An die Musik' is here transposed down two whole tones, giving it an unusual profundity. Schubert chose his keys very specifically (certain keys are allied to particular moods or themes in much of his music) but he himself transposed songs willingly enough (even sometimes for publication) and it is true that different styles of voice, pitch and interpretation can often bring out divergent qualities in the music. It is bound to be the case that (as with Mozart) Schubert will almost invariably be performed by artists older than the composer, and often they discover depths in the music that one wonders if Schubert even knew existed. Certainly he was a young man when he wrote 'An die Musik': he was lodging with Franz von Schober whose unconventional approach to life appealed to him, as did several of his poems, and though this one is nothing special it drew from Schubert a masterpiece of simplicity and pure beauty. (See p. 35)

Der Jüngling und der Tod (The Young Man and Death), D545

Also from March 1817, this song seems to have been written as a result of the success
of 'Der Tod und das Mädchen' (Death and the Maiden) from the previous month.
Where that song plumbed the depths, ending on a low D, this one is in a much
higher tessitura, so much so that even Fischer-Dieskau takes it down a minor third.
The theme of the poem is similar, that only death can bring relief from the troubles
of this earthly life, and Schubert introduces the dactylic rhythm (a figure of one long
note followed by two shorter ones) for Death's music. It is a rhythm he particularly
favoured and it was not entirely restricted to music about death. The opening
phrase, with the sun sinking, has an affinity with that passage in 'Der Wanderer'
in which the sun seems so cold to the poet (see CD2). This is the only known setting
Schubert made of words by his devoted friend Josef von Spaun.

*Dietrich
Fischer-Dieskau
(baritone),
Gerald Moore
(piano)*

Fischerweise (Fisherman's Song), D881

Schubert made seven settings of poems by Franz Xaver Schlechta between 1815 and
1826. The two remained friends until Schubert's death, though Schlechta, a civil
servant who rose to be head of a department in the Austrian Finance Ministry, was
almost too respectable to be a part of Schubert's artistic circle. This is one of the
1826 settings, and an excellent example of the 'modified strophic' song. In other
words the melody is essentially the same for each verse, though in the third verse
Schubert delays the entry of the voice at 'Dort angelt auf der Brücke', subtly pointing
up the words and giving room for 'Schlauer Wicht' to be uttered almost as an aside.
The bubbling accompaniment is as infectious as any of the brooks which flow
through Schubert's songs. (See p. 114)

*Dietrich
Fischer-Dieskau
(baritone),
Gerald Moore
(piano)*

Der Zwerg (The Dwarf), D771

Given the powerful nature of this setting and the majesty of 'Nacht und Träume'
(Night and Dreams), it is a great pity that Schubert did not set more poems by
Matthäus von Collin, Spaun's cousin and a link between Schubert's artistic circle
and the group of poets around Schlegel. Though it may have been written earlier,
we know that Vogl sang it at St Florian in the spring of 1823 and that it was published
by Sauer & Leidesdorf in May of that year. One can imagine that Vogl's no doubt
dramatic rendering made a considerable impact on an audience more attuned to
straightforward ballads than intellectually sophisticated art-songs. It is worth
reflecting for a moment, too, on the artistry Fischer-Dieskau brings to this song,
with that characteristically disembodied voice used to set the bleak scene on the

*Dietrich
Fischer-Dieskau
(baritone),
Gerald Moore
(piano)*

lake as the sun goes down, all the power being kept in reserve for release as the full horror of the situation becomes apparent. (See p. 84)

Symphony no. 5 in B flat major, D485

The London Classical Players, conducted by Roger Norrington

Once he had left school, Schubert seldom had access to an orchestra, and very few of his orchestral scores received any kind of performance, let alone a professional one. In 1816, however, he played viola (and his brother, Ferdinand, the violin) in an amateur orchestra led by the professional musician Otto Hatwig, and it was at Hatwig's house in the Schottenhof during the autumn that this symphony received its première, Schubert having finished the score on 3 October.

It is worth discussing briefly the nature of the performance heard here. The London Classical Players were formed in 1978 to perform orchestral music on authentic instruments. The first impression this makes is of a thinner, wiry sound compared with the suave, velvety tone produced by many leading orchestras today. If two orchestras, one modern, one period, were to play side by side, the modern one would overwhelm the period one, such has been the tonal development of the instruments and growth in personnel over nearly two centuries. In addition, the internal balance of a modern orchestra has changed so that with string numbers greatly increased and brass instruments very much more powerful, many conductors insist on doubling the woodwind in order to restore parity. The orchestra keeps growing and the sound gets thicker and richer. Schubert's orchestra on this occasion seems to have been seven first violins, six seconds, three violas, three cellos, two basses, one flute, and pairs of oboes, bassoons and horns – a mere twenty-eight players if they all turned up on the night. There are other, more subtle, differences such as the wooden flute with its recorder-like sound, stringed instruments with gut strings and bows of a different build, tension and weight giving a distinct tone and attack, horns without the mechanical aids of today, and so on. The pitch is not the same, about half a semitone below modern concert pitch, and those who play and conduct this music have all studied contemporary accounts of style and performance practice, affecting everything from speed to phrasing. The debate between the authentic and modern camps continues to be lively, but these days many players and conductors move readily between both performance worlds, bringing to either the enlightenment of the other's best practices. (See p. 32)

CD2   **Der Wanderer (The Wanderer), D489**

It is curious to note that this song, one of the greatest and best-known of Schubert's songs, and the famous piano fantasy to which it gave birth, arose from a fairly ordinary poem by an obscure doctor and public administrator, Georg Philipp Schmidt of Lübeck. The poem first appeared in a Leipzig publication of 1808, but it was a Viennese anthology of 1815 which brought it to Schubert's attention. In this it was entitled 'Der Unglückliche' (The Unhappy One) but Schubert gave it the title 'Der Wanderer' and changed the last line of the text to give greater emphasis to the word 'dort' (there). He made three settings of the words, all very similar except that the second version is transposed down a tone with the voice part written out in the bass clef (proof, if it were required, that one need have few qualms about transposing Schubert's songs into practicable keys). With its theme of the romantic desire for the unattainable the poem was sure to appeal to Schubert. His setting appealed to those who heard it, too. 'Der Wanderer' was published by Cappi & Diabelli in May 1821 as op. 4, no. 1, and along with 'Erlkönig' became the most successful of his songs during the composer's lifetime. In our own day Fischer-Dieskau has sung it many times and his several recordings bring out different aspects of the text and the music. This 1957 performance reveals an intimate approach, suggesting the poet musing alone upon the emptiness of his situation. Hope springs briefly with the thought of that ideal 'beloved land' sought by the romantic, but in the end the poet wanders on, silent and despondent. Note the rhythm of the piano accompaniment and the melody line at the words 'Die Sonne dünkt mich hier so kalt' (Here the sun seems so cold to me). These form the basis of the entire piano fantasy which follows. (See pp. 34 and 63)

Dietrich Fischer-Dieskau (baritone), Gerald Moore (piano)

Fantasy in C major ('Wanderer'), D760

Hearing the very positive mood at the opening of this quasi-sonata it is surprising to find that Schubert wrote it immediately after breaking off the B minor Symphony, the 'Unfinished', which (arguably) he had abandoned in distress at having learned that he had contracted syphilis. Perhaps the despair of his circumstances suggested to him the line in the song 'Der Wanderer', quoted above. This phrase, with its dactylic rhythm, he used as the starting-point for the emotional heart of the fantasy, the slow second section, and indeed nearly all the thematic material, including the powerful opening, derives from it, contributing greatly to the feeling that the music has simply evolved and flows naturally and inevitably from movement to movement. Almost certainly Schubert's problems in four-movement forms such as the symphony and sonata will have driven him to explore this device, whereby strength

Sviatoslav Richter (piano)

is gained from motivic congruity rather than the more conventional musical arguments. Later in the century the piece could have been published as a sonata – and in 1854 Liszt's Sonata in B minor, which owes so much to it in thematic structure, actually was – but in 1823 when it first appeared its form was too revolutionary to grant it this title. There is enough show and display in this fantasy to have attracted the attention of many pianists in the earlier part of this century, whereas the sonatas are only now beginning to become core repertory. (See p. 78)

Overture, *Die Zauberharfe*, D644

Vienna Philharmonic, conducted by Riccardo Muti

The incidental music for *The Magic Harp* by Georg von Hofmann was composed rapidly to commission in the summer of 1820; there were eight performances, making it comparatively one of the more successful of Schubert's dramatic offerings, a modest failure rather than a downright disaster. The overture was too good to be lost for ever so it is usually parcelled up with incidental music to *Rosamunde*, the very ineffectual dramatic collaboration of 1823. For this reason it has acquired the title of Overture to *Rosamunde*, but this it is most definitely not! It begins arrestingly with a portentous sequence of chords, but Schubert's essentially lyrical genius is soon to the fore, melodies 'good enough to sing' following each other in succession. In style the work belongs more to the tradition of the earlier symphonies than to the 'Unfinished' and 'Great' C major, so it is quite valid as well as instructive to make a comparison between the different sounds and textures of this recording by a modern symphony orchestra (and a greatly respected one at that) with those of the authentic performance of the Fifth Symphony on CD1. (See pp. 59 and 84)

Die Götter Griechenlands (The Greek Gods), D677

Dietrich Fischer-Dieskau (baritone), Karl Engel (piano)

The words come from an ode of 1788 by Friedrich von Schiller, which celebrates the glory of Greece and its mythology and laments the passing of what the romantics saw as the golden age. It was this regret for a lost paradise which attracted Schubert who, in 1819, set only one of the strophes, beginning with the words, 'Beautiful world, where are you?' It must be significant that he chose the key of A minor, for it was one of his favourites when he sought to represent uncertainty, exploiting the ambiguity of A minor and A major with that deft touch so characteristic of him. He took the opening phrase and its piano introduction as the material on which to base the third movement of the A minor Quartet (see below), continuing there to explore this tonal ambivalence. Here it is sung down a minor third. (See p. 56)

String Quartet in A minor, D804

The two great quartets composed in the early months of 1824 (the other is the D   *Alban Berg Quartet*
minor quartet, 'Death and the Maiden') are in many respects a summation of several
elements of Schubert's music to this date. Both are centred on slow movements
based on pre-existing material and, while in the case of the D minor this is by some
way the most substantial and weighty movement, in the A minor it is the shortest
of the movements, though by no means unimportant. The theme of this benign and
affecting Andante is the melody of the Entr'acte after Act III in *Rosamunde*. In the
theatre it was not just a means of filling the air with pleasant music before the drama
continued but was intended to indicate that the Princess Rosamunde would return
to renounce her regal past and live, instead, the life of a simple country girl. So, for
the moment, all is well with the world. But with the third movement, based on the
song 'Die Götter Griechenlands' (see above), the clouds gather, and it soon becomes
apparent that the whole quartet is concerned with expanding on this conflict
between an idyllic view of the past and an unattainable ideal in the present. Thus
the first movement begins with a restless accompanimental figure which continues
to provide a slightly disturbing undercurrent even when the opening A minor melody reappears in the apparent security of A major. The movement flits from major
to minor, from happiness to despair, calm to storm, its variety nevertheless wrought
from the simplest of material. The virility of the Alban Berg Quartet's playing brings
out the contrast between the light and shade in this movement splendidly. It is
reasonable to assume that before 1824 Schubert would have been troubled to find
a suitable Finale to conclude such a powerful and integrated work. Now he had the
confidence to allow himself some fun with one of his happy, gypsy-like tunes, in A
major at that. While it often threatens to break out into uncontrolled exuberance,
it never quite does, being restrained periodically with quiet and subdued passages.
Frequent excursions into the minor heighten the tension and serve as a reminder
of the conflict which underlies the whole work. The Alban Berg Quartet's approach
to the Finale emphasizes these aspects, where other performances might bring
out more of the rustic qualities – but then that is one of the great joys of music-
making at this level: there is always another angle from which to approach good
music. (See p. 92)

CD3   ## Ständchen (Serenade), D920

Brigitte Fassbaender
(mezzo-soprano),
This enchanting part-song, to words by Franz Grillparzer, was composed so that   *Capella Bavariae,*
Schubert's friend, Leopold Sonnleithner, could surprise his fiancée in the most   *Wolfgang Sawallisch*
romantic manner on her birthday. Grillparzer, a well-established dramatist and   *(piano)*

poet, clearly knew and respected Schubert's music, and Schubert probably met him through either the Fröhlichs or the Sonnleithners, to whom he was related. After the composer's death, Grillparzer was one of those most active in trying to establish a Schubert memorial, and he it was who wrote the epitaph carved on Schubert's tomb, 'The art of music here entombed a rich possession, but even far fairer hopes.'

The performance here is given by a female soloist with male chorus and piano, which is how Schubert wrote it, forgetting that Anna Fröhlich's pupils were girls. He quickly transposed it and both versions survive as valid alternatives. It is to be hoped that the inclusion of 'Ständchen' here might encourage those small groups of singers who have the right forces and a degree of expertise to investigate further the sadly neglected corpus of Schubert part-songs. (See page pp. 138–9)

Psalm 23, D706

Capella Bavariae,
Wolfgang Sawallisch
(piano)

Despite its Old Testament text, this is not a liturgical piece. Dating from December 1820, it was, like 'Ständchen', written for Anna Fröhlich's pupils at the Vienna Conservatoire, who performed it several times during the following year. The words are in German (in a version by Moses Mendelssohn, grandfather of Felix) and it was originally scored for female voices (two sopranos and two altos) with piano. The version heard here, then, is an arrangement, and though some may feel that the spacing of the chords works better an octave higher, the suave qualities of male professional singers undoubtedly add depth to the sound. The piece forms a very effective anthem when performed in a resonant church, the piano part easily transferring to the organ. (See p. 60)

String Quartet Movement (Quartettsatz) in C minor, D703

Borodin Quartet

It is the business of the professional record critic not only to draw attention to the differences between one interpretation and another, but also to provide an opinion on why one performance is superior to all others. Happily the author of this book does not have to make such agonizing decisions and, instead, can share with the reader a variety of styles of performance, perhaps occasionally pointing out the virtues of a particular approach, but not dismissing the rest. In the case of the so-called Quartettsatz there is an almost bewildering diversity of stances taken by performers and just one indication of this is the fact that the time taken to play the piece varies from a little under eight minutes to around ten. The Borodin Quartet are among those favouring the more expansive approach. One effect of this is to enhance the beauty and sweetness of the lyrical sections in strong contrast with the outbursts of violent energy and searing anger in the more fraught passages. The

Borodin players bring an elasticity of phrasing to bear on the melodic material, and their tone quality is much fuller than Schubert could ever have expected to hear: but as with Beethoven and Mozart, a romantic performance can be supremely rewarding, revealing aspects of the music which a more classical style might leave unexplored. (See pp. 61–2)

Fantasy in F minor, D940

Surely one of the very greatest piano duets ever written and in the first rank of keyboard music as a whole, the F minor Fantasy is thought to have been inspired by Schubert's association with Countess Karoline Esterházy. While individual movements from one or two of the solo piano sonatas or impromptus might qualify for the debatable accolade of 'Schubert's finest piano music', the effect of this fantasy as a whole is unique, its quality miraculously sustained from first note to last. Though it is laid out in four distinct movements they are designed to be played without a break, the second plunging dramatically into a remote minor key, the last (after the Scherzo) taking up the material of the opening section and developing it to a powerful conclusion. Unusually (and perhaps significantly, given Schubert's problems with sonata form), the work is built up of almost epigrammatic elements, yet they have an organic unity which suggests they were conceived as one. This may well have been the case, for the outline sketches from January 1828 show that the first two movements were already essentially complete. The third movement was less so, while the sketch for the Finale is found on different paper, though that, too, is close to its final form. It has been suggested that Schubert set the fantasy on one side while preparing for his show-case concert in March, returning to it only when the concert was out of the way. The one significant alteration was a considerable pruning of the third movement. Franz Lachner (soon to become conductor at the Kärntnerthor theatre) was Schubert's fellow pianist when the first performance was given at Bauernfeld's lodgings on 9 May 1828. After the performance Schubert took Bauernfeld off to hear Paganini in concert. (See pp. 131–3)

Christoph Eschenbach and Justus Franz (piano duet)

Heine songs from *Schwanengesang* (Swan Song), D957

It is reasonable to assume that Schubert was planning to write more than one song cycle when death overtook him. Sets of songs by Rellstab and Heine were under way and after Schubert's death his brother Ferdinand came to a business agreement with Haslinger to publish these songs along with 'Die Taubenpost' with words by Johann Seidl. This was not Schubert's own intention, neither was the collective title, *Schwanengesang*, nor the final order of songs, yet such is their emotional weight

Hans Hotter (baritone), Gerald Moore (piano)

that they are extraordinarily potent however they are grouped. The bonus here is the singing of Hans Hotter in 1954. The voice is deep, cavernous, resonant, dark and brooding, yet capable of enormous power, entirely appropriate to the bitterness and intensity of Heine's words and Schubert's settings of them in his last months.

The Atlas of mythology represents the heroic warrior who in defeat is made to groan under the burden of his punishment. The opening of the song is symphonic in conception and in the bass of the accompaniment is a hammer-blow theme made up of four notes (G, B flat, F sharp and G, here transposed down a minor third to suit Hotter's voice and range). These four notes recur throughout the Heine sequence, representing the irresistible force of destiny. Where 'Der Atlas' uses minor harmony to represent failure and suffering, 'Ihr Bild' (Her Picture) portrays loneliness and loss by use of a plain unison accompaniment (in essence even bleaker than minor harmony). The apparent simplicity of the barcarolle, 'Das Fischermädchen' (The Fisher-Maiden), is then the more telling, for what outwardly seems a naive song about the simple life of the girl provides the ideal vehicle for Heine's irony. It also serves to lull the ear, helping to set up an aural shock when the swirling mists of 'Die Stadt' (The Town) launch us on the terrifying journey into alienation. The cumulative effect of harmonic disorientation over the final three songs is profoundly unsettling (and a frustrating glimpse of what might have been had Schubert lived longer). 'Am Meer' (By the Sea) maintains this sense of disillusionment despite its straightforward strophic form. It could not more perfectly establish the right state of mind and emotion to begin to cope with 'Der Doppelgänger' (The Wraith), of which Fischer-Dieskau says: 'Fourteen years of resignation preceded this dramatic outburst at the end of Schubert's life, and he seems to have rid himself of a lifelong yearning with this one cry. Yet his confession ends in the major; it does not wallow in self-pity.'(See pp. 133–4)

Allegretto in C minor, D915

Artur Schnabel (piano)

It is fitting to include a Schubert recording (if brief) by Artur Schnabel for he did so much to bring Schubert's piano music before a wider public at a time when it was all but totally disregarded. Such is the acceptance of Schubert's piano music today that complete sonata cycles are relatively frequent occurrences (however complicated the programming of the many incomplete works). Schnabel's achievement was the more remarkable because it took place in an era in which piano recitals were predominantly concerned with show. What could be less showy than this miniature written as a gift for a civil servant, Ferdinand Walcher, a recent addition to the artistic circle who was departing on a posting to Venice? Walcher never again met Schubert. (See p. 124)

Der Hirt auf dem Felsen (The Shepherd on the Rock), D965

It is arguable whether this song or 'Die Taubenpost' was the very last song composed
by Schubert. Interestingly, they could hardly be more different, 'Die Taubenpost' a
return to the uncomplicated world of the strophic song, 'Der Hirt auf dem Felsen'
quite clearly an extrovert showpiece. The singer by whom it was commissioned, the
dramatic soprano Anna Milder-Hauptmann, gave the first performance in Riga on
21 March 1830. She was only in her early forties, yet she must have been in the
twilight of her career for the Berlin court opera dispensed with her services a year
later. It is doubtful, then, that she can have made as sweet or beautiful a sound as
Nancy Argenta does on this recording, her voice charmingly complemented by the
balmy tone of the wooden clarinet of the day. Melvyn Tan plays a modern copy of
a Viennese fortepiano of 1814. (See p. 142)

Nancy Argenta (soprano), Erich Hoeprich (clarinet), Melvyn Tan (fortepiano)

Die Taubenpost (Pigeon Post), D957, no. 14

There could be no more appropriate artists to conclude this anthology than Fischer-
Dieskau and Moore who between them did so much to broaden our knowledge of
Schubert song. Theirs was the first comprehensive collection of Schubert songs
on disc, compulsory study for serious students, Fischer-Dieskau's incomparable
combination of penetrating intellect, fabulous musicianship, vast range of vocal
colours and copybook diction all harnessed in the service of the music. There were
times, later in his life, when the demands of Dieskau's parallel opera career began
to threaten that delicacy of approach which had long characterized his best Lieder
singing, but even after forty-five years at the very pinnacle of the profession he could
still lift song on to a higher plane than (almost) anyone else. Here he is in 1957, still
a young man, though ten years after his debut recital in Berlin, the voice at its
freshest, each syllable given careful thought and appropriate articulation, yet with
no hint of technique or cerebral considerations imposing themselves on that finest
of musical inventions, a Schubert melody. It was for performances such as this that
Schubert's best songs were created. (See pp. 133 and 135)

Dietrich Fischer-Dieskau (baritone), Gerald Moore (piano)

Sehnsucht (Longing) Friedrich von Schiller

Ah, to leave this valley's depths	Ach, aus dieses Tales Gründen,
where the cold mist presses in;	Die der kalte Nebel drückt,
could I only find the way out,	Könnt ich doch den Ausgang finden,
then would I count myself as blessed.	Ach, wie fühlt' ich mich beglückt!
Far above are lovely hilltops,	Dort erblick ich schöne Hügel,
ever green and ever young!	Ewig jung und ewig grün!
Had I wings, oh had I pinions	Hätt ich Schwingen, hätt ich Flügel,
I would range among the hills.	Nach den Hügeln zög ich hin.
I can hear harmonious music,	Harmonien hör ich klingen,
sounds of sweetest heavenly peace,	Töne süßer Himmelsruh,
and the winds are lightly blowing	Und die leichten Winde bringen
balmy perfumes toward me.	Mir der Düfte Balsam zu.
Golden fruit I see there glowing,	Goldne Früchte seh ich glühen,
beckoning among the dark green leaves	Winkend zwischen dunkelm Laub,
and the flowers that blossom there	Und die Blumen, die dort blühen,
are not raped by winter's chill.	Werden keines Winters Raub.
Ah, how lovely it must be	Ach wie schön muß sich's ergehen
where the sun shines ever bright,	Dort im ewgen Sonnenschein,
and the air upon those summits –	Und die Luft auf jenen Höhen,
how soothing it must be!	O wie labend muß sie sein!
But the raging of the water	Doch mir wehrt des Stromes Toben,
bars my path with a grim tempest,	Der ergrimmt dazwischen braust,
high the waves rise up before me,	Seine Wellen sind gehoben,
fill my soul with nameless fear.	Daß die Seele mir ergraust.
Now, a boat comes rocking hither,	Einen Nachen seh ich schwanken,
but alas! no oarsman's there.	Aber ach! der Fährmann fehlt.
Quick, jump in, unhesitating!	Frisch hinein und ohne Wanken,
See, the sails are filled to go.	Seine Segel sind beseelt.
Faith and daring be the watchword,	Du mußt glauben, du mußt wagen,
since the gods will grant no pledge,	Denn die Götter leihn kein Pfand,
Miracles alone can bring you	Nur ein Wunder kann dich tragen
to that miracle-fair land.	In das schöne Wunderland.

Gretchen am Spinnrade (Gretchen at the Spinning-Wheel) Johann Wolfgang von Goethe

My peace is gone,	Meine Ruh ist hin,
My heart is heavy;	Mein Herz ist schwer;
I shall never, never again	Ich finde sie nimmer
Find peace.	Und nimmermehr.
Wherever he is not with me	Wo ich ihn nicht hab,
Is my grave,	Ist mir das Grab,
The whole world	Die ganze Welt
Is turned to gall.	Ist mir vergällt.
My poor head	Mein armer Kopf
Is crazed,	Ist mir verrückt,
My poor mind	Mein armer Sinn
Is shattered.	Ist mir zerstückt.

My peace is gone, *etc.*	Meine Ruh ist hin, *usw.*
I look out of the window Only to seek him, I leave the house Only to seek him.	Nach ihm nur schau ich Zum Fenster hinaus, Nach ihm nur geh ich Aus dem Haus.
His fine gait, His noble form, The smile of his lips, The power of his eyes,	Sein hoher Gang, Sein' edle Gestalt, Seines Mundes Lächeln, Seiner Augen Gewalt,
And the magic flow Of his words, The pressure of his hand And, ah, his kiss!	Und seiner Rede Zauberfluß, Sein Händedruck, Und ach, sein Kuß!
My peace is gone, *etc.*	Meine Ruh ist hin, *usw*
My bosom yearns For him. Ah, if only I could grasp him And hold him	Mein Busen drängt sich nach ihm hin: Ach dürft' ich fassen Und halten ihn
And kiss him As I would like, I should die From his kisses!	Und küssen ihn, So wie ich wollt', An seinen Küssen Vergehen sollt'!
My peace is gone, My heart is heavy!	Meine Ruh ist hin, Mein Herz ist schwer!

Freiwilliges Versinken (Voluntary Oblivion) Johann Mayrhofer

Whither, O Helios? In cool waters I will immerse my burning body, Inwardly certain that I can bestow New warmth upon the earth's fires.	Wohin? o Helios! wohin? „In kühlen Fluten Will ich den Flammenleib versenken, Gewiss im Innern, neue Gluten Der Erde feuerreich zu schenken.
I do not take; I am wont only to give. As prodigal as my life, My parting is bathed in golden splendour; I depart in glory when night draws near.	Ich nehme nicht, ich pflege nur zu geben; Und wie verschwenderisch mein Leben, Umhüllt mein Scheiden goldne Pracht, Ich scheide herrlich, naht die Nacht.
How pale the moon, how faint the stars, As long as I move on my powerful course; Only when I lay down my crown upon the mountains Do they gain strength and courage in the far distance.	Wie blass der Mond, wie matt die Sterne! So lang ich kräftig mich bewege; Erst wenn ich auf die Berge meine Krone lege, Gewinnen sie an Mut und Kraft in weiter Ferne."

An die Musik (To Music) Franz von Schober

Thou fair Art, in how many grey hours when the noisy activity of life had entangled me, has thou kindled my heart to the warmth of love, and carried me away into a better world!	Du holde Kunst, in wieviel grauen Stunden, Wo mich des Lebens wilder Kreis umstrickt, Hast du mein Herz zu warmer Lieb entzunden, Hast mich in eine bessre Welt entrückt!

Often a sigh, coming from thy harp,	Oft hat ein Seufzer, deiner Harf entflossen,
a sweet and holy chord of thine	Ein süßer, heiliger Akkord von dir
has opened up to me the heaven of better times –	Den Himmel bessrer Zeiten mir erschlossen,
thou fair Art, I thank thee for this!	Du holde Kunst, ich danke dir dafür!

Der Jüngling und der Tod (The Young Man and Death)
Josef von Spaun

(*The Young Man:*)	(*Der Jüngling:*)
The sun sets – would I could go with it,	Die Sonne sinkt, o könnt ich mit ihr scheiden,
escape with its last ray,	Mit ihrem letzten Strahl entfliehen!
ah! shun these nameless miseries	Ach diese namenlosen Qualen meiden,
and journey far into fairer worlds.	Und weit in schönre Welten ziehn!
O come, Death, and untie these bonds!	O komme, Tod, und löse diese Bande!
I smile at you, O skeleton –	Ich lächle dir, o Knochenmann,
lead me lightly away to lands of dream,	Entführe mich leicht in geträumte Lande!
O come and touch me!	O komm und rühre mich doch an!
(*Death:*)	(*Der Tod:*)
To rest in my arms is cool and gentle.	Es ruht sich kühl und sanft in meinen Armen,
You call! I will take pity on your misery.	Du rufst! Ich will mich deiner Qual erbarmen.

Fischerweise (Fisherman's Song) Franz Xaver Schlechta

Care does not assail the fisherman	Den Fischer fechten Sorgen
nor grief and pain.	Und Gram und Leid nicht an;
Early in the morning he unties	Er löst am frühen Morgen
his boat lightheartedly.	Mit leichtem Sinn den Kahn.
Round about him peace broods	Da lagert rings noch Friede
on every field and stream;	Auf Wald und Flur und Bach,
with his song he calls on	Er ruft mit seinem Liede
the golden sun to awake.	Die goldne Sonne wach.
At his work he sings	Er singt zu seinem Werke
with a loud, cheery heart.	Aus voller, frischer Brust
Work gives him strength,	Die Arbeit gibt ihm Stärke,
and strength makes him glad to be alive.	Die Stärke Lebenslust.
Soon there will be a gaudy shoal	Bald wird ein bunt Gewimmel
about in all the deeps,	In allen Tiefen laut
splashing through the sky	Und plätschert durch den Himmel,
reflected in the water.	Der sich im Wasser baut.
But he who would cast a net	Doch wer ein Netz will stellen,
needs clear, good eyes;	Braucht Augen klar und gut,
he must be as cheerful as the waves	Muß heiter gleich den Wellen
and as free as the flood.	Und frei sein wie die Flut.
There on the bridge fishes	Dort angelt auf der Brücke
the shepherdess. Sly baggage,	Die Hirtin – Schlauer Wicht,
give up your tricks!	Gib auf nur deine Tücke,
This fish you won't catch.	Den Fisch betrügst du nicht.

Der Zwerg (The Dwarf) Matthäus von Collin

In the gloomy light the hills are already fading;
the ship is suspended on the smooth sea-waves,
and on it are the queen and her dwarf.

She gazes up at the arched vault above,
upwards to the distant blueness interwoven with light
and palely interlaced with the Milky Way of heaven.

"Never, never have you yet lied to me, O stars!
(so she cries) And now I am soon to vanish,
for this you tell me. Yet I die willingly indeed."

Then the dwarf comes to the queen, and binds
round her throat the cord of red silk
and weeps, as though he would speedily become blind with
    remorse.

He speaks: "Thou thyself art guilty of this hurt,
since thou hast left me for the king;
and now your dying awakens only joy for me.

True, I shall hate myself for ever
who brought thee death with this hand –
yet now thou must vanish into an early grave."

She lays her hand on her heart, full of youthful life,
and the heavy tears run from her eyes
which she would fain lift in a prayer to heaven.

"Mayest thou get no sorrow through my death!"
she says; then the dwarf kisses her pale cheeks,
and immediately her senses depart from her.

The dwarf gazes on the woman, shut in by death;
he sinks her body deep in the sea with his own hands,
his heart so full of longing burns for her,
on no shore will he ever land again.

Im trüben Licht verschwinden schon die Berge,
Es schwebt das Schiff auf glatten Meereswogen,
Worauf die Königin mit ihrem Zwerge.

Sie schaut empor zum hochgewölbten Bogen,
Hinauf zur lichtdurchwirkten blauen Ferne,
Die mit der Milch des Himmels blaß durchzogen.

Nie, nie habt ihr mir gelogen noch, ihr Sterne,
So ruft sie aus, bald werd ich nun entschwinden,
Ihr sagt es mir, doch sterb ich wahrlich gerne.

Da tritt der Zwerg zur Königin, mag binden
um ihren Hals die Schnur von roter Seide,
Und weint, als wollt' er schnell vor Gram erblinden.

Er spricht: „Du selbst bist schuld an diesem Leide,
Weil um den König du mich hast verlassen,
Jetzt weckt dein Sterben einzig mir noch Freude.

Zwar werd ich ewiglich mich selber hassen,
Der dir mit dieser Hand den Tod gegeben,
Doch mußt zum frühen Grab du nun erblassen."

Sie legt die Hand auf's Herz voll jungem Leben,
Und aus dem Aug die schweren Tränen rinnen,
Das sie zum Himmel betend will erheben.

„Mögst du nicht Schmerz durch meinen Tod gewinnen",
Sie sagt's, da küßt der Zwerg die bleichen Wangen,
Drauf alsobald vergehen ihr die Sinnen.

Der Zwerg schaut an die Frau, vom Tod befangen,
Er senkt sie tief ins Meer mit eignen Händen,
Ihm brennt nach ihr das Herz so voll Verlangen,
An keiner Küste wird er je mehr landen.

Der Wanderer (The Wanderer) Georg Philipp Schmidt von Lübeck

I come here from the mountains;
the valley steams, the sea is stormy.
I wander silently and know little joy,
and always my sigh asks: Where?

Here the sun seems to me so cold,
the blood seems parched, life seems old;
and what they say is empty sound.
I am a stranger everywhere.

Where art thou, where art thou, my beloved land?
Sought for, suspected, and never known!
The land, the land so green with hope,
The land where my roses bloom,

Ich komme vom Gebirge her,
Es dampft das Tal, es braust das Meer.
Ich wandle still, bin wenig froh,
Und immer fragt der Seufzer: wo?

Die Sonne dünkt mich hier so kalt,
Die Blüte welk, das Leben alt,
Und was sie reden, leerer Schall,
Ich bin ein Fremdling überall.

Wo bist du, mein geliebtes Land?
Gesucht, geahnt und nie gekannt!
Das Land, das Land, so huffnungsgrün,
Das Land, wo meine Rosen blühn,

where my friends go wandering,	Wo meine Freunde wandelnd gehn,
where my dead are brought to life,	Wo meine Toten auferstehn,
the land which speaks my own language,	Das Land, das meine Sprache spricht,
O land, where art thou?	O Land, wo bist du?

I wander silently and know little joy,	Ich wandle still, bin wenig froh,
and always my sigh asks: Where? always where?	Und immer fragt der Seufzer: wo?
On ghostly breath the answer comes back to me:	Im Geisterhauch tönt's mir zurück:
"There, in the place where you are not, there happiness lies!"	„Dort, wo du nicht bist, dort ist das Glück!"

Die Götter Griechenlands (The Grecian Gods)
Friedrich von Schiller

Lovely world, where are you? Come again,	Schöne Welt, wo bist du? Kehre wieder,
fair flowering age of nature!	Holdes Blütenalter der Natur!
Ah, only in the fairyland of song	Ach, nur in dem Feenland der Lieder
survives the imprint of your fabled lore.	Lebt noch deine fabelhafte Spur.
The countryside laments its desert state;	Ausgestorben trauert das Gefilde,
no godly countenances meet my gaze.	Keine Gottheit zeigt sich meinem Blick,
Alas, of all that world so warm with life	Ach, von jenem lebenwarmen Bilde
only a shadow yet remains behind.	Blieb der Schatten nur zurück.

Der Atlas (Atlas) Heinrich Heine

Luckless Atlas that I am! A world,	Ich unglücksel'ger Atlas! Eine Welt,
the whole world of sorrows must I carry.	Die ganze Welt der Schmerzen, muß ich tragen.
I bear the unbearable, and break will my heart	Ich trage Unerträgliches, und brechen will mir das Herz
in my body.	im Leibe.

Proud heart, you willed it so!	Du stolzes Herz, du hast es ja gewollt!
You wanted to be happy, endlessly happy, or endlessly	Du wolltest glücklich sein, unendlich glücklich
wretched, proud heart,	oder unendlich elend, stolzes Herz,
and now you are wretched.	Und jetzo bist du elend.

Ihr Bild (Her Likeness) Heinrich Heine

I stood in dark dreams	Ich stand in dunkeln Träumen
and stared at her likeness,	Und starrt' ihr Bildnis an.
and my beloved's face	Und das geliebte Antlitz
started to secret life.	Heimlich zu leben begann.

Upon her lips	Um ihre Lippen zog sich
a wonderful smile played,	Ein Lächeln wunderbar.
and, as if from tears of melancholy,	Und wie von Wehmutstränen
her two eyes glistened.	Erglänzte ihr Augenpaar.

My tears too poured down	Auch meine Tränen flossen
from my cheeks;	Mir von den Wangen herab.
and ah, I cannot believe	Und ach! Ich kann es nicht glauben,
that I have lost you!	Daß ich dich verloren hab!

Das Fischermädchen (The Fisher Girl) Heinrich Heine

Lovely fisher girl,
drive your boat to shore;
come and sit down by me
and we will dally hand in hand.

Lay your head on my heart,
and do not be too afraid.
Every day you entrust yourself
to the wild sea and have no qualms.

My heart is like the sea,
it has its storms, its ebb and flow,
and many a lovely pearl
rests in its depths.

Du schönes Fischermädchen
Treibe den Kahn ans Land;
Komm zu mir und setze dich nieder,
Wir kosen Hand in Hand.

Leg an mein Herz dein Köpfchen
Und fürchte dich nicht zu sehr:
Vertraust du dich doch sorglos
Täglich dem wilden Meer;

Mein Herz gleicht ganz dem Meere,
Hat Sturm und Ebb' und Flut,
Und manche schöne Perle
In seiner Tiefe ruht.

Die Stadt (The Town) Heinrich Heine

On the distant horizon,
like a cloud-shape,
appears the town with its turrets,
veiled in twilight.

A humid breeze ruffles
the grey water;
with weary strokes
the sailor rows in my boat.

The sun rises once again,
beaming from the earth,
and shows me the place
where I lost my beloved.

Am fernen Horizonte erscheint,
Wie ein Nebelbild,
Die Stadt mit ihren Türmen,
In Abenddämmrung gehüllt.

Ein feuchter Windzug kräuselt
Die graue Wasserbahn;
Mit traurigem Takte rudert
Der Schiffer in meinem Kahn.

Die Sonne hebt sich noch einmal
Leuchtend vom Boden empor,
Und zeigt mir jene Stelle,
Wo ich das Liebste verlor.

Am Meer (By the Sea) Heinrich Heine

The sea was glittering far and wide
in the last rays of evening.
We sat by a lonely fisherman's hut;
we sat silent and alone.

The mist arose, the waters swelled,
the seamews flew back and forth.
The tears poured
from your loving eyes.

I saw them fall on to your hand,
and fell on my knees
and drank the tears
from your white hand.

From that hour my body has wasted away,
and my spirit is dying of desire.
The wretched woman has poisoned me
with her tears.

Das Meer erglänzte weit hinaus
Im letzten Abendscheine
Wir saßen am einsamen Fischerhaus,
Wir saßen stumm und alleine.

Der Nebel stieg, das Wasser schwoll,
Die Möve flog hin und wieder;
Aus deinen Augen, liebevoll,
Fielen die Tränen nieder.

Ich sah sie fallen auf deine Hand
Und bin auf's Knie gesunken;
Ich hab von deiner weißen Hand
Die Tränen fortgetrunken.

Seit jener Stunde verzehrt sich mein Leib,
Die Seele stirbt vor Sehnen
Mich hat das unglücksel'ge Weib
Vergiftet mit ihren Tränen.

Der Doppelgänger (The Ghost) Heinrich Heine

The night is quiet; the streets are still;
here in this house my dear one used to live.
She has left the town long since,
but the house still stands in the same square.

Another man stands there too, and stares into the sky,
and wrings his hands with the weight of his grief.
I am filled with horror when I see his face;
the moon shows me my own features.

You ghostly double, pale companion!
Why do you ape the pain of love
that tortured me in this place
full many a night in time gone by?

Still ist die Nacht, es ruhen die Gassen,
In diesem Hause wohnte mein Schatz;
Sie hat schon längst die Stadt verlassen
Doch steht noch das Haus auf demselben Platz.

Da steht auch ein Mensch und starrt in die Höhe,
Und ringt die Hände vor Schmerzensgewalt;
Mir graust es, wenn ich sein Antlitz sehe –
Der Mond zeigt mir meine eigne Gestalt.

Du Doppelgänger, du bleicher Geselle!
Was äffst du nach mein Liebesleid,
Das mich gequält auf dieser Stelle
So manche Nacht in alter Zeit?

Der Hirt auf dem Felsen (The Shepherd on the Rock)
Wilhelm Müller & Helmina von Chézy (?)

When I stand on the highest rock,
look down into the deep valley, and sing:
out of the deep dark valley far away
the echo soars up from the chasms.
The farther my voice carries
the brighter it comes back to me from below.
My sweetheart lives so far from me:
that's why I long so ardently for her over there.

I am wasting away in deep grief,
my happiness is ended,
earthly hope has left me,
I am so lonely here.
My song rang round the wood so longingly,
so longingly it rang through the night,
it draws hearts up to heaven
with wondrous power.

Springtime will come,
springtime my joy,
now I will get ready
to go on my travels.
The farther my voice carries
the brighter it comes back to me.

Wenn auf dem höchsten Fels ich steh,
Ins tiefe Tal hernieder seh, und singe:
Fern aus dem tiefen, dunkeln Tal
Schwingt sich empor der Widerhall der Klüfte.
Je weiter meine Stimme dringt,
Je heller sie mir widerklingt von unten.
Mein Liebchen wohnt so weit von mir,
Drum sehn ich mich so heiß nach ihr hinüber!

In tiefem Gram verzehr ich mich,
Mir ist die Freude hin,
Auf Erden mir die Hoffnung wich,
Ich hier so einsam bin.
So sehnend klang im Wald das Lied,
So sehnend klang es durch die Nacht,
Die Herzen es zum Himmel zieht
Mit wunderbarer Macht.

Der Frühling will kommen,
Der Frühling, meine Freud,
Nun mach ich mich fertig
Zum Wandern bereit.
Je weiter meine Stimme dringt,
Je heller sie mir widerklingt.

Die Taubenpost (The Pigeon Post) Johann Gabriel Seidl

I have a carrier pigeon in my service,
who is devoted and true to me.
She never falls short of the target I set her,
nor ever flies astray.

Ich hab eine Brieftaub in meinem Sold,
Die ist gar ergeben und treu;
Sie nimmt mir nie das Ziel zu kurz
Und fliegt auch nie vorbei.

I send her many thousand times
out on daily errands.
away to many a cherished spot
right up to my darling's house.

There she secretly looks in through the window,
and spies on how she looks and how she moves,
playfully gives my greetings
and takes my love's greetings away with her.

Now I have no more letters to write,
it is tears I give her;
and this she cannot bear,
so devotedly does she serve me.

By day, by night, in waking or dreaming,
it is all the same to her;
if she can only go afield
then she is more than rich.

She does not grow tired, she does not grow faint,
the way is always new to her;
she needs no decoy, she needs no wage,
the pigeon is so faithful to me.

So I too hold her so faithfully to my breast,
assured of the fairest prize.
Her name is "Longing" – do you know her,
the messenger of a faithful mind?

Ich sende sie viel tausendmal
Auf Kundschaft täglich hinaus,
Vorbei an manchem lieben Ort,
Bis zu der Liebsten Haus.

Dort schaut sie zum Fenster heimlich hinein,
Belauscht ihren Blick und Schritt,
Gibt meine Grüße scherzend ab
Und nimmt die ihren mit.

Kein Briefchen brauch ich zu schreiben mehr,
Die Träne selbst geb ich ihr:
O sie verträgt sie sicher nicht,
Gar eifrig dient sie mir.

Bei Tag, bei Nacht, im Wachen, im Traum,
Ihr gilt das alles gleich,
Wenn sie nur wandern, wandern kann,
Dann ist sie überreich.

Sie wird nicht müd, sie wird nicht matt,
Der Weg ist stets ihr neu;
Sie braucht nicht Lockung, braucht nicht Lohn,
Die Taub ist so mir treu.

Drum heg ich sie auch so treu an der Brust,
Versichert des schönsten Gewinns;
Sie heißt – die Sehnsucht!
Kennt ihr sie? Die Botin treuen Sinns.

Further Listening and Reading

Schubert is one of those composers, like Haydn, Mozart or Mendelssohn, who rarely fail to please. Though they may not always achieve the highest inspiration, you are unlikely to find yourself exclaiming: 'But this is simply awful!' So you can probably sample *any* Schubert you come across with reasonable confidence – and there is certainly plenty of it in the record catalogues. The choice of interpretations, however, can be bewildering. There are no rules. You may prefer the vintage performances of Beecham or Furtwängler in the symphonies, or of Schnabel in the piano works, or you may go for the modern approach, with period instruments and a generally less heavy, 'authentic' sound. It doesn't matter: if you find a style that appeals to you, stick with it and use that as your base. And, as a practising musician myself, I encourage you to support live performance too, whether at the highest professional level or the humblest amateur. After all, it was by amateurs that almost all Schubert's music was first performed, enjoyed and understood.

Turning first to the instrumental works, I should be inclined to suggest the 'Trout' Quintet as a starting-point – as irresistible a combination of tunefulness and joyful high spirits as exists anywhere in the chamber music repertoire. From there it is a short step to the Octet and either of the two Piano Trios, preferably both. The essential chamber list is completed with the profoundly moving String Quintet, the famous D minor String Quartet ('Death and the Maiden'), and the less famous, but magnificent, last quartet in G major. After that, perhaps, a look at the earlier quartets and the slight but charming solo violin repertoire.

Of the symphonies, the 'Great' C major (a casualty on this selection, like much of the chamber music, because of its length) probably needs the most preparation, and there is a certain logic to hearing them in numerical order, which leaves the 'Unfinished' eighth as the ideal preparation for the ninth. There is a similar logic to the piano sonatas, not forgetting the early incomplete ones which contain much beautiful music even if, in the end, they can only be seen as a rehearsal for the great late sonatas – of which the last, in B flat major, must take pride of place. The piano duet repertory is full of enchanting surprises.

As a singer I may have made too persistent a case for the songs, but the fact is that it was song which made the greatest impact in Schubert's lifetime, and it is song that lies at the heart of his creative inspiration. Clearly, the first need is to hear the two complete cycles, *Die schöne Müllerin* and *Winterreise* (both of which take over an hour in performance), but for the rest I can only suggest following my own preferences as expressed in this book. It would of course be wrong to imply that none of the other songs is worth hearing – far from it – but I *do* advocate a performance by the right kind of singer. In my opinion the standard is set by Dietrich Fischer-Dieskau. Among CDs only Graham Johnson's encyclopedic set with various singers provides an equal, and Johnson's notes give an insight into this music that few other bicentenary commentaries can approach.

*   *   *

Schubert is a composer about whom we know too little to make writing about him an easy matter. There will be any number of biographies produced during his bicentenary year, and each will hope to have something new to reveal. But the main known facts of Schubert's life remain more or less what they were in the three bibliographical masterpieces of Otto Erich Deutsch, published in English as *Schubert: A Documentary Biography* (1946; reprinted 1977); the *Thematic Catalogue of all his Works* (1951); and *Memoirs by his Friends* (1958).

The interpretations placed upon these facts vary from the classic but now out-dated account of George Grove, originally written for his dictionary in the 1880s but reissued separately in *Beethoven, Schubert, Mendelssohn* in 1951, to the *Critical Biography* (1958) and other writings on Schubert by Maurice J. E. Brown. I should be most inclined to value the opinions of John Reed whose *Schubert: The Final Years* (1972) disposes of a great many myths and presents the known facts in an objective view of exemplary scholarship. His exposition, *The Schubert Song Companion* (1985), is unsurpassed in its presentation of the songs, to be complemented only by the commentaries of Richard Capell (*Schubert's Songs*, 1928; revised Martin Cooper, 1973), Gerald Moore (*The Schubert Song Cycles*, 1975), and Fischer-Dieskau himself (*Schubert: A Biographical Study of his Songs*, 1976).

DATE	LIFE AND WORKS	MUSICAL CONTEXT	HISTORICAL BACKGROUND
1797	Franz Peter Schubert born, son of schoolmaster Franz Theodor Florian Schubert and Elisabeth née Vietz. Three older brothers who survive infancy are Ignaz (b. 1785), Ferdinand (b. 1794) and Karl (b. 1795).	Cherubini: *Medée.* Méhul: *Le Jeune Henri.* Grétry: *Anacréon chez Polycrate.* Birth of Donizetti.	French invasion of Austria; Peace of Campo Formio. Hölderin: *Hyperion* (to 1799); Goethe: *Hermann and Dorothea*; Schelling: *Ideas towards a Philosophy of Nature.*
1798		Beethoven: 2nd Piano Concerto completed; possibly 'Pathétique' Sonata. Haydn: *The Creation.*	Napoleon's expedition to Egypt; Nelson victorious at the battle of the Nile. Coleridge & Wordsworth: *Lyrical Ballads.* Schlegel brothers edit *Das Athenäum*, manifesto of German romanticism (to 1800).
1799		Salieri: *Falstaff.* Méhul: *Ariodant.* Haydn: Quartets op. 77.	Second coalition against France. Overthrow of Directory in France; Napoleon becomes First Consul. Schiller: *Wallenstein.*
1800		Beethoven: 1st Symphony, 3rd Piano Concerto and op. 18 Quartets completed. Cherubini: *Les Deux Journées.* Boieldieu: *Le Calife de Bagdad.*	Napoleon in Italy; Austrians defeated at Marengo. Further defeats at Hochstädt and Hohenlinden. Novalis: *Hymns to the Night.*
1801	Maria Theresia (Schubert's sister) born.	Haydn: *The Seasons.* Beethoven: 'Moonlight' and 'Spring' Sonatas.	Peace of Lunéville (Austria and France). Murder of Tsar Paul of Russia; accession of Alexander I.
1802	First attempts at the piano.	Beethoven's deafness brings him near despair, but he completes 2nd Symphony and 3 Piano Sonatas op. 31. Haydn: *Harmonie Messe.*	Concordat between France and Roman Catholic Church. Peace of Amiens (France and Britain). Napoleon appointed First Consul for life.
1803		Beethoven: 'Eroica' Symphony and 'Kreutzer' Sonata completed. Haydn: last Quartet (unfinished) op. 103.	Codification of Criminal Law completed (Habsburg empire). 'Recensoring' commission retrospectively bans 2500 books published 1780–92. Von Pergen builds up secret police.
1804		Beethoven: Triple Concerto and 'Waldstein' Sonata completed.	Napoleon crowns himself emperor of France. Code Napoléon promulgated. Francis II declares himself emperor (Francis I) of new Austrian empire. Schiller: *William Tell.*
1805		Beethoven: 1st version of *Fidelio* and 'Appassionata' Sonata.	Napoleon crowned king of Italy. Third coalition against France. Nelson victorious at Trafalgar. Battle of Ulm; French occupy Vienna. Austrian defeat at Austerlitz; Peace of Pressburg. Arnim & Bretana: *Des Knaben Wunderhorn* (to 1808).
1806		Beethoven: 4th Symphony and 4th Piano Concerto completed; also Violin Concerto, (Razumovsky) Quartets op. 59 and 2nd version of *Fidelio.* Cherubini: *Faniska.*	Napoleon's Federation of the Rhine; abolition of Holy Roman Empire. Prussians defeated at Jena and Auerstadt. Berlin and Warsaw occupied. Berlin Decrees: blockade of Britain declared. Archdukes Charles and John and Count Stadion preside over slightly more liberal regime in Austria (to 1809). Military reforms instigated.
1807	First soprano in Liechtental church choir, playing violin and composing songs, string quartets and keyboard works.	Beethoven: Mass in C. Spontini: *La Vestale.* Méhul: *Joseph.* Pleyel piano factory founded.	Russian defeats at Eylau and Friedland; withdrawal following Treaty of Tilsit. Fichte's *Addresses to the German Nation* (to 1808), Hormayr's *Handbook for a National History*

DATE	LIFE AND WORKS	MUSICAL CONTEXT	HISTORICAL BACKGROUND
1807 *cont.*			(20 vols. to 1814), a Habsburg commission to foster sense of patriotism. Britain abolishes slave trade. Turner: *Sun Rising in a Mist*; David completes *Coronation of Napoleon*. Wordsworth: 'Intimations of Immortality'; Hegel: *Phenomenology of Spirit*.
1808	Examination for and entrance into Imperial and Royal Court Chapel.	Beethoven: 5th and 6th Symphonies completed.	Abdication of Charles IV of Spain; fall of Madrid; Peninsular War begins. Austria obliged to accept Napoleon's 'Continental System'. A national *Landwehr* (militia) set up. Ingres: *The Bather*. Goethe: *Faust* (I).
1809		Beethoven: 'Emperor' Concerto, String Quartet op. 74. Spontini: *Fernand Cortez*. Birth of Mendelssohn. Death of Haydn. Weigl: *Die Schweizerfamilie*.	France and Austria (subsidized by Britain) again at war. Napoleon annexes Papal States. Tyroleans expel Bavarians but are crushed by French; execution of national hero, Andreas Hofer. Austrians challenge French invincibility at battle of Aspern, but are defeated at Wagram. Napoleon enters Vienna. Punitive Peace of Schönbrunn. Metternich becomes Foreign Minister.
1810	Fantasy in G for piano duet (D1).	Rossini: *La cambiale di matrimonio*. Hummel: *Mathilde von Guise*. Birth of Chopin and Schumann.	Marriage of Napoleon and Archduchess Marie Louise. Prussia abolishes serfdom. France annexes Holland, Hamburg and Bremen. Scott: *The Lady of the Lake*. Goya: *The Disasters of War* (to 1814).
1811	Early compositions including 'Hagar's Lament' (D5).	Beethoven: 'Archduke' Piano Trio. Weber: *Abu Hassan*. Birth of Liszt.	Civil Code introduced into Austrian empire, except Hungary, after 50 years of preparation. Austria declares state bankruptcy and devalues currency; rampant inflation continues throughout war years. Regency in Britain. Austen: *Sense and Sensibility*; Goethe's Autobiography (to 1814).
1812	Death of Schubert's mother. His voice breaks. Begins studying composition with Salieri.	Beethoven: 7th and 8th Symphonies completed. Rossini: *L'inganno felice*. Field: first *Nocturnes* published. Sonnleithner founds Gesellschaft der Musikfreunde (Philharmonic Society) in Vienna.	Napoleon invades Russia; battle of Borodino. Retreat from Moscow. Wellington takes Madrid. Davy: *Elements of Chemical Philosophy*. Byron: *Childe Harold* (I & II); Brothers Grimm: *Fairy Tales* (to 1815).
1813	Schubert's father remarries. Schubert leaves the seminary and enters teacher training college. First Symphony completed (D82).	Rossini: *Tancredi, L'Italiana in Algeri*. Cherubini: *Les Abencérages*. Birth of Verdi and Wagner.	War of Liberation opens (March); Austria joins in August. Napoleon overwhelmed by allied forces at Leipzig ('Battle of the Nations'). Wellington crosses Pyrenees into France. Death in action of poet Theodor Körner (his patriotic poems, *Lyre and Sword*, published in 1814).
1814	Mass in F (D105) performed. First opera, *Der Teufels Lustschloss*. String Quartet in B flat (D112). 'Gretchen am Spinnrade'. Meets Mayrhofer. In love with Therese Grob.	Beethoven: final version of *Fidelio*. Hummel has great success in Vienna.	Allies take Paris. Abdication of Napoleon and banishment to Elba. Restoration of Louis XVIII. Congress of Vienna (to 1815): Metternich's congress system seeks to determine European balance of power during next decade. Stephenson's first effective steam locomotive. Rückert: *Poems*; Scott: *Waverley*; Hoffmann: *Tales* (to 1815); Wordsworth: *The Excursion*.

DATE	LIFE AND WORKS	MUSICAL CONTEXT	HISTORICAL BACKGROUND
1815	Birth of half-sister Josefa Theresia. Schubert teaching at his father's school. Meets Schober. Over 200 compositions, including Symphonies no. 2 and 3, 2 masses, 4 dramatic works, c. 145 songs, amongst which are 'Heidenröslein', 'Dem Unendlichen', 'Erlkönig'.		Napoleon's 'Hundred Days'; defeat at Waterloo. Postwar settlement: Austria loses territory in Netherlands but gains Lombardo-Venetian kingdom. Holy Alliance of Austria, Prussia and Russia. Treaties of Paris: France maintains 1790 borders and pays war indemnity (150 million francs to Austria). In Austria a second police service directly under Metternich formed to crack down on intelligentsia. Catastrophic harvests and starvation: beginning of postwar depression. Uhland: *Poems*; Scott: *Guy Mannering*.
1816	Unsuccessful application to school in Laibach. Musical evenings at the house of Professor Watteroth. Schubert leaves home (and schoolmastering) to lodge with Schober. Symphonies no. 4 ('Tragic') and 5. Cantata *Prometheus* much acclaimed. 'Lied eines Schiffers an die Dioskuren', 'An Schwager Kronos', the 'Harper' Songs, 'Der Wanderer'.	Rossini: *Il barbiere di Siviglia, Otello.* Beethoven: *And die ferne Geliebte.* Hoffmann: *Undine.* Spohr: *Faust.* Death of Paisiello.	First Diet of newly formed German Confederation (39 independent states) under Austrian presidency, in competition with Prussia for dominance. National bank founded in Vienna. Coleridge: 'Kubla Khan', 'Christabel'; Shelley: *Alastor*.
1817	Schubert introduced to Vogl. Symphony no. 6, 2 Overtures 'in the Italian style', String Trio (D581). First completed piano sonatas. 'Der Tod und das Mädchen', 'Ganymed', 'An die Musik', 'Die Forelle', 'Gruppe aus dem Tartarus' (version 2).	Beethoven: first sketches for the 9th Symphony. Rossini: *La Cenerentola, La gazza ladra.* Rossini enjoys enormous popularity in Vienna. Hérold: *La Clochette.* Clementi: *Gradus ad Parnassum.* Death of Méhul.	Student societies (*Burschenschaften*) at German universities, notably Jena, promoting radicalism and nationalism: agitation reaches height during Wartburg festival. Grillparzer: *The Ancestress*; Coleridge: *Biographia Literaria*; Scott: *Rob Roy*.
1818	'Italian' Overtures performed at Schubert's first (secular) public concert. Living and teaching at his father's Rossau school. First visit to Zseliz (July) tutoring Esterházy daughters. Lodges with Mayrhofer on return to Vienna. First song in print ('Erlafsee'). Sonata for piano duet in B flat; 3 *Marches militaires*; 'Der Blumenbrief'.	Rossini: *Mosè in Egitto.* Donizetti: *Enrico di Borgogna.* Beethoven: 'Hammerklavier' Sonata. Birth of Gounod.	Congress of Aix-la-Chapelle: France readmitted to 'Concert of Nations'; allied troops withdrawn. Alexander I abandons liberal policies. Mary Shelley: *Frankenstein*; Keats: *Endymion*; Austen: *Northanger Abbey, Persuasion*; Grillparzer: *Sappho*.
1819	Introduced to Sonnleithner circle. Accompanies Vogl to Steyr. Composes 'Trout' Quintet and Piano Sonata in A (D664). 'Prometheus', 'Die Götter Griechenlands'.	Beethoven begins work on the *Missa Solemnis* (to 1822). Weber: *Invitation to the Dance.* Spontini: *Olimpie.*	Assassination of conservative playwright Kotzebue by student Karl Sand: backed by Prussia (Teplitz conference) Metternich retaliates with Carlsbad Decrees, designed to stamp out liberal opposition. First steps towards German customs union excluding Austria. Peterloo Massacre in England. *The Savannah* makes first steam crossing of Atlantic in 26 days. Géricault: *The Raft of the Medusa*. Byron: *Don Juan*, I & II; Schopenhauer: *The World as Will and Idea*; Scott: *Ivanhoe*; Goethe: *East-west Divan*.

DATE	LIFE AND WORKS	MUSICAL CONTEXT	HISTORICAL BACKGROUND
1820	Schubert introduced to Baron von Schönstein, Ladislaus Pyrker and the Fröhlich sisters. Police raid on Senn's lodgings. 23rd Psalm and Quartettsatz.	Beethoven: Piano Sonata, op. 109. Meyerbeer: *Margherita d'Anjou*. Birth of Offenbach. *Die Zwillingsbrüder* and *Die Zauberharfe* performed with little success.	Conference of Vienna: Metternich succeeds in modifying Federal Act to fix functions of the Diet and eliminate constitutional control within German states. Assassination of the duc de Berri, heir presumptive to French throne. Congress of Troppau: Great Powers agree to check revolutionary movements in Spain, Portugal and the two Sicilies. Shelley: *Prometheus Unbound*; Washington Irving: *The Sketch Book*; Lamartine: *Nouvelles méditations poétiques*.
1821	Unsuccessful application for court opera post. The first 'Schubertiad'. Schubert leaves Mayrhofer lodgings. Becomes friendly with Schwind. First publications of songs by Cappi & Diabelli. Summer visit to Atzenbrugg with Schober. Begins work on *Alfonso und Estrella* (to 1822) at Ochsenburg. 'Grenzen der Menschheit'. 'Geheimes'.	Weber: *Der Freischütz*; *Concertstück* for piano and orchestra. Erard patents revolutionary 'double escapement' action on piano.	Laibach conference: Austria authorized to suppress Neopolitan revolution. Insurrection in Piedmont suppressed. Arrest and life imprisonment of Count Confalonieri, head of liberals in Lombardy. Metternich appointed Chancellor (to 1848). Death of Napoleon. Greek War of Independence begins. Faraday discovers electro-magnetic rotation. Constable: *The Hay Wain*. Goethe: *Wilhelm Meister's Travels* (to 1829); Grillparzer: *The Golden Fleece*.
1822	Lodges with Schober. Meets Bauernfeld. Introduced to Weber. Schubert's 'Dream'. Probable date of contraction of syphilis. Returns to father's house. 'Unfinished' Symphony, Mass in A flat, 'Wanderer' Fantasy, 'Der Musensohn'.	Beethoven: Piano Sonatas opp. 110 & 111. Royal Academy of Music founded in London. Liszt, aged 11, makes debut recital in Vienna. Birth of Franck.	Congress of Verona. Suicide of Castlereagh, British Foreign Secretary: Britain's accelerated disengagement under Canning from Metternich's European system. De Quincey: *Confessions of an English Opium Eater*; Rückert: *Eastern Roses*. Heine: *Poems*.
1823	Very ill at start of year; admitted to hospital. Break with Cappi & Diabelli; first publications with Sauer & Leidesdorf. Opera *Fierabras* rejected by Barbaja. *Rosamunde* incidental music. *Momens musicals* (*sic*) begun. Piano Sonata in A minor (D784). 'Auf dem Wasser zu singen', 'Du bist die Ruh', *Die schöne Müllerin*.	Weber: *Euryanthe*. Beethoven: 'Diabelli' Variations. Rossini: *Semiramide*. Spohr: *Jessonda*.	French invasion of Spain. Meeting of Emperors Alexander and Francis at Czernovitz. Rothschilds (private bankers to Habsburgs) persuade British government to waive Austrian debt of £28 million. Monroe Doctrine extends US protection to newly independent South American republics. Faraday liquefies chlorine. Stendhal: 'Racine et Shakespeare'; Lamb: *Essays of Elia*; Cooper: *The Pioneers*.
1824	Second visit to Zseliz. Variations on 'Trockne Blumen'. Octet, Quartets in A minor – given a public performance – and D minor ('Death and the Maiden'), 'Arpeggione' Sonata, 'Grand Duo', Variations in A flat for piano duet.	Beethoven: *Missa Solemnis*, 9th Symphony, Quartet op. 127. Meyerbeer: *Il crociato in Egitto*. Donizetti: *L'ajo nell' imbarazzo*. Birth of Bruckner.	Repressive Carlsbad Decrees extended indefinitely (last until 1848). Death of Louis XVIII; accession of Charles X. Repeal of Combination Acts in Britain.

DATE	LIFE AND WORKS	MUSICAL CONTEXT	HISTORICAL BACKGROUND
1825	Moves to Wieden. Summer visits to Steyr, Linz, Gmunden and Gastein. Possibly 'Gmunden–Gastein' Symphony (identical with 'Great' C Major?) Sonatas in C ('Reliquie'), A minor (D845) and D (D850). 'Ellens Gesang III', 'Die Allmacht', 'Auf der Bruck'.	Mendelssohn: Octet. Beethoven: op. 132 Quartet. Berlioz: *Messe solennelle*. Auber: *Le Maçon*. Boieldieu: *La Dame blanche*. Bellini: *Adelson e Salvini*. Death of Salieri.	Austrian emperor agrees to reopening of Hungarian Diet after 13 years, to meet on a triennial basis. Accession of Tsar Nicholas I: Decembrist revolt suppressed. Stockton–Darlington railway, first passenger railway in Europe, opens (England). Faraday discovers benzene. Grillparzer: *King Ottokar's Success and Downfall*; Pushkin: *Boris Gudonov*; Manzoni: *The Betrothed* (to 1827).
1826	Fails to secure post as deputy music director of court chapel. Unsuccessful letters to publishers Breitkopf & Härtel and Probst. Vogl marries. String Quartet in G, Piano Sonata in G. 'Nachthelle', 'Totengräber-Weise', *Wilhelm Meister* songs, 'Fischerweise', 'Im Frühling', 'Ständchen' (Hark, hark the Lark), 'An Silvia'.	Weber: *Oberon*. Hérold: *Marie*. Mendelssohn: Overture to *A Midsummer Night's Dream*. Beethoven: Quartets opp. 130, 131, 135 completed, plus 'Grosse Fuge'. Berlioz: *Les Francs-juges* composed. Death of Weber.	Fenimore Cooper: *The Last of the Mohicans*; Eichendorff: *Aus dem Leben eines Taugenichts*; Hölderin: *Poems*; Heine: *Pictures of Travel*, I; Saint-Simon: *Nouveau Christianisme*; Casanova's Memoirs (to 1838).
1827	Lodging with Schober. Summer visits to Dornbach and Graz. Begins E flat major Piano Trio. Allegretto in C minor, 2 sets of Impromptus. 'Ständchen' (D920), *Winterreise*.	Death of Beethoven. Mendelssohn: *Die Hochzeit des Camacho*. Bellini: *Il pirata*.	Turks defeated by British, French and Russian fleets at Navarino. Niepce produces photographs on an asphalt-coated plate. Blake's illustrations to the Book of Job. Delacroix: *Death of Sardanapalus*. Heine: *Book of Songs*.
1828	Schubert Invitation Concert (March). Protracted dealings with publishers Probst and Schott. Moves to final lodgings with his brother Ferdinand (Sept). Counterpoint lessons with Sechter. Dies 19 Nov. Mass in E flat. Completes Symphony no. 9 in C (the 'Great'). String Quintet in C, 3 *Klavierstücke*, D946, Piano Sonatas in C minor, A and B flat (D958–60), Fantasy in F minor for piano duet. *Schwanengesang*, D957, 'Der Hirt auf dem Felsen'.	Rossini: *Le Comte Ory*. Hérold: *La Fille mal gardée*. Auber: *La Muette de Portici*. Marschner: *Der Vampyr*. Paganini takes Vienna by storm.	Ministries of Wellington (Britain) and Martignac (France) formed. Austria emerging from economic depression and embarking on early stages of industrial revolution. Wöhler's synthesis of urea founds organic chemistry. Andrew Jackson becomes US President. Webster's Dictionary first published. Mickiewicz: *Konrad Wallenrod*.

NOTES

1 Quoted in Marcel Brion, *Daily Life in the Vienna of Mozart and Schubert*, London, 1961. **2** Karl, Freiherr von Schönstein. **3** J. A. Westrup, *Schubert Chamber Music* (BBC Music Guide), London, 1969. **4** John Reed, *The Schubert Song Companion*, Manchester, 1985. **5** Hütten-brenner to Liszt, 1854. **6** Richard Capell, *Schubert's Songs*, London, 1928. **7** Letter from the Vienna Captaincy of the Civic Guard to the Lower-Austrian Government. **8** John Reed, *The Schubert Song Companion*, Manchester, 1985. **9** Quoted in A. J. B. Hutchings, *Schubert* (Master Musicians series), London, 3rd ed. 1976. **10** Geoffrey Sharp quoted by Maurice J. E. Brown in *Schubert Symphonies* (BBC Music Guide), London, 1970. **11** Holzapfel's Memoirs, 1858. **12** Josef von Spaun. **13** Maurice J. E. Brown, from the *New Grove Dictionary of Music and Musicians*, London, 1980. **14** Dietrich Fischer-Dieskau, *Schubert: A Biographical Study of his Songs*, London, 1976. **15** Josef Kenner. **16** Josef Karl Rosenbaum's Diary, 7 March 1821. **17** Letter from Moritz von Schwind to Franz von Schober, 7 January 1825. **18** Letter from Johanna Lutz to Leopold Kupelwieser, 7 March 1825. **19** Letter from Schubert to his father and stepmother, 25 July 1825. **20** Ferdinand Hiller. **21** Dresden *Abendzeitung*, 12 June 1828. **22** Letter from Johann Jenger to Marie Pachler, 4 July 1828. **23** Peggy Woodford, *Schubert*, London, 1978. **24** Andras Schiff, *BBC Music Magazine*, March 1997.

ACKNOWLEDGEMENTS

The Publishers gratefully acknowledge permission given by the following to reproduce illus-trations and photographs:
AKG London vi (Gesellschaft der Musikfreunde, Vienna/Erich Lessing) & 11 (Historisches Museum der Stadt Wien/Erich Lessing) & 27 (Neue Pinakothek, Munich) & 37 & 67 (Histor-isches Museum der Stadt Wien/Erich Lessing) & 68 (Schubert-Museum der Stadt Wien) & 69 (Historisches Museum der Stadt Wien) & 86 & 90 (Historisches Museum der Stadt Wien) & 102 × 2 (Schubert-Museum der Stadt Wien/Erich Lessing) & 117; Bildarchiv der Öster-reichen Nationalbibliothek, Vienna x, 5, 10, 18, 21, 38, 54, 64, 80, 105, 130, 148; Archiv der Gesellschaft der Musikfreunde, Vienna 6, 65, 77, 110, 120; Franz Schubert Institut/from Ernst Hilmer: Schubert, Akademische Druck- und Verlagsanstalt, Graz 1989 16, 41, 109; Historisches Museum der Stadt Wien 17, 30, 45, 95, 106, 118, 130, 151; Ullstein 58, Oberösterreichisches Landesmuseum, Linz 58 Graphische Sammlung Albertina, Vienna 125; Wiener Stadt- und Landesbibliothek 126, 152; Getty Images 135. Quotations by permission of J. M. Dent & Sons (O. E. Deutsch trans. Erich Blom, *Schubert: A Documentary Biography*); Mrs Gita Holroyd-Reece (Deutsch trans. Blom, *Schubert: Memoirs by his Friends*); Dietrich Fischer-Dieskau and Cassell plc (*Schubert: A Biographical Study of his Songs*). Song translations are reproduced by courtesy of EMI Classics: 'Sehnsucht', 'Der Jüngling und der Tod', 'Fischerweise', 'Die Götter Griechenlands', 'Der Hirt auf dem Felsen' and the six Heine songs from *Schwanen-gesang* tr. William Mann; 'Gretchen am Spinnrade' and 'Freiwilliges Versinken' tr. Richard Wigmore; 'An die Musik', 'Der Zwerg', 'Der Wanderer' and 'Der Taubenpost' tr. Arthur Jacobs.

Key to Schwind's 'Schubert evening at Josef von Spaun's'